Walking as Artistic Practice

Walking as Artistic Practice

ELLEN MUELLER

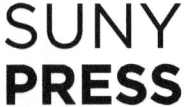

Cover Credit: Kate Gilmore, *Walk the Walk*, 2010. Performance for Public Art Fund, New York. Courtesy of the Artist. Photo: Adi Shniderman.

Published by State University of New York Press, Albany

For information, contact State University of New York Press, Albany, NY
www.sunypress.edu

Library of Congress Cataloging-in-Publication Data

Name: Mueller, Ellen, 1982– author.
Title: Walking as artistic practice / Ellen Mueller.
Description: Albany, NY : State University of New York, [2023] | Includes
    bibliographical references and index.
Identifiers: LCCN 2022059400 | ISBN 9781438494814 (hardcover : alk. paper) |
    ISBN 9781438494821 (ebook) | ISBN 9781438494807 (pbk. : alk. paper)
Subjects: LCSH: Walking as art.
Classification: LCC N7433.99 .M84 2023 | DDC 702.8—dc23/eng/20230724
LC record available at https://lccn.loc.gov/2022059400

10 9 8 7 6 5 4 3 2 1

Contents

List of Illustrations   vii

Acknowledgments   ix

Introduction   1

Chapter 1   History of Walking as Artistic Practice   5

Chapter 2   Analyzing Walking Works   21

Chapter 3   Observational Walking   45

Chapter 4   Leading Versus Following   65

Chapter 5   Who Gets to Walk and Where?   89

Chapter 6   Rituals   117

Chapter 7   Place   139

Chapter 8   Activism   155

Chapter 9   Connections to Drawing   175

Chapter 10   Embodiment   191

vi | Contents

Appendix   207

Notes   221

Index   243

Illustrations

Figure 1.1   *The Menhir di Ussano.*   6

Figure 1.2   *Dada Excursion to Saint-Julien-le-Pauvre.*   12

Figure 2.1   Sarah Cullen, *The City as Written by the City*,
             2004–ongoing.   23

Figure 2.2   Map diagram.   24

Figure 2.3   John Schuerman, *Precinct Perimeter*, 2020.   30

Figure 3.1   Fran Crowe, *Walking to Save Some Sea—My 46,000
             Challenge*, 2006–2007.   49

Figure 3.2   *Lickable Cities* by MJ Hunter Brueggemann,
             Vanessa Thomas, Ding Wang.   58

Figure 3.3   Marsad Drâa, *Project Qafila [second stage]*, 2017.   60

Figure 4.1   Camille Turner, *Miss Canadiana Heritage and
             Culture Walking Tour*, 2011.   77

Figure 4.2   Ben Kinsley & Robin Hewlett, *Street with a View*,
             2008.   86

Figure 5.1   Stuart McAdam, *Lines Lost*, 2013–2014.   93

Figure 5.2   JeeYeun Lee, *Walking Detroit*, 2017–2018.   103

Figure 5.3   Nando Messias, *The Sissy's Progress*, 2014.   106

Figure 6.1   Caspar David Friedrich, *Wanderer Above the Sea
             of Fog*, 1817.   119

Figure 6.2a   Explanation for constructing cup-and-rings marks
               and labyrinth.   127

Figure 6.2b   Explanation for constructing double meander.   127

Figure 6.2c   Explanation for constructing Cretan labyrinths.   127

Figure 6.3   Zig Jackson, *Entering Zig's Indian Reservation*, 1997.   135

Figure 7.1   Kate Green, *Watershed Line*, 2021.   146

Figure 7.2   Lucia Monge, *Plantón Móvil*, 2011.   148

Figure 8.1   Gandhi leading the famous 1930 nonviolent
               resistance Salt March.   156

Figure 8.2   Amish Morrell, *On the Land, in the City: Snowshoe
               on Niwa'ah Onega'gaih'ih (The Humber River)*, 2019. 171

Figure 9.1   Anna Campbell, Still from *Saddledrag: Trail*, 2006. 178

Figure 9.2   Barbara Lounder, *Stamp Sticks*, 2007.   186

Figure 10.1   Diane Borsato, *Your Temper, My Weather*, 2013.   196

Figure 10.2   Hiwa K, *Pre-Image (Blind as the Mother Tongue)*,
               2017.   203

Figure 10.3   Martin Kersels, *Tripping photos #1 (A) Beverly
               Center*, 1995.   204

Acknowledgments

This book came together through a lot of care and curiosity over many years. I first encountered the idea of walking as artistic practice in 2008 as a graduate student. I was learning from Rozalinda Borcilă who had subverted a course at the University of South Florida, entitled *Site/Performance*, to focus solely on walking as an activity that organizes our understanding of space. Thinking of myself somewhat narrowly as a performance artist at the time, I signed up for the class hoping to glean guidance in the realm of performance. Delightfully, the course focused very little on performance and much more on the city of Tampa, Florida, as a lab that we used to explore how our environment could be understood, both as individuals and collectively as a community.

Since that time, I have kept an eye out for an opportunity to further indulge in this area of study, which disrupts conventional notions of categorization and is partly why I am drawn to it. When I encountered the open call for class proposals at the Minneapolis College of Art and Design (MCAD) Continuing Education department, I knew it could be my chance to dive back into a subject that has sustained my own practice, something that I was eager to share with others.

The wonderful students who took my three-week workshops at MCAD during the summers of 2019 (in person), 2020 (online), and 2021 (online) were vitally important to the formation of this text. All these students jumped into this topic and the accompanying exercises with impressive enthusiasm, producing beautiful and unexpected work that inspired much of this book. Those workshops were joyful and inspiring, and I hope readers will bring that same spirit of adventure to their interactions with the text.

I'd also like to thank my acquisitions editor Richard Carlin who supported this project from the beginning. Thanks to those who reviewed the proposal, Karen Gergely, Rae Goodwin, and Kevin McKelvey. Special thanks to the MCAD Library staff who ordered many books to support this research, processed interlibrary loans, put books on reserve, or checked out even more for me. This was no small task. Additionally, I'd like to thank everyone who read portions of the book in its draft stages, including Wakáŋyaŋkéwíŋ/Liz Cates, Jen Caruso, Genevieve DeLeon, Laura Schweitz, Vida and Paul McCollam, Janice Mueller, and Keven Mueller. Thank you most of all to Phil McCollam, who spent huge amounts of time on this project, whether it was creating illustrations, researching birth years of artists and scholars online, compiling information on spreadsheets, or reading drafts. The book would not have been possible without him.

Introduction

Walking as artistic practice has been a niche topic with cyclical levels of interest in various art worlds over the past century, with particular interest in the past few decades. Author and artist **Francesco Careri** (1966–) traces early predecessors of artistic walking's history back to the wandering hunters of the Paleolithic period.[1] Such long-lasting interest, from Paleolithic times to the current moment, both inside and outside the various art worlds, makes walking a compelling topic for personal artistic practice, general walking enthusiasts, as well as teaching.

Walking disrupts conventional notions of categorization, which is partly why it is ripe for contemporary art studies, providing a path for walkers, artists, and students of wide-ranging lived experiences, hoping to connect to the larger world where boundary-crossing and critical thinking are necessary for solving the complex problems we all face in the current globalized moment. To this point, throughout this text, issues related to identity and lived experience are highlighted, including my own: I am a cisgendered white woman, and I don't have any disabilities at the moment. I have received artistic training through institutionalized educational spaces, which has brought me to this interest in walking as artistic practice. While I have consulted with other artists and scholars on this book and worked to reduce bias, it is important to be open about my own lived experience for those considering this text. Walking is a complex topic with varying levels of accessibility, and everyone experiences it differently.

As an introduction to walking as artistic practice, this book begins with a history of walking, starting with wandering philosophers and activists, moving on to mid-twentieth-century art movements, and arriving at current day participatory and social practices. Establishing this foundational background will help people better understand the remaining content of the book. Readers then encounter a chapter on analyzing walking works, where they will become more familiar with approaches to documentation and popular conceptual topics used in walking projects. Finally, readers will be introduced to the language used to formally, conceptually, and contextually review these works. That language is then used to describe examples throughout the remaining chapters.

The next chapters walk through various themes that frequently appear in walking as artistic practice, such as observational walking, which pays attention to sensory experience and notions of "the everyday." Issues of leading versus following, as well as who gets to walk and where, bring with them theories of tourism, leisure, surveillance, race, gender, and disability. Further chapters examine rituals and concepts of place, where sub-topics of pilgrimages, parades, labyrinths, notions of home, environmentalism, and urban versus rural spaces all take on new meaning.

Activism has its own chapter where reenactments, performances, attire/props, and demonstrations are all reviewed. There is a chapter on connections to drawing, which highlights relationships to land art, performance, technology, and architecture. Lastly, a chapter focuses on embodiment and the meditative qualities of walking, with which non-artists will likely be most familiar.

There are appendixes providing tips and resources for various documentation approaches in case readers are new to using photography, video, or audio. There are also sample syllabi for structuring classes or workshops, as well as suggested walking readings and resources for seeking out further exercises. Brainstorming tips are included to help new artists come up with ideas. Similarly, community engagement tips are included for those who might be trying socially engaged work for the first time. Additionally, tips for travel-based walking have been added, as walking is frequently included in tourism experiences. Lastly, there is a list of different types of walking to inspire further examination of the field.

Exercises and vocabulary sidebars are included throughout the text to help engage walkers and apply the concepts detailed in the chapters. Artists, writers, and various groups are bolded on first mention in the book, and birth/death dates are included whenever possible to help contextualize the works on a timeline, given that some of the artists and writers are from hundreds of years ago, while others are still living. Indigenous artists and writers have their Native affiliation noted as available. Walking project examples are mentioned in every section, and while most of the examples could be mentioned under several of the sections, specific choices were made to help include as many examples as possible.

After reading this book, walkers should be able to create and discuss new walking works that are meaningful within their own creative practices and contexts, while also referencing the histories and creators who have come before them.

Chapter 1

History of Walking as Artistic Practice

Early Records of Walking

Walking as an artistic practice, or the use of walking in artworks, has a long history, and much of it is not art-specific. However, there are material, scale, and durational similarities between some of these early historical walking practices and contemporary artistic walking projects. For example, scholars such as Francesco Careri (1966–) trace walking history back to the earliest known nomads and wanderers, for whom walking was a way of life. He cites hunter-gatherer or shepherding Indigenous groups across Africa, Asia, South and North America, Australia, and Europe who walked to follow food sources and material sustenance. In selected locations, some nomadic communities, such as the Tuareg of the Saharan regions of North Africa or the Kochi in Afghanistan continue these traditions in the present day.[1] These walking practices can be linked to some contemporary artistic walking projects.

Careri also specifically calls out large-scale stone path markers and their variants, sometimes called menhirs, erected in the Neolithic landscape throughout Egypt, Ancient Greece, and Western Europe (see figure 1.1). The menhirs have widely-debated possible purposes connected to walking, such as "sacred paths, initiations, processions, games, contests, dances, theatrical and musical performances."[2] Careri highlights menhirs as early architectural objects used by nomadic hunters and shepherds—people who relied heavily on walking.[3] Similarly debated in terms of their purpose, ancient labyrinths are also large-scale walking-related built structures in the landscape. Scholars note wide-ranging functionality, from dancing to

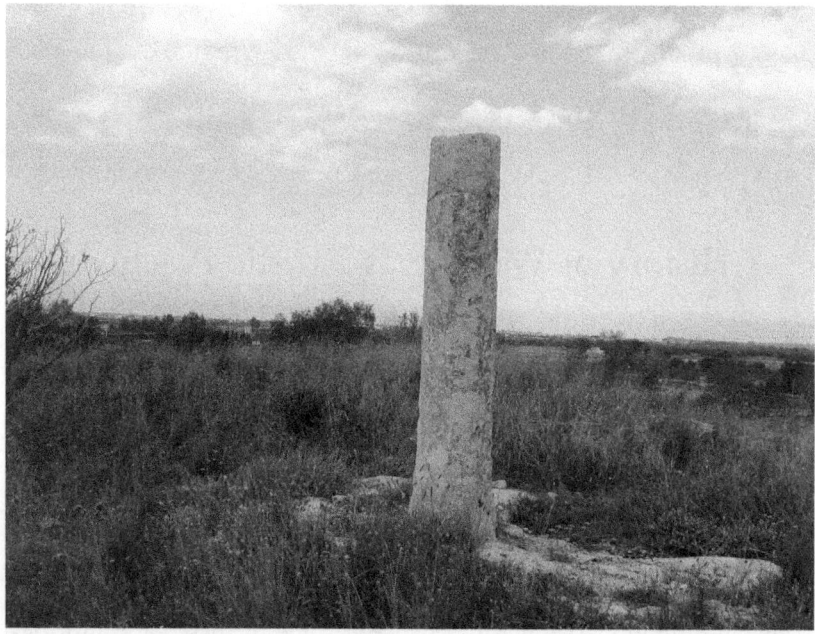

Figure 1.1. *The Menhir di Ussano*, dating back approximately 4000–5000 years, the Menhir di Ussano is located approximately 5 km from the town of Cavallino, Province of Lecce, Italy. *Source*: Wikimedia Commons, public domain.

rituals to religious reflective practices (further discussion of labyrinths in chapter six). The scale and stone materials used with menhirs and selected labyrinths are linked to some current artistic walking practices.

These historical examples might not seem immediately or directly linked to walking as artistic practice, but as one studies the field more deeply, one can spot material, scale, and durational connections between these walking practices and various artistically driven manifestations of walking throughout the twentieth and twenty-first centuries.

EXERCISE: Reflective Preparatory Writing

Why do you walk—what drives you to do so? Is it a need or a want? Where do you typically walk? Where would you like to walk? How do you walk? (fast, slow, etc.) Do you walk alone or with others?

Thinkers and Walking

One might next examine thinkers who used walking to help facilitate reflection. Similar to the early records of walking discussed above, connections to contemporary artistic practice might not seem immediately apparent. However, many current walking projects build on the ideas of thinking, perspective taking, meditating, and reflection as laid out in the historical examples that follow.

To begin, an early example of walking-based thinking is **Aristotle** (384–322 BCE) who founded the Peripatetic school in Athens, where his students would walk as they held their discussions. Moving forward in time, philosopher and Japanese haiku master, **Matsuo Bashō** (1644–1694), similarly had students, however he left them behind to go on a great walking journey near the end of his life. He kept a travelogue, *Oku-no-hosomichi* (*Narrow Road to the Deep North*) (1702), in both poetry and prose. This text covered his five-month 1,200-mile journey in 1689, mostly on foot from Edo (modern-day Tokyo) to the Tohoku region. In one of its most memorable passages, Bashō suggests that "every day is a journey, and the journey itself home."[4] This concept of journeying is a common through line in many contemporary walking works.

From Bashō, one can travel to the eighteenth-century Romantic movement in Europe, a time when poets and philosophers were engaged with walking as a method for thinking and perspective taking. This movement foregrounded solitary experiences in nature as a cure for a corrupt society, and creativity as a unique gift of talented individuals. One of the founders of the Romantic movement was Genevan philosopher **Jean-Jacques Rousseau** (1712–1778), who wrote *Reveries of the Solitary Walker* (1782), which was published shortly after his death. It consists of ten chapters called "walks" containing anecdotes and reflections inspired by his walks on the outskirts of Paris. Additionally, in *Emile* (1762), he writes: "To travel on foot is to travel in the fashion of Thales, Plato, and Pythagoras. I find it hard to understand how a philosopher can bring himself to travel in any other way."

Leaping forward in time a few decades, and moving from France to England, **Samuel Taylor Coleridge** (1772–1834), an influential and controversial figure of English Romanticism, recorded a weeklong solo walking tour in 1802 that followed a circular route including the Cumbrian mountains. He wrote, drew, and mapped the physically strenuous journey in his notebook, which is now kept in the British Library.[5] Variations on writing, drawing, and mapping later become frequently used modes of documentation in contemporary walking works.

Not long after, in 1818 **Dorothy Wordsworth** (1771–1855) wrote an account of recreationally ascending and closely observing Scafell Pike in England. Later her brother, English Romantic poet **William Wordsworth** (1770–1850)—also a friend of Coleridge—used this account (unattributed) in his popular guidebook to the Lake District, which inspired many other countryside explorers. The sister and brother duo lived together for much of their lives, and were committed to daily extensive walks for nearly four decades, which was unusual for women at the time, and opened the door for future women walkers.[6] One such walker was writer **Sarah Stoddart Hazlitt** (1774–1843) who published *Journal of My Trip to Scotland* (1894) after taking two unaccompanied walking trips across the Highlands of Scotland (approximately 170 miles in seven days, and 112 miles in five days) during a particularly stressful time when her husband bullied her into a divorce so he could be with his mistress.[7] Another such walker was the openly-lesbian wealthy landowner diarist **Anne Lister** (1791–1840), who went on to be the first documented woman to ascend Mont Perdu (1830), and later the first documented person to climb Mont Vignemale (1838), both located in the Pyrénées mountains on the border of France and Spain.[8]

A few decades later, **Henry David Thoreau** (1817–1862), the Massachusetts-based naturalist and author of *Walden* (1854), a book reflecting on simple living conditions in a nature setting, also published an essay entitled "Walking" (*The Atlantic*, 1862). In this piece, Thoreau considers "the virtues of immersing oneself in nature and lamented the inevitable encroachment of private ownership upon the wilderness."[9] He was active during the American Romantic Period alongside **Ralph Waldo Emerson** (1803–1882; the owner of Walden Pond) and held transcendentalist beliefs that people and nature are inherently good, while society and its institutions corrupts the purity of the individual. Transcendentalists grew out of English and German Romanticism, among other modes of thought,[10] noting divine experience in the everyday, and believing people are at their best when they are self-reliant and independent. In this way, one can see a clear connection from French Romanticism to English and American interpretations, as well as Romanticism's ongoing ties to walking.

One could next revisit France and examine the concept of flânerie, which was first developed by the poet **Charles Baudelaire** (1821–1867) in his essay "The Painter of Modern Life" (1863). He defines the flâneur as a dilettante observer or dandy moving through Parisian streets, an idle wanderer and a symbol of modernity. The term continues to carry a number of associations, such as stroller, loafer, a man of leisure, the idler, or the urban explorer.[11] One can observe depictions of the flâneur in various impressionist paintings created around the same time, which have led to stereotypes of the flâneur as a melancholy male artist or writer collecting observations for new works. Since then, authors such as **Rebecca Solnit** (1961–) (*Wanderlust: A History of Walking*, 2000) and **Lauren Elkin** (1978–) (*Flâneuse: Women Walk the City*, 2016) have pointed out problematic gender issues surrounding this masculine-centric stereotype.

German Jewish philosopher and cultural critic **Walter Benjamin** (1892–1940) went on to further develop and popularize the idea of the flâneur by connecting it with Marxist ideas of escaping capitalist control. Scholar **Aggie Toppins** (1979–) describes his twist as, "Benjamin saw solitary wandering through the city as a way of exerting one's embodied will or liberating oneself from capitalist control."[12] In Benjamin's unfinished *Arcades Project* (1927–1940), he amassed a collection of writings reflecting on life in Paris in the nineteenth century, with particular focus on the well-known iron-and-glass–covered walkways. He brought focus to the sights, sounds, and smells of the city, which can be at once exciting and overwhelming. By alternating between Benjamin's own flâneur-like reflections, and quotations from widely-varying texts, the form of the text in *Arcades Project* reflects the overwhelming and fragmented quality of sensory overload one might encounter walking in the city.[13]

Much has been said about the flâneur, and in some ways it is like a blank canvas onto which society projects its desires and anxieties. For example, some describe the flâneur as a recreational, contemplative slothful person, or a dawdling observer in the city who has a joy for walking. Others emphasize the obvious aspects of privilege the flâneur must hold, such as sufficient wealth to wander and hang out in cafés all day while watching people work and play. Others emphasize the hedonistic elements, including doing nothing, gossiping, and looking out for manifestations of the unusual or absurd. Some go further and say the flâneur is a conman or a club lounger seeking refuge in the crowd.

EXERCISE: Flânerie

Consider the various interpretations of flânerie. Select one, and let it define a solo walk for yourself. Afterwards, journal your observations and reflections.

While the concept of the flâneur might be the most recognizable and frequently referenced from these walking thinkers, many other philosophers and writers followed and built on the idea of linking bodily movement to contemplation. For example, Virginia Woolf (1882–1941) wrote "Street Haunting" (1930), which "combines urban exploration, early psychogeography and a sense of women's bodies in urban spaces," according to poet Alice Tarbuck.[14]

Another example, **George Santayana** (1863–1952), a Hispanic-American philosopher who taught at Harvard, wrote "The Philosophy of Travel" in the *Virginia Quarterly Review* (1964). In this essay he compared plants and animals, drawing attention to animals' ability to move, when he states, "The roots of vegetables (which Aristotle says are their mouths) attach them fatally to the ground, and they are condemned like leeches to suck up whatever sustenance may flow to them at the particular spot where they happen to be stuck. Close by, perhaps, there may be a richer soil or a more sheltered or sunnier nook but they cannot migrate, nor have even the eyes or imagination by which to picture the enviable neighboring lot." The difference being that animals can move, experience more of the world, and imagine alternatives thanks to their locomotion.[15]

Another thinker who built on these ideas was French Jesuit philosopher and social theorist **Michel de Certeau** (1925–1986) who wrote *The Practice of Everyday Life* (1980), which contains a chapter entitled "Walking in the City." In this essay he elaborates on an analogy between urban systems and language, with improvisational walking (shortcuts, wandering, desire lines, etc.) acting like turns of phrase, inside jokes, or stories. He states, "The act of walking is to the urban system what the speech act is to language or to the statements uttered." He describes the city as "a space of enunciation,"[16] where walkers demonstrate possibilities through their walking choices. He states, "The walking of passers-by offers a series of turns and detours that can be compared to 'turns of phrase' or 'stylistic figures.' There is a rhetoric of walking."

Thinkers and philosophers continue to reflect on walking into the twenty-first century, with landmark works such as Solnit's *Wanderlust: A History of Walking*, which highlights an eclectic collection of intersections between walking, history, culture, and thinking, or more recently, *Wanderlust: Actions, Traces, Journeys 1967–2017* (2017) curated and edited by **Rachel Adams** (1982–), which is an exhibition catalog featuring thoughtful essays and reflections on wide-ranging works. Additionally, artists have been publishing on this topic, from *Walking Art Practice: Reflections on*

Socially Engaged Paths (2018) by **Ernesto Pujol** (1957–) to *Walking's New Movement* (2015) by **Phil Smith** (1956–) to *Prompts for Participatory Walks* (2019) edited by **Todd Shalom** (1976–); all of which take a first-hand experience-based approach to walking as artistic practice.

Through careful examination, one can clearly trace connections from early thinkers who celebrated walking, to contemporary practices of artistic walking, and notice how they are often still intertwined.

Walking and Activism

Another recurring and impactful use of walking throughout history is activism via protest marches, walk-off strikes, fleeing enslavement, and walking occupations. The first recorded labor strike occurred in 1159 BCE under the rule of Ramesses III in Egypt. Tomb-builders had been waiting eighteen days beyond their payday and decided to march toward Deir el-Medina to stage a sit-in near the temple of Thutmose III.[17] Similarly, Ancient Rome saw walk-offs multiple times as they had a small wealthy upper class, a large lower class, and no middle class. In 494 BCE the lower-class workers walked out of the city to Mons Sacer ("sacred mountain") while labor negotiations took place.[18]

Moving forward in time, **Harriet Tubman** (~1820–1913) was an escaped enslaved woman in the United States who led many enslaved people to freedom. After her own escape in 1849, she helped lead many of her relatives and friends to freedom through the Underground Railroad, a network of people offering shelter and aid to help enslaved people in southern states escape to free, northern states and Canada from the early 1800s to 1865. As a conductor on the Underground Railroad, Tubman helped people walk at night to avoid detection, leading them to freedom.

Around the same time in the 1830s and 1840s, the working-class English held protest marches for Chartist movement,[19] putting forth a charter of six demands related to voting rights and political representation. While these marches were unsuccessful at the time, they eventually led to a great deal of governmental reform. Later, further marches led to the voting rights (suffrage) of women in the United States (1920) and England (1928), although it must be mentioned that women's suffrage in the US excluded women of color, who were effectively banned until the Voting Rights Act of 1965. These marches continued across the globe and into recent history, which will be covered in greater detail in chapter eight.

Art Movements

We start to see walking used as a medium for artistic experimentation in the 1920s with the Dada movement, which consisted of a group of artists reacting to the horrors of the first World War (three million people died between 1914 and 1918) with a focus on antagonizing audiences with the absurd and unexpected via anti-art experiences. There was a belief that art reflected life, and in the face of all the deaths from WWI, they aimed to reflect back the nonsensical nature of the war and protest against the oppressive intellectual rigidity of art and life through cynical and ugly art. Their works focused on simultaneity, chance, irrationality, and the nonsensical by rejecting rules and logic.

For example, on April 14, 1921, a group of Dada participants met to go on a mock guided tour at Saint-Julien-le-Pauvre churchyard in Paris (see figure 1.2), a space the organizers deemed to have no reason to exist (per the poster advertisement for the event). On this tour **André Breton** (1896–1966) read a manifesto, and **George Ribemont-Dessaignes** (1884–1974) read arbitrary definitions from a dictionary as keys to mon-

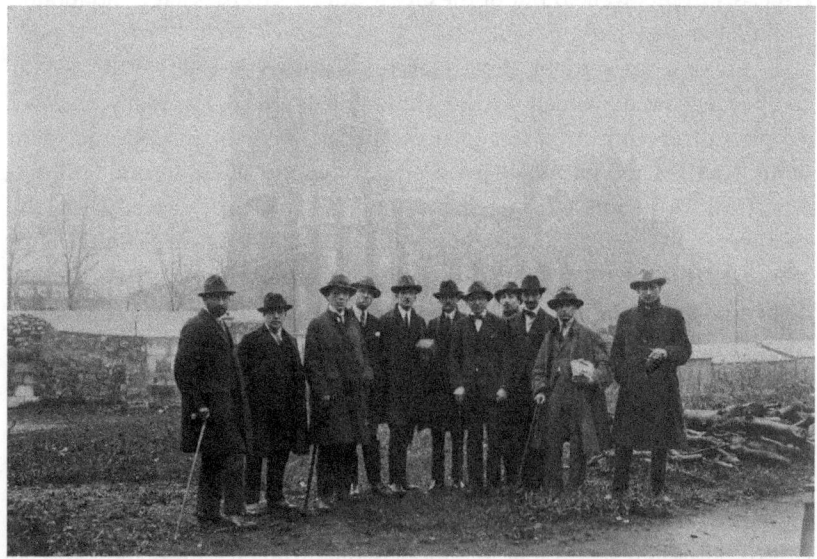

Figure 1.2. *Dada Excursion to Saint-Julien-le-Pauvre*, anonymous photographer, April 14, 1921. *Source*: Public domain.

uments in the churchyard. Other absurdist elements of the event were canceled due to rain. This event was meant to reject art's assigned urban spaces by engaging with a space that was considered banal (the street), and establishing the walk as art, or anti-art.

EXERCISE: Absurdist Tour

Taking inspiration from the Dadaists, think of a place that has no reason to exist (from your point of view). Give an absurdist tour of that place. How do you recruit people to your tour? What are the participants' reactions?

Then in 1924, the Dada movement started to morph into Surrealism, marked by the release of Breton's first Surrealist manifesto. This movement explored the inner workings of the mind, dream states, the irrational, play, chance, collaboration, the poetic, and the revolutionary. Breton went on another walk, this time for ten days in the countryside with three colleagues. Breton described this walking and conversing for many consecutive days as an "exploration between waking life and dream life." Surrealists used the term *deambulation* or *errance* to describe this newly defined disorientation via purposeless undirected wandering. The goal was to unleash the collective unconscious while walking as a small private group, with emphasis on unplanned chance encounters. After returning from the walk, Breton wrote one of the first Surrealist manifestos.[20]

EXERCISE: Chance or Random Principle

Taking inspiration from the Surrealists, gather a small group of walkers, and strive to wander in a purposeless and disoriented fashion, letting chance encounters guide your walk. It could help to pick a random principle to guide your walk (reminder to stay safe). For example, maybe you will only make right turns at each fork in your path, or you determine your path by throwing dice, or you will use a map from a different place to navigate this one.

What is easy and what is hard about this mode of walking? Who might be more or less able to wander in this way? Read more about who gets to walk and where in chapter five.

It is important to acknowledge the Surrealists built on the ideas of Dadaists by taking an interest in outmoded places and objects, or trivial and underappreciated locations by tapping into the unconscious, which we now recognize as riddled with subjective biases. Further, Surrealists were one of the first groups to celebrate following "magnetic" people, specifically prostitutes, in the name of getting lost and disoriented in urban spaces. Undoubtedly, this was an unwelcome approach that lacked the consent of sex workers, and unfortunately was later mimicked by future artists. Through contemporary eyes, we can recognize the problematic nature of this methodology, although at the time it was celebrated as a revolutionary method of chance encounter. Following and consent is covered in more depth in chapter four.

Next, the Situationist International (also known as the Situationists), a revolutionary group of European artists and writers that operated from 1957–1972, took up the act of walking as a way to subvert capitalism. Situationists wanted art without artists or artworks and were fans of the ephemeral. There was support for rejecting representational art and the concept of personal talent, and instead favored the directly lived moment. They aimed to develop objective methods of exploring the city and studying the terrain, which was a failure in some regards because they overlooked subjective personal and societal biases throughout their processes. For example, their own member, **Abdelhafid Khatib**, wrote the article "Attempt at a Psychogeographical Description of Les Halles" (1958), which detailed how he struggled with the restrictions on North Africans walking freely at night, and was arrested twice attempting to do so. In other ways, the Situationists succeeded by innovating with new forms of walking and critically thinking about everyday urban spaces by emotionally disorienting oneself, as detailed below.

Perhaps the most famous Situationist was Marxist group leader **Guy Debord** (1931–1994), who published information about the dérive (some also use the term drifting), describing it as walking as a scientific experiment or tool in urban walking, as opposed to a chance-based operation. The idea of the dérive formed out of the Situationist collective, including member, novelist, and critic **Michèle Bernstein** (1932–) who was an avid drifter, who claimed the dérive "wasn't a hobby, [the SI] wanted to make it a way of life."[21] The Situationists believed the dérive had the potential to be a playful, constructive technique for moving around the city while paying attention to the space's psychological influence, drawing attention to boundaries between public and private, and pointing out commodification, privatization, and security of space. The dérive is a small-group walking exercise,[22] and through this joint experience, the Situationists wanted pedestrians to become more aware of their overlooked urban surroundings and begin to see new possibilities.[23]

EXERCISE: Drawn and Repelled

Considering the critical stance of the dérive and its emphasis on heightening awareness of overlooked surroundings, go for a destination-less exploratory walk and record the ambiances and atmospheres where you feel drawn to certain places and repelled by others. Why might you be experiencing those particular subjective associations, emotions, and behaviors? How did the architecture, topography, and space affect your experience? How does that relate to class, gender, race, ability, and other markers of identity? How could you imagine a better experience of the route you walked?

The Situationists also outlined the theory of psychogeography as a discipline that "could set for itself the study of the precise laws and specific effects of the geographical environment, consciously organized or not, on the emotions and behavior of individuals."[24] Debord emphasized ". . . the evident division of the city into zones of distinct psychic atmospheres; the path of least resistance which is automatically followed in aimless strolls . . . the appealing or repelling character of certain places . . ."[25] While these directives for paying closer attention to one's impulses during walking continue to be useful for individual walking experiences with heightened awareness, they also gloss over a great deal of nuance based on identity and context. For example, to say that any division of the city is "evident" assumes a universal experience of walking in the city, which we know is not the case as noted by Khatib, and we will delve into this idea further during chapter five.

It is important to note that contemporary scholars acknowledge the word psychogeography has taken on many different meanings to different groups of people and may not be the most useful or descriptive term due to its lack of specificity in contemporary practice. Scholar **Merlin Coverley** (1971–) states in the preface to the 2018 edition of his seminal text, *Psychogeography*, that the term has fallen into disfavor and is "overused to the point of exhaustion."[26] **Morag Rose** (1974–) of the Loiterers Resistance Movement goes further, explaining how contemporary walkers have built on the broad term: "Psychogeography has now evolved into a rich and diverse body of art and literature. Psychogeographers use walking in creative ways to explore, experience and map the city."[27]

Around the same time as the Situationists started experimenting with the dérive in the late 1950s, the Japanese avant-garde group Gutai started developing a number of performances and conceptual pieces, with several examining or including walking. Take for instance *Please, walk on here (Kono ue o aruite kudasai)* (1955) by **Shozo Shimamoto** (1928–2013), which consists of a bridge-like structure on the ground. Participants were asked to walk on the structure and sense the structure's instability or imminent collapse as they are walking.

Also in the late 1950s, artist **Allan Kaprow** (1927–2006) was developing the first happenings, which are defined as a call or invitation for artists to abandon hierarchy, exclusion, and sellable object-based practices for limitless investigation of relationships between ideas, acts, or everyday life. These events were a major contribution to the field of performance art in the 1950s and beyond. Happenings did not always include walking, but some did because of the overarching focus on the everyday, which could include an array of ways that people move around (see chapter three for further discussion of the everyday).

Also around this timeframe, an important technological development took place in the mid-1960s—the availability of personal video equipment. This allowed walks to be documented in a new way, beyond photography, drawings, or other previously used archiving methods. Artists played with this new medium in exciting ways that highlighted audio and visual opportunities of repetition, speed, and light, among others. For example, in *Walk with Contrapposto* (1968), artist **Bruce Nauman** (1941–) recorded a sixty-minute black-and-white video of himself walking up and down a narrowly constructed corridor, striking poses with each step, drawing attention to the space via his body.[28]

The 1960s and 1970s saw a huge influx of experimental practices, from conceptual performances to process art, ready-mades, and the joining of art and life. The United States economy was on the rise post-World War II and many members of the European avant-garde had relocated to the US. It is also when Fluxus, Art Povera, and land art developed. Common threads between these experimental movements included elevating active participation over passive spectatorship, and the urge to move art outside the traditional gallery as a means of institutional critique. One example is Fluxus artist **Robert Filliou**'s (1926–1987) hat-based exhibition space, entitled *Galerie Légitime* (1962) in which he walked around predetermined paths and engaged with people, showcasing the artworks that fit in his hat.[29] This work demonstrates active engagement with chance passersby in wide-ranging ways at non-traditional places, all common elements of these experimental practices.

Fluxus, a movement that officially ran 1962–1978, but arguably began in the 1950s and continues today, included a range of creative practices, such as artist multiples, newspapers, newsletters, films, installations, events, concerts, banquets, and manifestos. Experimental composer and music theorist, **John Cage** (1912–1992), was a central influence on much of their work. Key figures in Fluxus included **George Maciunas** (1931–1978), **George Brecht** (1926–2008), **Yoko Ono** (1933–), **Mieko Shiomi** (1938–), **Benjamin Patterson** (1934–2016), and **Nam June Paik** (1932–2006).

Fluxus artists experimented with scores (sets of directions), street theater and impromptu performances, as well as walking tours that involved blindfolds, street sounds, visiting sidewalks and public restrooms, and so on. A simple example of one of their scores is Ono's piece, *City Piece* (1961), which simply states, "Walk all over the city with an empty baby carriage." This set of directions could be completed in wide-ranging ways depending on the location and the person executing it, which is part of the appeal of Fluxus's work. They even had a word for this expectation that something different might happen with each iteration: "implicativeness,"—each new work implies many others.

Implicativeness is one of the twelve criteria for a flux-work, as defined by Fluxus members **Dick Higgins** (1938–1998) and **Ken Friedman** (1949–). The other eleven criteria are globalism, unity of art and life, intermedia, chance, experimentalism, playfulness, simplicity, exemplativism, specificity, presence in time, and musicality.[30] Art critic **Lori Waxman** (1976–) outlines how these twelve criteria help illuminate the ways in which Fluxus was similar to Surrealism. For example, both used poetry as a mode of thought, research as practice, art as process rather than an end, embraced non-specialization and non-professionalization, and a belief in play.[31] These approaches also overlap several of the other experimental practices of the 1960s and 1970s.

Art Povera developed primarily in Italy and used humble, cheap, or reused materials in an effort to free the artist from conventions of the art market and the corporatization of art, while also disavowing singular makers. Perhaps one of the most famous walking pieces from this movement was **Michelangelo Pistoletto**'s (1933–) *Walking Sculpture* (1967), in which Pistoletto rolled a ball made of newspaper down the streets and beckoned for the participation of the whole community, creating an impromptu procession.

Modern dance also underwent profound shifts in the 1960s and 1970s as artists began to incorporate walking and other daily activities into their performances. *Walking on the Wall* (1971) by **Trisha Brown** (1936–2017) was one such work and consisted of her troupe walking on the vertical wall using a system of mounted tracks, ropes, and harnesses. Similarly, *Trio A* (1978) by **Yvonne Rainer** (1934–) was a highly influential solo performance of everyday movements, such as tapping, kneeling, and walking. **Steve Paxton** (1939–) simply sent a group of people to walk across the stage at different intervals in *Satisfying Lover* (1967). All of these artists were founding members of **Judson Dance Theater** (1962–1964), along with **Lucinda Childs** (1940–), and **David Gordon** (1936–2022), and the group was known for its collaborations with visual artists such as **Robert Rauschenberg** (1925–2008) and **Andy Warhol** (1928–1987).

Land art developed out of Minimalism in 1966–1967. Minimalism had an emphasis on clean simple forms that forced the observer to share space with the objects and addressed the presence of the body in time and space. Land art built on these ideas, moving out of traditional art spaces, and involving large-scale interventions in landscapes. A notable bridging moment between Minimalism and land art was **Tony Smith** (1912–1980) giving a December 1966 interview in *Artforum*, where he discussed the idea of a path as both an object and experience. That interview was quickly followed by **Richard Long**'s (1945–) important work, *A Line Made by Walking* (1967), in which he used walking to leave the trace of a line in the grassy landscape. This work was followed by another often-cited *Artforum* article, "A Tour of the Monuments of Passaic, New Jersey" (December 1967), by **Robert Smithson** (1938–1973), who drew further attention to site-specificity and the passage of time via his walk along the river and industrial sites, captured in photographs and written reflection.

From there we see many artists begin to intervene in landscapes such as **Nancy Holt**'s (1938–2014) *Sun Tunnels* (1976), which includes an arrangement of cement tunnels in the desert with strategically placed holes that align with celestial events. The work is not activated until a participant walks into and around the artwork. Similarly, **Jeanne-Claude** (1935–2006) and **Christo**'s (1935–2020) *Wrapped Walk Ways* (1977) (project for Jacob L. Loose Memorial Park, Kansas City, Missouri) directly ties to the concept of walking by simply wrapping sidewalks throughout the park with saffron-colored nylon fabric. Another example of pivotal land art is *Marsh Ruins* (1981) by **Beverly Buchanan** (1940–2015), consisting of three concrete and tabby forms planted in Georgia, near the remote site where a group of enslaved people died by suicide in 1803. The forms were covered in a layer of tabby, an impermanent mixture of sand, water, and lime that was used in the construction of plantations and slave living quarters in the US South. The remote location in the Marshes of Glynn necessitates walking and careful looking to witness them, as the site is unmarked, and the materials are steadily eroding and sinking back into the earth.[32]

In land art, the work includes many things, such as the place itself, the inviting of others, the act of making the journey, the photos, videos, maps, and writings, and so on. We can easily see how walking as artistic practice intersects and grows from land art with its connections to place and process.

Contemporary Practices and Collectives

More recently, walking as artistic practice has intersected with social practices, reenactments, durational works, museum education, and many other contemporary topics and art forms, many of which are explored in more depth in the following chapters. One intersection of particular interest is the trend towards collective organizing and practicing. This trend towards working in groups mirrors and builds upon the approaches of past cohorts, such as Dadaists, Surrealists, Situationists, Gutai Art Group, Fluxus, and others.

For example, the **Walking Artists Network** (2008–) operates an active website for walking artists from across the globe to connect both online and in person. The online platform **walk · listen · create** (2019–) is for walking works and events that intersect with sound, place, and technology. Similarly, more localized place-based collectives have formed, including several in the United Kingdom, such as Manchester-based **Loiterers Resistance Movement** (2006–), *Walking Institute* (2013–) in Huntly, Scotland, and **walkwalkwalk** (2005–2010) in London's East End, to select just a few. Groups in different parts of the world include the female-led **Jalan Gembira** (2016–) in Yogyakarta, Indonesia, **Mother Earth Water Walks** group (2003–2017) headed by Anishinaabe leaders focused on the perimeter of the Great Lakes in North America, and **Walking Lab** (2018–), which emerged in the 2000s with directors based in Canada and Australia plus collaborators from across the world, among many other collectives.

Summary

In this chapter, early records of walking were highlighted to show the long history of walking in relationship to human experience and to point out material, scale, and durational connections between these early walking practices and contemporary artistic projects. Next, thinkers and activism were examined to demonstrate how future artistic walking projects build on this legacy. Finally, walking was traced in relationship to various art movements, including contemporary practices. Throughout the rest of this text, readers will learn about wide-ranging approaches to walking that build on the foundations presented in this chapter.

EXERCISE: Timeline

Using a free online timeline tool (a quick internet search will reveal several options), lay out the events summarized in chapter one to visually understand the scope of walking as artistic practice. Then research three to five more walking works to add to the timeline. Consider working in small groups to make the process more interactive.

Chapter 2

Analyzing Walking Works

To analyze walking works, look to other creative practices with similar features, such as performance or participatory social practices. Walking works are similarly durational or time-based, so viewers or participants might analyze as they take part in a walking work, or they might be looking at documentation of the work. In chapter four there is further discussion of liveness, and in chapter eight there is discussion of reenactments and reprising works. In this chapter, readers will learn about different modes of documenting or archiving work, the vocabulary of the formal elements and principles of design (two-, three-, and four-dimensional), different types of content or meaning, and the importance of context.

Documenting and Archiving Techniques

Artist **Laurie Anderson** (1947–) reflects on her evolving attitude towards documentation in her foreword to the book *Performance: Live Art Since the 60s* (2004),

> I myself used to be very proud that I didn't document my work. I felt that, since much of it was about time and memory, that was the way it should be recorded—in the memories of viewers—with all the inevitable distortions, associations and elaborations. Gradually I changed my mind about making records of events because people would say things like, "I really loved that orange dog you had in that show!" And I've never

had an orange dog ever. I started to keep track of things after
that. I just didn't want it to disappear.

Being a participant or witness to the live event is quite different from
looking at or experiencing documentation or an archive of a work after
the fact (see chapter four for further discussion of liveness). In part, this
difference is because of the wide range of archival practices that an artist
might undertake.

While mapping, photographs, video, and written reflections might
be some of the most common forms of walking documentation, they are
certainly not the only ones. Artists also rely on audio recordings, collected
objects/souvenirs, traces left behind, drawings, sculptures, artist books,
installations, interviews, reprises or reenactments of past works, and more.
Documentation itself can go on to become an artwork separate from, or
shown alongside, the original walking work.

Some artists will show multiple forms of documentation in combination to better convey the experience. For example, Francesco Careri
analyzing Robert Smithson's practice states, "A series of elements (the place,
the journey, the invitation, the article, the photos, the map, the earlier and
subsequent writings) combine to constitute its meaning and, as in all of
Smithson's works, the work itself."[1] This same combined and overlapping
approach can be used to convey the complexity and multifaceted nature
of any walking piece.

Maps and Mapping

One form of archiving that can stand on its own but is also often used in
combination with other forms of documentation is mapping. For example,
Fallen Fruit (2014–), a collaboration between **David Allen Burns** (1970–)
and **Austin Young** (1966–), has an ongoing project entitled *Public Fruit
Maps* (2004–), which consists of visiting neighborhoods and mapping all
the fruit trees that grow over public space. These maps exist not only as
images to display in art settings, but also as functional maps that can be
downloaded from their website and used by people on the streets.

While maps provide visual representation of walking, it is important
to acknowledge that maps in the West are often created as tools of domination, outlining "lands to conquer, divide, sell, and use."[2] Writer **Lucy
Lippard** (1937–) goes into further detail, stating "The 'naturalization' of

maps—the myth that maps show the world the way it really is—veils the fact that maps are cultural and even individual creations that embody points of view. They map only what the authors or their employers want to show; resistance is difficult."[3]

Keeping these communication and domination challenges in mind, maps can also be useful for capturing invisible or intangible qualities. For example, mapping scents (discussed further in chapter three), is a way of capturing the odors of a particular walking path at a particular time of day, during a specific seasonal time. There are also more abstract maps, such as *The City as Written by the City* (2004–) by **Sarah Cullen** (1979–), which are created by a special drawing box carried by hand while walking, via a handle that comes out of the top of the box (see figure 2.1). It allows a pencil to hang just above a piece of paper, so with each footstep, a map of a person's particular gait and pace is recorded through specific marks left behind on the paper. While the maps created this way might be incomprehensible to the untrained eye, study of the maps reveals the uniqueness of each person's walk and patterns between people and paths.

Within mapmaking practices, also known as cartography, there are some recognized elements of a map that help orient the reader (see figure 2.2).

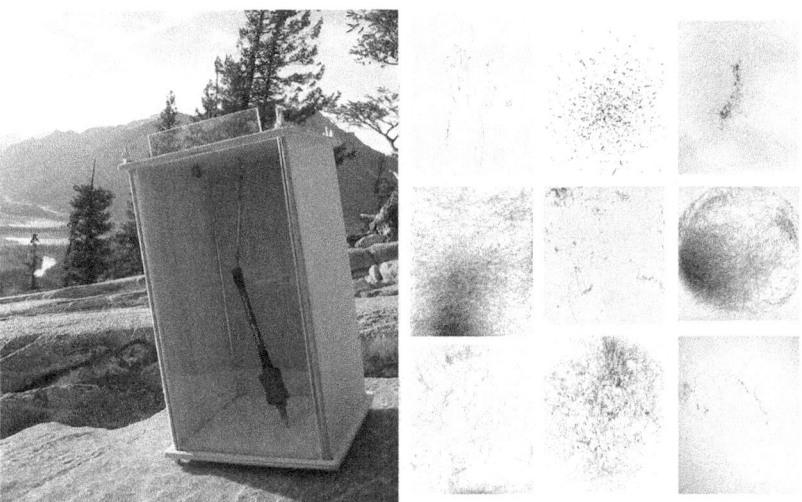

Figure 2.1. Sarah Cullen, *The City as Written by the City*, 2004–ongoing, wood box, hardware, pencil, paper, © Sarah Cullen. *Source*: Courtesy of Sarah Cullen.

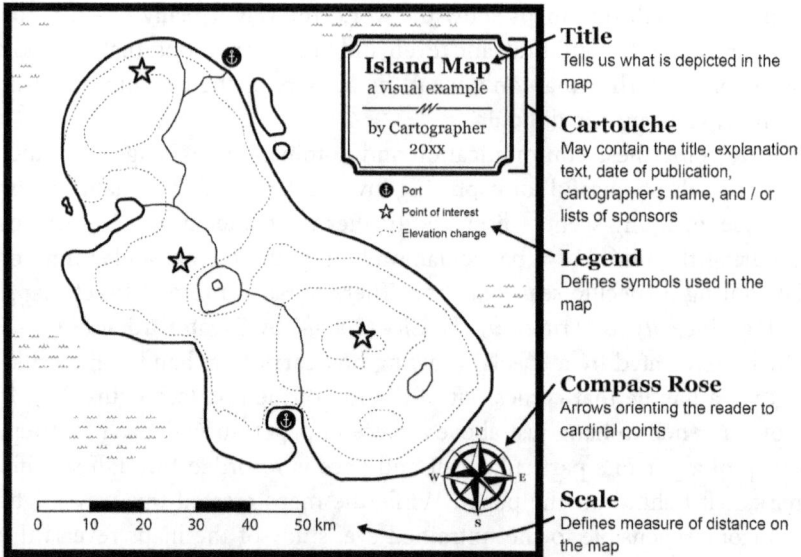

Figure 2.2. Note the most commonly used parts of the map, © Phil McCollam. *Source*: Courtesy of Phil McCollam.

EXERCISE: Draw a Map by Hand

While there are plenty of quick and easy GPS mapping apps available, a hand-drawn map can convey a certain intimacy that might be valuable to some artists depending on their goals and audience.

Think of one of your favorite walks and draw a map from start to finish of the walking path. Include the standard elements of a map. Think about how color, line quality, and shape can convey meaning to the reader.

When it's finished, share it with someone else, and see if they are able to understand and use the map. If there is feedback on how to improve the map, create a second draft with the fixed elements.

Photography

Photography can take the form of photojournalism, capturing key moments, places, and interactions from the walk, or be reconfigured in various ways to act as stand-alone artworks unto themselves. For example, photo documentation of Trisha Brown's *Walking on the Wall* (1971) presents a descriptive view of what occurred during the walking performance, and what it looked like from multiple angles. In this work, Brown used mountaineering equipment to support performers' bodies as they walked perpendicularly to the gallery wall, emphasizing concepts of embodiment and effort towards normalcy. The photographs showcase specifically what happened during the walking event.

In contrast, **Roberley Bell**'s (1955–) *Still Visible After Gezi* (2015) centers photography as the work itself. The photos capture trees the artist encountered on walks through Istanbul in 2010, and then tried to revisit in 2015 after the 2013 Gezi Park protests. In this case, the carefully selected photos are arranged into specific groupings that describe the trees, or their absence, making the photographic arrangements into the work itself, rather than a *document of* live work that occurred in the past. This use of the photo helps emphasize the importance of the memories, as well as their ephemeral nature.

Video / Film

Another frequent form of archiving is video or film, which, similar to photography, can aim to capture and represent live events, or be edited to exist as a piece unto itself. An example of using video to document and represent a live walking work is **Pat Naldi** (1964–) and **Wendy Kirkup**'s (1961–) *Search* (1993), which consists of silent video footage borrowed from a surveillance system, documenting a synchronized walk in the city center of Newcastle-upon-Tyne. The documentary nature of this video is heightened by the fact that it includes time and location stamps across the footage, also a central part of the meaning of this work. Conversely, **Milli Chen**'s (1962–) *Tour* (2014) is a wall-sized video installation showcasing walks across genocide sites that no longer show visual evidence of the atrocities that occurred there. It includes audio of lullabies from the countries represented in the work. While this work includes video documentation of walks, it is the combination of sound, scale, and edited footage that makes the work a unique experience from the initial walks themselves.

Audio

Sounds can be recorded and shared in a wide range of ways, including providing evidence of a walk that has already happened, or act as the artistic medium of a live walking event. To explain, in **Carrie Schneider**'s (1979–) *Hear Our Houston* (2012–2015), members of the public were invited to record audio walking tours of the city. Each recording was hosted on a website for the public to download and listen to while retracing the steps of the amateur tour guide. The audio in this case provides interactive evidence of walks that have already occurred and can take place again with a new participant. In contrast, **Phil Kline**'s (1953–) *Unsilent Night* (1992–) is an annual event in New York City that orchestrates a promenade of people with boomboxes (or anything that amplifies music) playing four different tracks, creating an experimental electronic musical piece. The audio is a central medium of the work, rather than a document of the experience. While video documentation exists, the liveness of the audio walk is embraced and performed in many locations each year; since its inception, the walk has been performed in 101 cities and four continents.

EXERCISE: Walking Soundtrack

Think of all the songs or audio tracks that mention walking or walking-related topics and make a big list. Then curate the list into a selection of tracks that equal approximately thirty minutes. Take the tracks with you on a walk via a mobile device, walking and listening for the full thirty minutes (select a route that is safe for listening to audio). How did each track affect your walking? What did you notice as you walked?

Resources: Check out the walking-related songs collected in Lure of the Lost (2016) by **Anthony Schrag** (1975–).

Written Texts

Many walking artists rely on written words as a way of archiving walks, whether that's through journalistic reflection, graphically designing text for display or distribution, or publishing manifestos, artist's books, or scores (sets of directions) to instigate further works. For example, **Sophie Calle**'s (1953–) *Suite Vénitienne* (1980) included extensive reflection on her experiment of following a man to Venice. This urban expedition also included photography, but the written text contained a great deal of detail that helps the viewer contextualize this walking work. Similarly, **JeeYeun Lee**'s (1971–) *Walking Detroit* (2017–2018) leans on a written recounting of collected walks, in addition to photography, to touch on site-specific issues of memory, identity, architecture, and more.

A different use of written text is the display of carefully graphic-designed words, such as **Hamish Fulton**'s (1946–) *Melting Glacier* (2005), along with many of his other works. Similar to a mural or billboard, he creates large prints or wall-based installations of text related to the walks he went on. **Andrea Carlson** (1979–, Grand Portage Ojibwe) works in a comparable fashion, developing large-scale carefully designed installations and projections featuring Indigenous text in publicly walkable spaces, such as *You Are on Potawatomi Land* (2021–),[4] (see further information in chapter five).

This tie to graphic design can also be found with the common practice of developing walking-themed artist books and zines, which are independent publications often produced in small batches and distributed in non-traditional ways. Examples include *Weird Walk*, described as a multiple-issue journal of wanderings and wonderings out of the British Isles,[5] or international collaborative projects like the zine *Parallel Walking: Between Here and There, Between the Seen and Unseen* (2022), which brought together **Walkspace** (2020–) collective in Birmingham, UK, and the female-led Jalan Gembira walking group in Yogyakarta, Indonesia, for a cultural creative exchange through the act of walking.[6]

Another use of written text is the development of manifestos and scores, which can act as both archival material and pieces unto themselves. A manifesto lays out an archive of particular ideas and beliefs and opens up the possibility of new creations within those guidelines. Similarly, artistic walking scores can be displayed as an artifact of a walk, while also providing directions for future walking experiences. Both the manifesto and the score might be published and displayed in a gallery space, online, or as physical copies. This practice has been common from the earliest artistic walking groups and projects. **Hugo Ball** (1886–1927) published a Dada manifesto in 1916; as mentioned in chapter one, André Breton published a manifesto of Surrealism in 1924; the Situationists published their founding manifesto in 1957; George Maciunas (1931–1978) published a Fluxus manifesto in 1963.

EXERCISE: Manifesto Writing

Find and read three artist manifestos (they don't need to necessarily be related to walking). While there are multiple books of artist manifestos available, many are also searchable online. Next, write your own artist manifesto in relation to walking. Think of a who, what, where, why, when, and how format in relationship to your ideas about walking and art. Compare and contrast your walking manifesto with someone else's walking manifesto.

Online Presence

A popular mode of sharing a walking piece is through an online presence, whether that is a website, blog, or social media profile. These sites of interaction expose the project to a much wider audience and also act as an archive for the project. The informal setting of an online presence allows the documentation to represent what happened, while also inviting others to try reprising the work or similar walking approaches themselves (chapter eight has more information about reprises and reenactments).

This online presence approach is particularly popular for walking collectives, such as the Walking Artists Network, **Global Performance Art Walks,** The Loiterers Resistance Movement, and many others because an online presence is available wherever an internet connection exists. Additionally, it is easy to embed or link to online maps, participatory maps, videos, photo galleries, and descriptive texts via an online presence, which makes walking works more available to others. Further, online discussion is available in these spaces, connecting people from all over the world and disseminating ideas to anyone seeking access to them.

One example is *One Block Radius* (2004) by **Glowlab (Christina Ray** and **Dave Mandl** [1959–]), which was a website documenting the block on which the New Museum was built in New York City. This site archived reflections from city workers, children, street performers, and an architectural historian using videos, blogs, field recordings, and interviews. The site was divided into three categories: observation, interaction, and response. This project also highlights the challenges of maintaining online presences in a long-term way. Website URLs can expire, social media sites can shut down, institutions hosting projects can close, and so on. Even though this work was associated with a well-known institution, the New Museum, it was never fully archived on the New Museum's site (or if it was, it is not publicly available), and it disappeared from public view after the project's independent domain expired. Sadly, the Internet Archive also did not collect any data or snapshots of their website, so one cannot even look back at a skeletal version of the site or the exact date it disappeared. The project is gone, aside from some writings that mention an overview of the work. Not all projects need to or should exist forever, but it is important to be aware of these potential limitations and consider them during the process of making informed archival choices.

Sculptures and Objects

Objects and sculptures are also popular ways to document walking works. Some of these three-dimensional pieces exist in traditional gallery settings on pedestals, while others are participatory works, or items collected from the act of walking. For instance, **Brian Thompson**'s (1950–) *Sun Gate at Machu Picchu* (2012) takes the form of a traditional sculpture made from gilded oak wood; however, the form is derived from maps, which are traced and cut in a tapering pattern to create the precious looking object for consideration. In contrast, *Piedra que cede (Yielding Stone)* (1992) by **Gabriel Orozco** (1962–) features a Plasticine ball equal to the artist's weight, which was rolled in the street, collecting imprints and detritus from the participatory journey. This object does not have nearly the same precious quality as Thompson's work due to the surface quality and scale, but is still a sculptural object representing an archive of physical marks from a walk. Lastly, some sculptural objects are made specifically for interaction, such as **Krzysztof Wodiczko**'s (1943–) *Alien Staff* (1993–1994). This work is a form of portable public address equipment for immigrants, which didn't become fully activated as a work until it was taken to streets and used to communicate in unfamiliar cultural environments with unfamiliar languages.

Installation

Another common approach to archiving any walk is to create an installation, which can be located in any number of locations. A traditional gallery-based installation focused on walking is *Live-Taped Video Corridor* (1970) by Bruce Nauman (1941–). This constructed space consisted of two walls forming a narrow corridor with two monitors at the end of the arrangement. As participants would walk down the corridor, one monitor showed the participant from behind growing smaller as they approached, while the other one did not show the participant at all, creating an eerie or unsettling effect throughout the walk into the installation. In comparison, other walking installations might take place outdoors, such as *The Gates* (1979–2005) by Jeanne-Claude and Christo, which consisted of 7,503 fabric panels hanging from sixteen-foot-tall orange gates throughout New York City's Central Park. Regardless of location, installations can be an immersive means of engaging participants in a walking work.

Drawing and Painting

Sketching along the walking path, or afterwards, has been a human impulse going back hundreds of years. Take artist **Gao Qipei** (1660–1734), known for painting landscapes, animals, and people using his fingers and nails rather than a brush, or **Utagawa Hiroshige** (1797–1858) who created *The Fifty-Three Stations of the Tōkaidō* (1833–1834) as a series of woodcut prints reflecting on the eastern sea highway linking Edo (present-day Tokyo) and Kyoto in Japan. Representational oil painters such as **Gustave Caillebotte** (1848–1894) have captured moments of urban walking, as in *Paris Street; Rainy Day* (1877). In contemporary walking practice, drawing and painting can be broadly interpreted to be anything from journal sketches, like *Precinct Perimeter* (2020) by **John Schuerman** (1961–), a series of drawings made in response to the murder of George Floyd (see figure 2.3), to abstract paintings, like those from **Brendan Stuart Burns** (1963–), created in response to his walking experiences along the Pembrokshire coast. Other drawing approaches range from GPS map-based

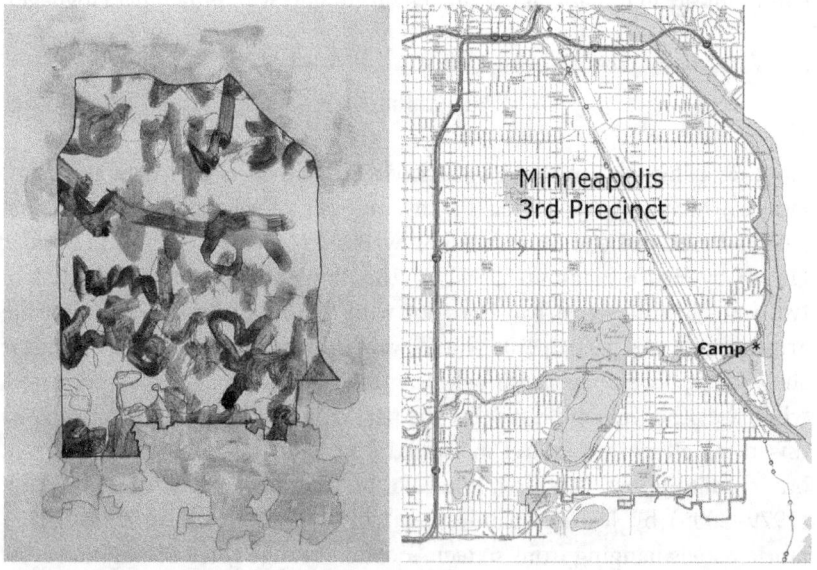

Figure 2.3. John Schuerman, *Precinct Perimeter*, July 23, 2020, Left: drawing with arsonist ashes and ink on paper. Right: Map of walking route, © John Schuerman. *Source*: Courtesy of John Schuerman.

EXERCISE: Direct Experience Versus Observed Experience

This exercise requires a group of people. Divide the group in half. The first half will execute a walking exercise and document and write about the experience, while the second half will document and write about their works as observers. Afterwards, compare and contrast the documentation and written reflections from the participants versus the observers. How are they similar? How are they different? What might this tell us about direct experience versus observed experience?

drawings to traces left on the landscape, and everything in between. Read more on the body as a drawing instrument in chapter nine.

Form, Content, Context

To take in and analyze different forms of walking as artistic practice, one needs to understand the language of form, content, and context. Once a person understands this vocabulary of formal, conceptual, and contextual analysis, they can clearly and concisely articulate their views as participants or observers during and after a walking work.

FORM

To begin, analysis of form is the examination of the sensory experience of a work. As mentioned above, this could describe a live participatory experience, or examination of documentation of an event that has already occurred. Thus, one might encounter two-, three-, or four-dimensional (time-based) experiences. Each of these dimensions has some specific elements and principles.

Two Dimensions

Two-dimensional work generally refers to drawings, maps, prints, paintings, and other items that consist mainly of height and width. These could be presented vertically on the wall or hanging from a structure, or presented horizontally on shelves, pedestals, the ground, and so on. This chart outlines elements and principles viewers can recognize in two-dimensional work.

Elements of Two-Dimensional Work	
Line	A line is the path of a point, or the connection between two points. Lines can be made on their own, or they can be created where two shapes meet. There is also "implied line," where a line doesn't really exist, but appears to be present.
Shape / Space	Shape is a perceivable area (think silhouette). Shapes can be created by lines or by color or value changes that define edges. The shape itself is the positive space, and the space around the shape is the negative space.
Value / Tone	Value or tone is the relative lightness or darkness of an area.
Texture	Texture is the perceived look, feel, or quality of a surface. Texture can be actual (tactile) or implied.
Color	Human perception of different wavelengths of visible light; component parts include hue (the name of the color; example: blue), saturation (purity or intensity of the color), and value (relative lightness or darkness of the color).
Principles of Two-Dimensional Work	
Balance	Balance is the equalizing of the visual weight of elements. There are three types of balance: symmetrical (one half mirrors the other), asymmetrical (dissimilar items balance each other out), and radial (elements are spread out circularly from a central point).
Repetition / Rhythm	Repetition is a repeating visual element (line, shape, pattern, texture, movement), and rhythm is its flowing and regular occurrence. Both repetition and rhythm are often found in patterns.
Focus / Emphasis	The focus or emphasis is the object or element that first catches our attention. Contrast in elements is one of the most common ways to create focus.
Unity / Harmony	Unity or harmony is the visually satisfying effect of combining similar, related elements to create a sense of oneness, wholeness, or order in a work of art.
Scale / Proportion	Scale is the overall size of something. Proportion is the relative size of objects within a work. For example, a caricature exaggerates the proportion of one or more facial features.
Contrast	Contrast is the relative difference between elements. Bright vs. dark; heavy vs. light; rough vs. soft; etc. The greater the difference between light and dark areas, the more attention the area attracts.
Movement / Hierarchy	Movement is the visual path our eye follows. Hierarchy is a manipulation of elements to create movement through a work.

To demonstrate how one might apply these elements and principles, here is a sample formal analysis of *All GPS Traces in Berlin in 2011–2012* (2012), an artwork by **plan b** (**Sophia New** [1974–] and **Daniel Belasco Rogers** [1966–]):

This two-dimensional work is laser engraved on acrylic and has stark contrast between the black lines and the white background. There are not many other values than black and white. The lines move in and out of a central area with loose radial symmetry. The density of the lines towards the middle creates focus with the color contrast. There is repetition of various shapes, though they are all different scales.

EXERCISE: Two-Dimensional Formal Analysis

Find a walking work that has two-dimensional documentation or archiving. Write a three-sentence formal analysis of the work using at least five vocabulary words from the elements and principles of two-dimensional design.

Three Dimensions

Three-dimensional work generally refers to sculptures, collected objects or souvenirs, installations, and other items that consist mainly of height, width, and depth. These could be presented in any number of arrangements. This chart outlines elements and principles viewers can recognize in three-dimensional work.

Elements of Three-Dimensional Work	
Space	A continuous area or expanse surrounding or enclosed by mass (holes and cavities).
Form / Mass	An enclosed volume or three-dimensional body of matter making up the area of an object.
Line	A line is the path of a point, or the connection between two points. Lines can be made on their own, or they can be created where two shapes meet. There is also "implied line," where a line doesn't really exist, but appears to be present.
Plane	A flat surface.
Texture	Texture is the perceived look, feel, or quality of a surface. Texture can be actual (tactile) or implied.

continued on next page

Elements of Three-Dimensional Work (continued)	
Color	Human perception of different wavelengths of visible light; component parts include hue (the name of the color; example: blue), saturation (purity or intensity of the color), value (relative lightness or darkness of the color).
Light / Value	The relative lightness or darkness of an area. Light and value help provide a sense of space and depth around an object. Light sources can be ambient (circumstantial daylight), or specific/task oriented (spotlights, accent lights, key/back/fill lights). Light can also be reflected or diffused to control brightness.
Principles of Three-Dimensional Work	
Balance	Balance is the equalizing of the visual weight of elements. There are three types of balance: symmetrical (one half mirrors the other), asymmetrical (dissimilar items balance each other out), and radial (elements are spread out circularly from a central point).
Repetition / Rhythm	Repetition is a repeating visual element (line, shape, pattern, texture, movement), and rhythm is its flowing and regular occurrence. Both repetition and rhythm are often found in patterns.
Focus / Emphasis	The focus or emphasis is the object or element which first catches our attention. Contrast in elements is one of the most common ways to create focus.
Unity / Harmony	Unity or harmony is the visually satisfying effect of combining similar, related elements to create a sense of oneness, wholeness, or order in a work of art.
Scale / Proportion	Scale is the overall size of something. Proportion is the relative size of objects within a work. For example, a caricature exaggerates the proportion of one or more facial features, while installations in sculpture gardens often have a very large scale.
Contrast / Variety	Contrast is the relative difference between two or more elements. Variety is the relative diversity and change throughout a piece.
Movement / Hierarchy	Movement is the visual path our eye follows. Hierarchy is a manipulation of elements to create movement through a work.

To demonstrate how one might apply these elements and principles, here is a sample formal analysis of *Missa* (1992), an artwork by **Dominique Blain** (1957–):

This three-dimensional work features repetition as 100 pairs of army boots hang from a ceiling grid via monofilament, creating a hovering plane in space. The shoes hover just above the floor, creating tension in the space between the shoes' soles and the surface of the floor. There is implied movement as each pair of shoes is arranged as if it is marching. The regular placement in a grid creates a strong sense of uniformity—no one pair of shoes stands out, and instead the emphasis is on the sameness. The shiny texture of the shoes stands out under the bright lights of the gallery.

EXERCISE: Three-Dimensional Formal Analysis

Find a walking work that has three-dimensional documentation or archiving. Write a three-sentence formal analysis of the work using at least five vocabulary words from the elements and principles of three-dimensional design.

Four Dimensions

Four-dimensional work is time-based or durational. Four-dimensional work generally refers to experiential or participatory work, video or screen-based work, sound works, socially engaged installations, and other items that take place over time. This chart outlines elements and principles viewers can recognize in four-dimensional work.

Elements of Four-Dimensional Work	
Time	The progression of events and existence from the past, through the present, and into the future. Categories of time include measured, experienced, edited, running, biological, linear, non-linear, and digital among others. Time of day and seasonal time can affect smells, light, and sounds.
Architecture / Topography	Architecture consists of buildings or structures. Topography consists of the relief features or surface configuration of an area.
Shape	The outline of a form. Shape in four-dimensional works is most common in relationship to architecture, topography, light, and movement. Shape can be organic (rounded or soft), geometric (linear/ angular), or a combination.

continued on next page

Elements of Four-Dimensional Work (continued)	
Space	A continuous area or expanse within which a work can take place. Four-dimensional space can be digital (screen-based) or analog (in relationship to environment, architecture, or topography). Positive space is a form, or area of focus, within a larger environment. Negative space is the area surrounding the form or area of focus. Space can also be described with various atmospheric air qualities such as temperature, humidity, or pressure.
Color	Human perception of different wavelengths of visible light; component parts include hue (the name of the color; example: blue), saturation (purity or intensity of the color), value (relative lightness or darkness of the color). Light can also have different colors or temperatures (cool versus warm).
Light	A form of radiant energy that reflects off the world around us and into our eyes, allowing us to see our environment and color. Light sources can be ambient (circumstantial daylight), or specific/task oriented (spotlights, accent lights, key/back/fill lights). Light can also be reflected or diffused to control brightness. Shadows, projections, and silhouettes also utilize light.
Movement	A shift or variation in the location of an object, light, or sound. Stillness is movement's opposite. Gestures or isolations are movements by a part of a whole.
Sound	Vibration that can be perceived by the ear. Its opposite is silence. Sound has three basic parts: an attack (onset, growth, birth), sustain (steady-state, duration, life), and decay (fall-off, termination, death).
Smell	The detection of airborne molecules by the olfactory cleft located on the roof of the nasal cavity. Smells are described with and affected by the principles of intensity, direction, causality, duration, juxtaposition, spatial relationships, atmospheric qualities, and transitions.
Taste	The detection of molecules dissolved in liquid via taste buds across the surface of the tongue, roof of mouth, and back of throat. Taste has five basic types: sweet, salty, sour, bitter, and umami or savory.

Principles of Four-Dimensional Work	
Value / Brightness	The relative lightness or darkness of an area as caused by a light source. Low-key environments with little light have a different sense of brightness than high-key environments with a great deal of existing light.
Balance	Balance is the equalizing of the visual weight of elements, and is often referenced in relation to movement, sound, light, architecture, topography, space, and time. There are three types of balance: symmetrical (one half mirrors the other), asymmetrical (dissimilar items balance each other out), and radial (elements are spread out circularly from a central point).
Contrast / Variety	Contrast is the relative difference between two or more elements or stimuli. Variety is the relative diversity and change throughout a piece.
Direction / Reflection	The course along which light, sound, or movement moves. For example, light has specific names for directional lighting, such as side-light, back-light, down-light, and up-light. Direction can also apply to touch (feeling the direction of wind), smell, or sound (identifying the source).
Repetition / Rhythm	Repetition is a repeating visual element (line, shape, pattern, texture, movement), and rhythm is its flowing and regular occurrence. Looping is a specific type of continuous repetition in time-based work. In chapter ten, the rhythm of walking is analyzed as an aid to thinking.
Scale / Proportion	Scale is the overall size of something. Proportion is the relative size of objects within a work. For example, a caricature exaggerates the proportion of one or more facial features, while installations in sculpture gardens often have a very large scale.
Causality	Everything has a cause and effect. This principle is especially important in narrative works. Causality is also central to smell, taste, touch, and sound, which all have sources that cause these sensations.
Duration	The length of time something continues or exists.
Energy Dynamics / Intensity	The amount and type of energy felt by the viewer or participant at any given moment. Intensity can also apply to scent and taste.

continued on next page

Principles of Four-Dimensional Work (continued)	
Interactivity	The exchange of information between two or more entities; influencing or having an effect on each other. There are several categories of interactivity, such as cognitive, social, contextual, participant-centered, creator-centered, activity-centered, and system-centered.
Musicality	The characteristic parts or principles of music and sound. Every sound has pitch (the frequency of a sound vibration), tone (the quality of a sound vibration), and amplitude (loudness, volume in decibels). Musical sounds also have timbre (quality), melody (procession of tones that create a tune), and harmonics (selection of tones played simultaneously to create a chord).
Simultaneity / Juxtaposition	Simultaneity describes two or more things happening at the same time. Juxtaposition describes the comparison of two or more possibly contrasting elements or subjects to create new meaning.
Spatial Relationships	Relative locational ideas such as high, middle, low, far, and near. Additional relationships include interlocking, adjacent, clustered, gridded, among others. In film and video, there are special terms such as background, middle ground, and foreground, as well as a variety of different framing shots.
Atmospheric Qualities	Ways the air around a human can be altered, such as temperature, humidity, or pressure.
Tempo / Speed	The rate at which time, sound, light, or movement passes. Common terms include slow, fast, accelerate (speed up), and decelerate (slow down). In chapter ten, pace of walking is analyzed as an aid to thinking.
Transitions	Move participants from one energy dynamic to another, allowing for change and development over the course of a work.

To demonstrate how one might apply these elements and principles, here is a sample formal analysis of *Violin Phase from Fase: Four Movements to the Music of Steve Reich* (1982), an performance by **Anne Teresa De Keersmaeker** (1960–):

This four-dimensional work features a single person moving repetitively and rhythmically through space on a sandy topography, leaving traces of a circular shape divided into eight slices. The duration is sixteen minutes and includes minimalist music accompaniment. The work is not very interactive, as the audience watches the work unfold, although the energy intensity is high as the performer moves throughout the space and spins repeatedly. The use of light is simple, with the circular area and performer illuminated evenly, and the audience remains darker.

EXERCISE: Four-Dimensional Formal Analysis

Find a walking work that has four-dimensional documentation, archiving, or participation. Write a three-sentence formal analysis of the work using at least five vocabulary words from the elements and principles of four-dimensional design.

CONTENT

Content analysis is the examination of the meaning, message, or concept the artist intends to communicate, or that others infer from the work. Direct participants in the work might have a different impression of the content than others who review documentation afterwards. In some cases, the documentation is the only opportunity to engage with the work, especially if the work was made by the artist alone.

There are three types of content: physical, emotional, and intellectual. Physical content affects the body and biological functions. For example, if you are engaged in a walking work, and much of the activity is headed uphill, participants will experience increased physical challenge. Emotional content causes an emotional reaction in the participant. For example, if a walking work takes place on the shoulder of a highway and cars are flying by, it might cause participants to feel anxious or scared of being hit by a vehicle because it is not a safe space for unprotected bodies. Intellectual content engages the thought process. For example, in *A Common Third* (2010) by **Simon Pope** (1966–), he invited guests to walk with him to places neither of them were familiar with. This situation required both Pope and the guest to make spontaneous decisions and negotiate their route together, thereby engaging intellectually.

Context

Lastly, contextual analysis is the examination of the set of factors surrounding the creation and display of a walking work. This could include place, identity (positionality), power relationships related to privilege and difference, and history among other factors.

Place

Place is a key part of context because of its cultural, political, and geographic associations as well as its histories. In fact, the entirety of chapter seven focuses on the concept of place because it has such a profound role to play in walking works. Place could refer to either where the work was created, or where it is later displayed or experienced. For example, when **Milan Knížák** (1940–) and critic **Jindřich Chaulupecký** (1910–1990) hosted several Fluxus artists from democratically free countries to perform their scores in 1966 communist Prague, the works had a very different effect and meaning than they would have in other contexts. An example of one of those works is Knížák's *Walking Event* (1965), which stated,

> On a busy city avenue, draw a circle about
> 3m in diameter with chalk on the
> sidewalk. Walk around the circle as long as
> possible without stopping.

In Prague at that time, society was policed at all hours, organizing an unofficial public gathering was not allowed, and not following rules of conduct could result in jail time. This work would be received very differently in a country with fewer social restrictions. In this way, the sociopolitical element of place is very important to the context of a work.[7]

Identity

Identity (sometimes also called positionality) includes elements that affect how we receive and process information, such as class, race, gender, sexuality, age, ability, appearance, nationality, language spoken, religion, and so on. Some elements of identity provide people with privileges or can result in oppressive treatment. Here, we are talking about privilege as an unearned advantage, right, or perk that is not available to everyone, but only a specific group. Identity/positionality take into account the attributes of both the maker and participants. Artists decide how much of their identity to publicly share and when; this can be a tricky balancing act.

Vocabulary: Identity and Positionality

One's identity and positionality can have a profound effect on how a walking work is developed and interpreted because it affects where and when a person can walk (see chapter five). There are many elements of identity and positionality, and these are just a small selection.

- **Privilege:** an unearned advantage, right, or perk that is not available to everyone, but only a specific group; to be privileged is to be advantaged.

- **Class:** sorting people by perceived status (social and economic).

- **Race:** "a group sharing some outward physical characteristics and some commonalities of culture and history."[8]

- **Ethnicity:** "your nationality, heritage, culture, ancestry, and upbringing . . . something you acquire based on where your family is from and the group which you share cultural, traditional, and familial bonds and experiences with."[9]

- **Gender:** a social construct based on cultural norms, behaviors, and psychological traits or roles typically associated with one sex; gender varies and evolves across societies and over time, and is generally categorized as male, female, or nonbinary; see also vocabulary listed in chapter five.

- **Sexuality or sexual orientation:** "refers to the enduring physical, romantic and/or emotional attraction to members of the same and/or other genders, including lesbian, gay, bisexual and straight orientations"[10]; see also vocabulary listed in chapter five.

- **Disability:** "a physical, mental, cognitive, or developmental condition that impairs, interferes with, or limits a person's ability to engage in certain tasks or actions or participate in typical daily activities and interactions."[11] However, disabled people have adapted, added onto, or otherwise defined the term to suit their lived experiences. See also vocabulary listed in chapter five.

- **Citizenship:** status of being "a native or naturalized person who owes allegiance to a government and is entitled to protection from it."[12] This is different from **nationality**, which refers to where a person was born. See also vocabulary listed in chapter five.

Power Relationships

Contextual analysis also includes consideration of power relationships. For example, where is the work available? Is it available beyond traditional art galleries, museums, and other established institutions, or is it aimed at predominantly upper class and educated audiences? Additionally, has any form of cultural appropriation taken place? If yes, does it consider and call out historical power relationships?

History

Contextual analysis also looks into the art and design history that has led to this work. It considers who has been previously working this way, and how these ideas and approaches have developed over time.

Not all of these elements will always be present in a walking work—they might be mixed and matched, and there are likely other contextual elements that could be brought forward. Also, context is not static. The artist changes, the work changes, where it is presented changes, and all of these factors shift the contextual analysis.

To demonstrate how one might apply contextual analysis, consider *Slave Rebellion Reenactment* (2019) by **Dread Scott** (1965–):

This work's context is closely tied to place because it showcases the reenactment of the German Coast Uprising of 1811, which took place in the river parishes just outside New Orleans, a very specific location. Additionally, identity is inextricably linked to this work's context because it is centered on a group of enslaved people who are predominantly Black. Further, power relationships are key here because the enslaved people were fighting for both their own freedom and the end of slavery as a whole. Additionally, the reenactment took place in public (outside of established art institutions). Lastly, this work calls on the ongoing history of artists engaging with reenacting, activism, and protest.

Critique Guide

Use this helpful set of reminders when critiquing a walking artwork. If you address these three components for any walking piece you are analyzing, even if it's just one or two details per component, you will be able to engage in conversation and analysis.

1. Form (elements/principles as appropriate for 2D, 3D, 4D)

2. Content (physical, emotional, intellectual)

3. Context (place, identity/positionality, inherent power relationships, and history)

Summary

In this chapter, various forms of documenting walks were covered, including mapping, photography, video, audio, writing, online presences, sculpture, and installation. Exercises for practicing these approaches were included. By examining a range of documentation approaches, artists are provided with more choices for creating new works. Additionally, analysis guidelines were covered, with attention to form, content, and context. These key words and definitions will help walking artists to more deeply examine their work, and the work of others, by pushing them to analyze beyond their first impulses. Readers are encouraged to use the critique guide to examine walking works and ensure all formal, contextual, and content elements are addressed.

Chapter 3

Observational Walking

One of the most common and accessible modes of walking as artistic practice is observational walking, or paying attention to one's sensory experiences, including seeing, hearing, feeling, smelling, and tasting. Architect and researcher Francesco Careri describes walking in terms of observation when he states it is ". . . simultaneously an act of perception and creativity, of reading and writing the territory . . ." Observational walking is open and adaptable to many people, in one form or another, regardless of which senses they have access to, or how the terrain is crossed (further discussion of disability and walking is available in chapter five).

Practitioners have been leaning on observational methods since the earliest records of walking. It's clear that heightened observation was, and continues to be, a popular way to process and share the act of walking, from Matsuo Bashō's closely observed walking haikus ("Listen! a frog / Jumping into the stillness / Of an ancient pond!" *Spring Days*, 1686)[1]; to Dorothy Wordsworth's visual observations of ascending Scafell Pike in 1818 (". . . hardly a cushion of moss, & that was parched & brown; and only growing rarely between the huge blocks & stones which cover the summit . . ."); to the walking/running work by **Lenka Clayton** (1977–), *The Distance I Can Be From My Son* (2013), in which she records on video how far she is able to allow her young son to venture from her before she feels the need to chase after him.

EXERCISE: Observational Portrait of a Neighborhood

This is a group walking exercise due to the length of the line and the need for multiple portraits to create a group of work to analyze.

1. Take a moment to draw a straight line approximately ½ mile long (.8 km) on a map of your neighborhood.

2. Walk along that line and make note of five everyday things, people, or experiences.

3. Create a portrait of this everyday experience in any media you like (drawing, audio, video, photo, etc.).

4. Post everyone's neighborhood portraits as a group and analyze similarities and differences.

This exercise is inspired by *Composition 1960 #10* by **La Monte Young** (1935–), which simply states, "Draw a straight line and follow it."

Observation is also central to several of the art historical movements mentioned in chapter one. For example, flânerie is simply defined as the act of a solo urban walker who observes and explores, paying attention to the sights, sounds, and smells of the city. The dérive is similarly urban and observation-based but is completed in small groups "guided by the attractions of the terrain and the encounters they find there."[2] Fluxus scores often combine a sense of play with close observation, as in *#185* (date unknown) by **Bob Lens** (1939–), "Wind materials you find / Around objects you find on a walk / Leave them along your path."

Contemporary art walking tours also rely heavily on guided observation. Take for example, **Pamela Z's** (1956–) *Site Reading* (2011) in which she asks a group of walkers to look carefully at the skyline and use the heights of buildings as a way to interpret vocal pitch as they spend four minutes completing one 360-degree rotation of their body, creating an experimental musical piece of vocal intonation. Through close observation, the group is interpreting and playing the neighborhood[3], experimenting with volume, musicality, energy dynamics, spatial relationships, and interactivity.

To get a better sense of the breadth of observational walking, this chapter will examine examples of walking that engage with each of the senses and look at some of the more frequently referenced concepts that intersect with observational walking.

The Senses

Historically in Western European settings, five senses have been most recognized: sight, sound, touch, taste, and smell. However, scientists recognize several other sensitivities, including senses of balance, directional spatial sense (also known as cognitive mapping)[4], proprioception (awareness of the body in space, such as the hip, knee, and ankle joints while walking)[5], various body regulation senses (body temperature, carbon-dioxide content in the blood, etc.), echo-location, and more.[6] Additionally, some people experience a phenomenon called synesthesia, in which a person experiences one type of sensation through a different one. For example, a person might read the word "shoe" and taste lemons, or they might see letters and numbers in specific colors.

To narrow the field, we will focus on the previously mentioned five senses. At first glance, the five senses might seem straightforward, but like any other part of contemporary life, they are intertwined with systems of privilege and difference based on complex histories and ways of living. For example, scholar **Victoria Henshaw** (1971–2014) pointed out that since Greek and Roman times, sight or sound have been considered the most valuable sensory experiences in Western cultures.[7]

We will examine all five senses below and pay special attention to how each one can enhance observational walking practices, how the senses affect one another, and how they are related to larger social systems. It is also important to keep in mind that emphasizing certain sensory experiences can unintentionally create barriers for some participants. Additional information about disability and sensory limitation is covered in chapter five.

SIGHT

To see is to perceive relative lightness, darkness, and color. Light is a form of radiant energy that reflects off the world into people's eyes[8], allowing people who are sighted to see their environment and to see colors.

Walking and seeing often go hand in hand for basic safety reasons, such as not tripping over obstacles in the topography or not running into things. Sight is also tied to perceiving light, color, and reflections in the surrounding environment, alerting walkers to important contrast, repetition, and spatial relationships that can inform their experience. One can visually sense changes in the scale and proportion of surroundings, giving clues about transitions in the environment related to nearness and farness. Walkers also use sight during group walks to notice changes in energy dynamics and interactivity with others. Sight combined with any of the other senses can amplify or enhance the experience. For example, if one is on a foraging walk, there is a popular saying, "You eat with your eyes first," which implies that alluring visuals can enhance a taste experience. Altogether, sight can take a very central role in a walking piece.

One example is *Head Sculpture* (1973) by **Efrat Natan** (1947–), which took place in Tel Aviv the morning after the Israel Independence Day military parade and consisted of a T-shaped sculpture that sat over the walker's head, creating a very specific and narrowed point of view to the front and two sides. This limited the sight of the walker and also drew a great deal of attention to Natan due to the scale of the sculpture, which would have stood out as irregular on the busy urban corner of Frishman and Dizengoff streets. The reduction of vision poses conceptual questions about belonging and nonconforming, which further resonated with the timing of the piece after the military parade.

Sight can also be an integral part of socially engaged walking works that embrace slow looking, such as bird watching or mushroom hunting, or observing a single site over long periods of time. For example, *Vedute Manoeuvre* (2011) by **Tim Brennan** (1966–) asked participants to take a handful of "view cards" on a walk around Venice to explore specific physical and psychological views of an environment, considering how they might affect collective knowledge of a place. The tour also asked participants to read quotes on the back of the card simultaneously, creating a moment of noise to bring attention to the built environment. Either way, as a card holder or a passerby, looking is centered in this walk.

Walking projects that rely on sight can also intersect with larger social systems and challenges, such as environmental destruction. For instance, *Walking to Save Some Sea—My 46,000 Challenge* (2006–2007) by **Fran Crowe** (1956–) was a project of looking and collecting plastic garbage from a beach for one full year (see figure 3.1). Crowe would take photographs of the collected plastic garbage and eventually published a book from her collection walks. She also creates huge installations with the found material, building recognizable shapes (circles, rectangles, lines, etc.) and using color sorting to create visual interest while conveying the sheer volume of the plastic garbage.

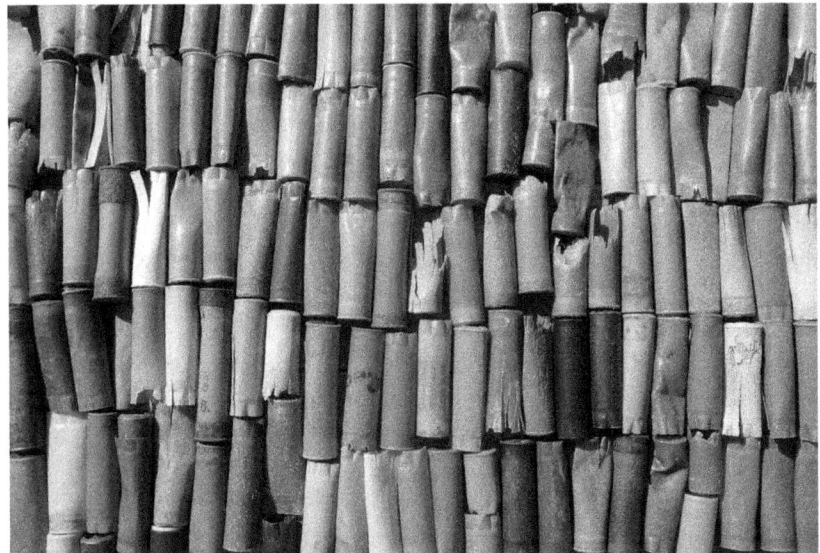

Figure 3.1. Fran Crowe, *Walking to Save Some Sea—My 46,000 Challenge*, 2006–2007, photograph, © Fran Crowe. *Source*: Courtesy of Fran Crowe.

EXERCISE: Bird Watching Walk

Go on a bird watching walk. Bird watching builds skills in observation, and highlights chance encounters. As **Jenny Odell** (1986–) mentions in *How to Do Nothing: Resisting the Attention Economy* (2019), "Bird-watching is the opposite of looking something up online. You can't really look *for* birds; you can't make a bird come out and identify itself to you. The most you can do is walk quietly and wait until you hear something, and then stand motionless under a tree, using your animal senses to figure out where and what it is" (8).

1. Select a regionally appropriate beginner's bird watching book or mobile app. Feel free to do further research online or a local library.

2. Identify at least three different birds while on your bird watching walk.

3. Do not trespass on private property (be safe).

4. While you were bird watching, what else (beyond birds) did you notice about the path of your walk through your slow looking process? Write down your observations to share with the group.

SOUND

After sight, listening might be the second most commonly used sense that observational walking projects rely on. Sound is vibration moving through a medium, such as air, that can be perceived by the human ear. Those who are deaf or hard of hearing cannot perceive sound or are not able to hear sounds well. Sound is unlike vision in that it is passive or involuntary—a person can't close their ears the way they close their eyes.

Listening of any kind during a walk requires attention to contrast, repetition, and duration of various sounds. Walkers might notice causality, juxtaposition, or interactivity between sounds they hear and other things in the environment depending on their spatial relationships. One might begin to notice some of the musical qualities of various sounds, such as pitch or loudness. The speed of the walk can also dramatically influence what is heard or not. Further, sound combined with smell or touch can create strong walking impressions and memories, such as the combination of seagulls squawking and the feel of sand underfoot, or a combination of moving trucks beeping in reverse as street food vendor scents waft along the sidewalk.

Some artists might take dramatic action to home in on sound, such as **Patrick Gillespie** (1980–) in his performative walk, *Prosthetic for Public Space* (2008) in which he donned a suit made of sheepskin that limited his sight and ability to speak. As he marched wearing this suit in a parade curated by **Fritz Haeg** (1969–), entitled *East Meets West Interchange Overpass Parade* (2008), he mainly relied on sound and directions from others to make his way, discovering new people and objects. In this way, energy dynamics, interactivity, contrast, and spatial relationships all affected the direction Gillespie walked as he moved with the parade.

There are also recognized modes of deep listening ("the difference between the involuntary nature of hearing and the voluntary, selective nature of listening")[9] and active listening ("making a conscious effort to hear, understand, and retain information that is being relayed to you")[10] that fit nicely with walking. Composer **Pauline Oliveros** (1932–2016), who coined the term *deep listening*, left us with several listening scores in her 1974 *Sonic Meditations*, including this walking-specific one: "Take a walk at night. Walk so silently that the bottoms of your feet become ears."[11]

Active listening, on the other hand, comes into play more often when discussion or conversation with others is a key focus of the walk.

For example, with **Jaime Koebel's** (1978–, Cree-Métis, Lac La Bich, AB) company **Indigenous Walks** (2014–), the emphasis is on active listening as Indigenous guides walk and talk through downtown Ottawa, Canada, to bring awareness to social, political, and cultural issues, while exploring monuments, landscape, architecture, and art.[12] The juxtaposition of the storytelling with the urban setting creates opportunities for participants to understand new meanings and histories, balancing the words with the surroundings.

EXERCISE: Sound Archive

We will familiarize ourselves with the popular concept of a sound walk. A sound walk, or walking piece, is any walk that focuses on listening to the environment, with or without the use of technology, or adds to the experience through the use of sound or voice. This can include a scripted or choreographed score or work that has additional audio elements.[13]

For this exercise, you will archive sounds you hear on a ten-minute walk. The act of sensing and archiving sounds will sharpen our observational skills. Sharing the archives will enhance our sense of community.

1. Select a walking path that is about ten minutes long. Be mindful of safety—avoid walking where you don't feel safe.

2. As you walk, record the sounds you encounter in any way that feels appropriate (audio recording, written notes, map making, photographs, videos, collected objects, etc.). Be specific and detailed as you archive.

3. When you return, arrange your archive in a way that you can share with others. Be ready to explain the sounds and your archival choices.

TOUCH AND PHYSICAL SENSATION

Touch is the physical sense of pressure, temperature, weight, texture, pain, vibration, tickle, itch, and further sensations, generally in the skin. There are a variety of different receptors in the skin for detecting these stimuli. Sometimes the word *haptic* is used to describe these touch-based sensations.

When one thinks about touch or physical awareness in relation to walking, one might think about embodied sensations related to feeling the ground beneath the feet, weight in the joints, the tactile sensation of air passing by the skin, or the stretching of muscles and tendons. It could be feeling the warmth or coolness of the surrounding environment as you pass in and out of light, or move closer or further away from buildings, trees, and other substantial objects. It might also be an awareness of physical feelings such as the heart rate speeding up, or a sensation of fatigue. When touch is combined with other senses, it can affect one's experience of a walk. For example, when walking in a hot environment, an iced beverage can engage both taste and haptic temperature sensations.

Take for example, **Okwui Okpokwasili**'s (1972–) *Market Thrum* (2016) in which she facilitated a slow walk of nine people through the Gold Coast Trading Company (an African market in the South Bronx) encouraging heightened sensory awareness of the self, the group, and the surroundings. In order to move slowly as a group, all participants had to pay very close attention to how it felt to move through space in this specific spatial relationship. Careful attention must have been paid to speed (feeling air move around and between members), the surrounding architecture (market shelving and displays), and any irregularities in the topography. Walkers also had to manage fatigue and strive to remain connected to the group's energy dynamics and cohesive interactive movement. The participants were challenged to follow the overall direction of the group (when they were turning or staying the course) and when they were making corrections.

Touch is also very important for blind or partially sighted walkers. In *Blind Field Shuttle* (2010–) by **Carmen Papalia** (1981–), groups of up to ninety people line up behind Papalia, put their hand on the shoulder of the person in front of them, and shut their eyes for an approximately one-hour walk through various terrains. The exercise heightens nonvisual senses like touch and builds awareness for Papalia's proposal for *Open Access* (2015), "a relational model for accessibility that centers considerations of agency and power in relation to the social, cultural, and political conditions in a given context."[14] After the walk, participants create a sensory map reflecting on what they just experienced.

EXERCISE: Texture Archive

You will archive textures you feel on a ten-minute walk. The act of sensing and archiving textures will sharpen our observational skills. Sharing the archives will enhance our sense of community.

1. Select a walking path that is about ten minutes long. Be mindful of safety—avoid walking where you don't feel safe.

2. As you walk, set a one-minute timer. After one minute, pause to observe the possible textures around you, and select one to feel and record. You can record the textures you encounter in any way that feels appropriate (taking rubbings, audio recording, written notes, map making, photographs, videos, collected objects, etc.). Be specific and detailed as you archive.

3. Repeat this exercise ten times (ten minutes total), using the timer to facilitate chance encounters along your route.

4. When you return, arrange your archive in a way that you can share with others. Be ready to explain the textures and your archival choices.

SMELL

Humans detect smell with the olfactory cleft located on the roof of the nasal cavity, and can discern more than one trillion scents.[15] Artist **Kate McLean** (1965–) adds, "Smell is possibly the ultimate repetitive sense; it is through a series of sniffs that we ingest olfactory information in discrete, repeated units to form an overall experience."[16] Researchers, such as **J. Douglas Porteous** (1943–), have studied combining the sense of smell with walking and mapping and identified the term *smellscape*, which is defined as the "qualitatively perceived spatial and temporal characteristics of the olfactory landscape."[17] McLean has deeply explored the concept of smellscape and developed a freely available project called *Smellfie Kit* (2015–), which orients participants to three categories of smell and three modes of smelling.

EXERCISE: Smellfie Pair Walk

Visit Kate McLean's website to download the Smellfie Kit. Identify a partner to go walking and smelling with. Follow the directions.

1. What are McLean's three categories of smell?

2. What are McLean's three modes of smelling?

3. Where will you walk?

   a. Bring water (smell needs moisture) and sniff your skin if your sense of smell wanes.

4. Consider walking the route a second time in reverse to confirm your perception of your recorded smells.

5. Compare your smellnotes (a term from McLean) charts during and after the walk. How are they different or similar?

In general, smell is not as frequently referenced in walking artworks, but is often present whether one is consciously aware of it or not. This phenomenon is due, in part, to the subjective and ephemeral nature of smells. Smell can be affected by what a walker sees, hears, feels, or tastes around themselves. The duration and intensity of a smell can also affect how one perceives it. For example, if one briefly walks past a neighborhood bakery, it might momentarily bring back a memory of eating a pastry with a friend, whereas if one is walking along the edge of a bread crumb factory's grounds on the periphery of a city, the immersion in the smell of bread for that length of time, and in that setting, will yield a completely different smell experience and set of associations.

As noted previously, in Western cultures, sight and sound have been considered more valuable than smell. In contrast, non-Western cultural understandings and descriptions of scent vary, and scholar **Constance Classen** (1957–) reminds readers that processing scent is personal and value-coded by the members of any given society.[18] Scholar **Jim Drobnick** uses the term *odorphobia* to describe making cultural or class assumptions based on foul smells as "a moral intolerance towards others, especially workers, immigrants, non-Western peoples and the poor."[19] Walking artists can counter these assumptions and biases by drawing participants' attention to them, and providing examples or generative questions to help enhance a more nuanced understanding of smell.

A great example of this approach to odorphobia and countering assumptions is *The Olfactory Chambers of Ward 88* (2014) by the **Maraa Collective** (2008–). This walk took place in Bangalore, India, and used the format of a tourism walk to critically examine the processing of waste and the caste system. The walking route was led by odor and followed the same route as the street sweepers and waste sorters, most often members of the Dalits caste, which has been traditionally responsible for clearing excrement. These individuals were falling victim to injury and death on the job. By using the format of a walking tour and drawing attention to the smells of this incredibly difficult work, Maraa Collective hoped to retell narratives of everyday waste and its accompanying smells, highlighting the social injustice of the situation. This work may remind some of *Touch Sanitation* (1978–1980) by **Mierle Laderman Ukeles** (1939–), in which she shook the hand of every sanitation worker in New York City, shining a light on their labor and demonstrating respect for their work.

A different facet of smell is the ability to discern spatial relationships from scents based on their contrast and direction. Urban and rural spaces often have different smells, and the speed with which smells arrive and fade away can also help a walker hypothesize about causes, location, time of day, and more. Smells can carry in the air, but also are ". . . embedded in surfaces and within the materiality of urban structures and fabrications as well as the natural world."[20] Additionally, smell also has strong ties to memory and emotion due to the brain's anatomy, which walking artists can use to their advantage.[21] For example, in *Procession* (1974) by **Teresa Murak** (1949–), the artist wore a coat made of cress seed (a small, fast-growing plant with a distinctive smell) as she walked through the streets of Warsaw, Poland. On this walk, she was introducing an unignorable Mother Nature figure into this urban environment, highlighting issues of femininity through her labor of growing the coat prior to the event. Scent, and its relative intensity according to spatial relationships with the coat, helped heighten the experience.[22]

EXERCISE: Smellscape Mapping

Make a smellscape walking map of an area you are familiar with.

1. Select an area with at least three distinct smells (for example, food, emissions, nature, animals, waste,[23] etc.) to create a walking tour map.

2. Go to the places where you remember the smells, and walk up and down the streets and paths, taking notes of where the smells are the strongest (intensity), time of day, wind direction, temperature, humidity or other weather elements, and any other factors that would affect a future walker's experience. Note duration of smells, identifying if they feel like general background smells or temporary episodic smells, and try to identify their sources. Note spatial relationships by examining how far can you go from the sources of the scents before the smell disappears. How can you mark those shifts in intensity on the map? Be as descriptive as possible.

   a. Bring water (smell needs moisture) and sniff your skin if your sense of smell wanes.

3. Now make your smell map. You could draw it by hand or use a tool like Google Maps. Either way, you will turn in an 8½" × 11" PDF, visually summarizing your map. What colors, symbols, mark-making, line qualities, and descriptive labels will you use and why?

4. The group will combine all the PDFs into a collaborative zine for distribution.

TASTE

Taste is the chemical perception of sweetness, sourness, saltiness, bitterness, and umami/savoriness through taste buds on the tongue, throat, epiglottis, nasal cavity, and esophagus. Smells and textures can also influence the human sense of taste.[24] "Taste is one of our most complex senses. It is resistant to quantification, profoundly situated, individual, ephemeral, and difficult to replicate."[25] Perceptions of taste can also be influenced by cultural understanding.

Taste might not be one of the first things a person thinks of when contemplating walking; however, drinking or eating often accompany a walk. Take for example *Walking Lunches* (2010–2020) by **Claudia Zeiske** (1959–). On these walks, Zeiske provided an agenda, sandwiches, and tea to a lunch partner who took three photos on the walk. Zeiske wrote notes to accompany the images for an archive. Here, the walking practice would be incomplete without the sense of taste, which was in juxtaposition to the conversation and photography, affecting the atmospheric quality of the walk, and acting as a point of transition or causality on the walk. Pausing to eat can interrupt the repetition of the walk or enhance the rhythm if one eats or drinks while walking.

Foraging for food is also closely tied to walking, often including tasting along the way. In this way, taste may also be one of the more dangerous senses to engage while walking, as you have to invest in your education to avoid plants or other materials that could cause harm. Beyond the required knowledge to avoid harm, foraging is valuable for the way it changes the speed at which people walk (people walk more slowly to more closely observe the topography) and changes their relationship to the ground and spaces they are walking through, as well as their spatial relationship to each other.

A foraging walk is a highly interactive walk with an acute focus on observation, not only through taste, but all the other senses, too. Visually, a foraging walker is on the lookout for shape, color, contrast, the direction of light, repeated patterns, and many other combinations of indicators of the edible. In terms of sound, one might look for quieter areas in urban settings, or certain animal sounds in rural areas. One might feel for hotter or colder spots depending on the food sources they are seeking. A foraging walker might use smell to determine a good location or discern one type of plant from another. All of this is in addition to the sense of taste.

One example of this approach is the design lab **SPURSE**, which has hosted many urban foraging walks, especially around their book *Eat Your Sidewalk* (2017), which they describe as "a manifesto and a call to action. We want to inspire you to find wonder and ecological possibilities directly underfoot. We want to launch a sidewalk-to-table revolution that changes our cities and gives us a new sense of community and place."[26] The book encourages urban foraging as a mode of deeply connecting to urban spaces. The use of food in social practice works like this is a common way to engage the often-overlooked sense of taste, as well as build relationships with others.

EXERCISE: Dandelion Taste

The act of researching, finding, and tasting will sharpen our observational skills. Talking with community members to find a safe-to-eat dandelion will enhance a sense of community.

1. Select a walking path to a dandelion that you know has not been treated with pesticides (this may take some research), and that you may dig up and investigate. Be mindful of safety—avoid walking or digging where you don't feel safe.

2. When you arrive at the dandelion, dig out the plant, including roots.

3. Take a nibble of different parts of the plant: leaves, blossom, stem, root.

4. Write down the differences in the flavors. Be ready to share your observations with others.

Lastly, and somewhat unexpectedly due to the dangerous nature of the practice, some researchers have actually gone on tasting walks in which they lick their surroundings. Such is the case with **MJ Hunter Brueggemann** (1987–), **Vanessa Thomas** (1985–), and **Ding Wang** (1989–) in *Lickable Cities* (2014–2017), a research project in which they licked surfaces, objects, flora, and fauna on walks in cities around the world (see figure 3.2).[27] Of

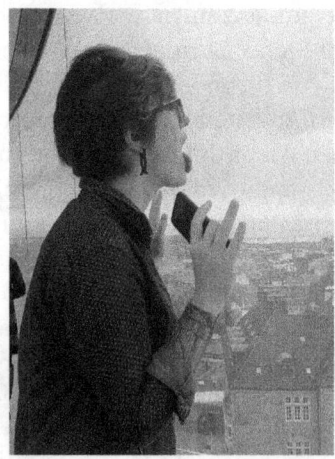

Figure 3.2. *Lickable Cities* (MJ Hunter Brueggemann, Vanessa Thomas, Ding Wang), photograph; photo by Zoe Luski and Vanessa Thomas. *Source*: Courtesy of Vanessa Thomas.

course, contamination and safety were challenges, and predictably, near the end of the project, one of the researchers became very ill. However, the project did highlight interesting theoretical questions about what it might be like to design with, and for, taste. The researchers posed questions about how biased expectations might affect one's sense of taste based on "neighborhood demographics and urban investment."[28] They also asked, "How will we include or exclude super-tasters and non-tasters? How will we cope with certain flavors that do or do not travel across cultures, ages, or social classes? What might we lose by ignoring these dimensions of taste?"[29] These questions of accessibility are relevant not only for the sense of taste, but also for the other four senses, in their own ways.

EXERCISE: Five Senses

Having reviewed these five senses, craft a walk that includes all five. Where will you go? Who's invited? In what ways will you engage all five senses? When will you take the walk? Why did you make these choices? Afterwards, reflect on how it went. How would you change the walk if you did it again?

The Personal Experience

One can also pay attention to the overall personal experience during observational walking, paying special attention to the feelings, memories, and thoughts the observations from the walk brings to the surface. Sensory input is deeply personal, with certain scents, imagery, temperatures, humidities, pacing, flavors, etc. associated with specific and potent memories or emotions. Additionally, walking can be a way of personally knowing a place by embodying certain distances, turns, and topography as one regularly walks certain paths. Ritualistic walking, such as daily walks, is covered in chapter six, and ways of knowing places are covered in depth in chapter seven.

Sometimes the term *phenomenology* is used to discuss first-person experiences via sensory and bodily awareness, memory, thought, behavior, and emotion.[30] This idea is directly related to observational walking, thinking of it as a mode of learning more about the self and place. Scholar **Luis Carlos Sotelo-Castro** (1968–) builds on this idea when he reflects on walking and mapping, "it is the subject-who-takes-part who has been mapped, not space. . . . It is through the act of sharing the spatial autobiographical narratives that result out of the participation process, that the participants may be enabled to position and map the self."[31] Other scholars working in the vein of phenomenology include German philosopher and mathematician **Edmund Husserl** (1859–1936), and French philosopher **Maurice Merleau-Ponty** (1908–1961) who wrote *Phenomenology of Perception* (1945) and saw the body as the primary site for understanding the world.

A phenomenological approach was referenced by the research group **Marsad Drâa** (2013–) in their project *Project Qafila [second stage]* (2017), an interdisciplinary research trip, including a walking residency with a Spanish artistic association, **CerCCa**, focused on caravan culture in the Saharan desert (see figure 3.3). The researchers used phenomenological walking to understand their surroundings, group dynamics, and themselves as they moved through the desert together. The trip resulted in a publication and an installation of visual materials, with focus on "issues related to slave trade, draawa social contracts, the valley political ecology, [I]ndigenous and Islamic epistemologies, colonial legacies, and [B]lack radicalism."[32] *Project Qafila* is just one of several projects and conferences that have been hosted by Marsad Drâa since 2013 when it was founded by **Carlos Pérez Marín** (1971–), with the aim of studying lifestyles and cultures of desert regions.

Another example of centering this personal experience during observational walking is *Poema Volcánico* (2014) by **Eduardo Navarro** (1979–), in which he documented an Ecuadorian volcano by walking into it with

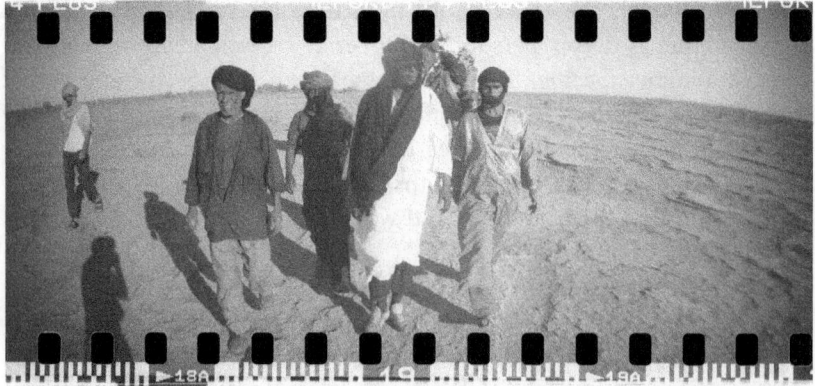

Figure 3.3. Marsad Drâa, *Project Qafila [second stage]*, 2017, an interdisciplinary research trip focused on caravan culture in the Saharan desert, photo by Carlos Pérez Marín. *Source*: Courtesy of Carlos Pérez Marín.

protective gear and creating drawings via litmus paper tests of the acidity of the air. The walk was inspired by his personal memories growing up near a volcano, and he completed multiple treks to directly experience the challenges of the topography of the crater and the physicality of the protective suit. Through Navarro's phenomenological walking research, he developed methods to document and interpret the volcano's gasses, resulting in an archive of grid-like drawings of the experience.

The element of personal experience, reflection, and discovery as an element of observational walking is expansive and has long been recognized and utilized in human rituals, pilgrimages, and labyrinth practices, which are covered in more detail in chapter six. Similarly, observational walking is closely tied to a heightened personal mind-body awareness, which is covered in more detail in chapter ten. What is described here is just a brief introduction to these ideas related to personal experience and observation.

EXERCISE: Seven-Day Walk

Go for a walk seven days in a row and document your experience of the weather using all your senses. Long durational walks build patience and expand awareness over time. Changes in weather can be subtle or severe, heightening sensory experiences.

1. Select a ten-minute route and a time of day you can walk for seven days in a row. Be safe.

2. As you're walking, think about all your senses. You will record your reflections **after** the walk each day.

3. Diligently record your sensory impressions of the weather after each walk. This could be written, audio or video recordings, or other approaches.

4. Be ready to share your archive and discuss your overall personal experience of the weather with the group.

The Everyday

Artist Allan Kaprow stated, "Pollock, as I see him, left us at the point where we must become preoccupied with and even dazzled by the space and object of our everyday life, either our bodies, clothes, rooms, or, if need be, the vastness of Forty-Second Street. Not satisfied with the suggestion through paint of our other senses, we shall utilize the specific substances of sight, sound, movements, people, odors, touch."[33]

Artist **Meghan Moe Beitiks** (1979–) points out, "Walking is not always a beautiful, existential meditation on nature, wellness and place. It is sometimes long, boring, and painful, and those, too, are generative experiences."[34] Beitiks is pointing to the concept of "the everyday" in walking; observational walking has long-standing connections to the concept of the everyday (see chapter one), which consists of the mundane, ordinary, and often overlooked aspects of daily life.[35]

For example, the mid-1800s concept of the flâneur/flâneuse was simply a person (most often an upper class man at this time) who strolled the city in order to experience it as a passive observer with a disengaged point of view.[36] Similarly, the mid-1900s concept of the dérive, or drift, was a playful technique for wandering rapidly through cities, not for commuting or leisure, but to experience the attractions or repulsions of the topography, architecture, and the atmosphere of a place.[37] While the dérive, in one way, tries to escape elements of the everyday by experiencing the familiar in new ways, the exercise itself is very much in response to everyday surroundings. Additionally, in the post-war 1950s and 1960s, elevating elements of the everyday, such as walking—a time-based intangible practice—was a way to push back against art collectors and the monetization of the art world, which was a common thread at that time (see chapters one and eight).

Geographer **David Seamon** (1948–) contends that most places are the product of everyday, mundane practices, and routines,[38] like walking to one's favorite local restaurant. To that point, *Chip Shop Tour of E8* (2007) by the collective walkwalkwalk focused on exactly this facet of the everyday. This walking piece started with a map available from the Transition Gallery and sent participants outside to explore the E8 postcode of greater London by visiting a selection of chip shops. The invite read, ". . . Navigate your own route to a Chippy and you can then sample their fare in one of three specially designed commemorative chip paper wrappers. Witness live the under-rated art of chip wrapping and poke-folding. . . ."[39] Later photographic documentation of walking to these seemingly mundane shops was collected on a blog as an archive. Both the lower-class and relatively inexpensive nature of the chip shops, in combination with free transportation (walking), emphasized an elevation of the everyday.

Other walking artists document their everyday walks, such as commuting, running errands or dog walking, as a form of personal archive. These types of ritualized daily walks are covered in more depth in chapter six. For example, artist **On Kawara** (1933–2014) traced all his movements on maps for twelve years in a piece entitled *I WENT* (created 1968–1979, published 2007). There were twelve books of these maps with 4740 pages total. Each daily trip is traced in a red line on a map and is dated. When taken collectively, the books convey the enormity of the passage of time and the breadth of physical distances—issues often overlooked when considering ordinary activities.

A slightly antagonistic use of walking and the everyday was *Tilted Arc* (1981) by **Richard Serra** (1939–). For this site-specific wall-like installation, Serra wanted to disrupt the everyday flow of people walking across the plaza in front of the Jacob K. Javits Federal Building in New York City, creating a contrast with stereotypical urban figurative monuments that people pass by without really looking closely, or experiencing physically. He said he wanted the sculpture to "encompass the people who walk on the plaza in its volume."[40] The 120-foot-long and twelve-foot-high rusted steel wall caused such a disturbance in everyday foot traffic that the public demanded it be removed, and it was. This interactive installation not only highlighted walking and the everyday, but it also drew so much attention that it caused its own demise.

EXERCISE: Star Gazing

1. Go for a walk at night (select a place where you feel safe—take a fellow walker with you) and ensure there aren't any clouds obscuring your view of the stars.

2. Look up at the stars as you're walking (be safe—remember to also watch your step).

3. Note what you observe. How does the everyday look different to you walking at this different time of day? How does your experience of walking shift when your point of view is mostly upward towards the sky? How does it affect walking speed? If you pause, where do you tend to choose to pause and why? How are you affected by the darkness?

Chance

Chance, or the uncertainty of a specific outcome, is intertwined with observational walking because the walker can't control what they will encounter, and there is a great deal of the unknown involved. The Surre-alists recognized this fact and built on the idea of flânerie by conducting experiments that purposefully involved randomness and chance in order to overcome the everyday mundanity of one's surroundings. For example, they would recommend using a map from a different city to navigate the current one, which would heighten awareness of elements that might have escaped one's awareness otherwise.[41] Fluxus artists were also highly reli-ant on chance events. For example, in *Theatre Music* (1964) by **Takehisa Kosugi** (1938–2018) consisted of an extremely simple score, "Keep walking intently," which is open to all sorts of interpretation and chance encoun-ters. Some might consider it an individual directive, while others might apply a more collective understanding. The work gives no sense of time ranges or limits, nor location(s). It implies a persistent movement, but no definition of direction, interactivity, or speed. Indeed, the majority of this score is left up to chance.

Many observational walking projects also rely on dialogue, which itself relies on chance due to the unpredictable nature of talking to another person. Take for example *A Common Third* (2010) by Simon Pope in which he invited guest walkers to places that neither he nor the guest knew. Then they worked together to figure out the route together through discussion. Their choices were influenced by weather, familiarity with the terrain, and other chance conditions. Afterwards the participants created reflective audio recordings describing both the mental and physical paths taken.

Summary

In this chapter observational walking was examined with attention to sen-sory experience, personal experience, the everyday, and chance encounters. Observational walking is important because it is often regarded as easily accessible and adaptable to different people with different sensory abilities, although it can also raise challenges of ability (discussed in chapter five) and privilege (discussed in chapter two). The concept of phenomenology was introduced and tied to the sensory and personal experience. These approaches are helpful for crafting new works for either individuals or participatory groups. Exercises throughout help the reader explore these ideas in greater depth.

Chapter 4

Leading Versus Following

As social creatures, humans will always have to negotiate leading and following, as socializing is integral to human emotional and physical health.[1]
Walking practitioners have been embracing the roles of leader and follower
since the earliest records of walking. From neolithic builders using tall rock
menhirs to mark paths and lead walking people to their destinations, to
the Australian Aboriginal walkabout rite of passage following paths across
the land and sky, to various protest marches since Roman times, it is clear
that leading and following are deeply human experiences.

Leading and following also bring up ideas of mirroring, mimicry,
and simulation, which are all ways that humans learn from each other.
Children follow teachers, or each other, as they move from one space
to another. Students follow directions for various activities or take turns
leading a group. Adults are also accustomed to leading and following,
whether that is getting in line at a store, guiding a coworker, or taking
part in tourism experiences in new places. This familiarity across age
groups makes leading and following an easy point of access for bringing
people into a walking artwork.

Digging deeper into leading and following, complex issues arise,
such as consent regarding one person following another, group dynamics
when walking together, leading without being physically present, or the
topic of "liveness" and archiving for participants versus witnesses before
and after an event. Here we will explore various examples to get a better
sense of these subtopics, as well as the breadth of leading and following
in artistic walking practice.

Following and Consent

The act of following someone should include consent, which is clear permission or agreement from the person who is being followed. However, that has not always been the case throughout art history. For example, Surrealists and Situationists would often follow people without consent, in particular sex workers, throughout the city in the pursuit of the unknown or unfamiliar as an act of "drifting."

More specifically, in October 1969 **Vito Acconci** (1940–2017) created his famous *Following Piece*, which consisted of him leaving his apartment every day for twenty-three days to follow random people on the street until they entered a cab, residence, or other private space. Along with taking photographs and written notes, he typed up descriptions of these acts of following and sent them to arts professionals. Some interpret this piece as an exploration of public versus private space, while others point out the problematic power dynamics and similarities to stalking, due to the lack of consent.

Yoko Ono and **John Lennon** (1940–1980) similarly made a video work in 1969 entitled *Rape*, in which a young walking woman was followed without consent to create a seventy-seven-minute film. While Ono and Lennon intended the work as a commentary on the lack of privacy celebrities endure, it is an ethically problematic work because the woman who was filmed was not allowed to opt out of the following experience, thus perpetuating the very concept it was intending to critique.

Sophie Calle also has multiple walking works that center around the act of following with varying levels of consent, such as *Suite Vénitienne* (1980) and *The Shadow* (1981). While the gender roles are flipped in *Suite Vénitienne*—Calle follows a man from Paris to Venice—the lack of consent is still obvious. Calle's ultimate intentions in this piece are never completely clear, with topics of persistence, investigation, and the personal versus anonymous all having prominent roles in the photographs, phone calls, and notes that make up this narrative project. In *The Shadow* (1981), Calle requests her mother hire a detective to follow her and photograph her without her knowledge (the detective did not know that Calle knew he was following her).[2] While Calle initiated this project, and clearly provided consent, the project still examines the ideas of watching and being watched without knowing when and where it's happening. She later exhibited the photographs and descriptions, continuing to ask questions about public and private control, as well as voyeurism, exhibitionism, and chance.[3]

The examples above mostly focus on issues of gender as it relates to public and private space, but consent-to-follow also intersects with issues of surveillance, race, and perceived public safety. In chapter five, readers will explore how people of color encounter challenges with surveillance, safety, and walking in various locations.

Consent is just one of several elements that affect walking with groups. Below, readers will examine many other considerations for successful participatory walking projects such as group dynamics, tourism, and participation.

Group Walking Dynamics and Tips

The art of wandering is followed by the art of meeting.

—Francesco Careri

To lead or follow implies a group activity of at least two or more people. Working in groups brings about wonderfully unpredictable results, which is why collaborative walking projects can be such a fruitful exercise. Similarly, walking in groups can present challenging group dynamics, which people can prepare for by reviewing some best practices in preparation, communication, and collaborative decision making.

Preparation

Todd Shalom in *Prompts for Participatory Walks* (2019) has a substantial section on planning group walks similar in format to those from *Elastic City* (2010–2016), a collaborative project focused on participatory group walks. Shalom's book includes tips for how to craft instructional prompts, ethical considerations, recommended duration (seventy-five to ninety minutes), route planning, and number of people (six to twelve). Shalom recommends rehearsing leading the walk with a friend or two to get feedback and tweak the experience before the scheduled group walk. Other organizations with more rural group walks, such as **Deveron Projects**' the *Walking Institute* in Scotland, provide detailed lists of what to prepare, from mindset (know your limits, leave no trace, etc.) to supplies (shoes/boots, camera, backpack, snacks, etc.).

The collaborative research group **iLAND (interdisciplinary Laboratory for Art Nature and Dance)** (2004–) recommends considering the varied histories and ecosystems of a place before engaging with it. In their "gathering information" tips, they specifically recommend finding documents (books, articles, journals, maps, etc.) to research conceptual frameworks related to the site. They also recommend informal oral interviews and on-site observation and data collection. After completing this preparatory research, the artist might also consider developing a diagram and/or map to illustrate the relationships discovered between the concepts and systems related to the place.[4] iLAND's recommendations echo protocols in the natural sciences, much like **Karen O'Rourke**'s (1951–) recommendations in *Walking and Mapping: Artists as Cartographers* (2013), where she suggests all walking scores include safety and equipment recommendations, procedural instruction including objectives and methods, as well as reporting standards.[5]

In Phil Smith and **Simon Persighetti**'s (1954–) book, *A Sardine Street Box of Tricks* (2012), they recommend finding a way, or ways, to bind the group together for the duration of the walk, such as a joint action (like a high five), a stamp on the hand, everyone carrying a flag or stick, handing out matching shirts, etc. Additionally, they recommend adding a tiny ritual to different parts of the walk. For instance, participants could purposefully walk around an object in a particular way, or stir water whenever it is encountered, jump over cracks, touch rocks, use a pointing stick, cut a ribbon at a certain point, or bring chalk to mark certain areas. These shared moments create community. Read more about rituals in chapter six.

Artist Kate McLean provides specific advice for working in pairs in her *Smellfie Kit* (discussed in more detail in chapter three), including a recommendation to consider walking in silence when entering an unfamiliar area to help home in on the activity of smelling, much like one would on a listening-focused walk.[6] Then, schedule breaks so partners can rest their olfactory concentration, and share reflections. During these pauses, additional information can be provided by a walking leader, including anecdotes from past walks, which may help alleviate any participant concerns.[7] This advice mirrors some of the methods used by the **Walking Reading Group** (2013–), which also uses a pair-based structure to walk and discuss readings. One difference is that the Walking Reading Group approach involves switching conversation partners several times during the walk. Depending on the focus of a given walk, in this case smelling versus reading, an artist can adjust the group walking approach accordingly.

Accessibility concerns are also a central part of group walk planning, and as artist and scholar Morag Rose reminds, "If possible design in access and inclusion from the beginning of a project, don't try and add it on later."[8] Accessibility activist **Emily Ladau** (1991–) points out several suggestions that could be applied to group walks, such as sending any written materials in advance to give people extra time to process and decide whether or not to participate, making sign language interpretation available as needed, considering seating and resting options throughout, checking for mobility equipment accessibility along the route, and offering large-print and braille materials as needed.[9] These accessibility accommodations will benefit everyone, and there is a name for this phenomenon: The curb cut effect. When curb cuts were installed in sidewalks for wheelchair access, they ended up also benefiting people with baby strollers, shopping carts, wheeled suitcases, roller skates, and more.[10] When you add accessibility features to your walking project, everyone will benefit.

Be clear in your descriptions and promotions (if there are any) of what participants should expect. Be sure to address the who, what, where, when, why, and how of the experience, and pair it with a compelling descriptive image. Communicate anything that needs to be prepared ahead of time, any costs, or any items the walkers should bring with them. If you plan on documenting the walk, or asking participants to document, let them know ahead of time. Be mindful of different people's abilities and be transparent about duration, terrain, and anything else that could affect someone's ability to participate in the walk.

If you are planning to lead a walk through a place with which you are less familiar, take the time beforehand to familiarize yourself. Meet people from the community if possible. Identify places people can use a restroom or a resting spot if needed.

Planning Guide

1. Who

   a. Who is invited? Can anyone sign up? Are there any prerequisites? How many people to expect?

   b. Are you partnering with an organization?

2. What

    a. Provide a clear description of what to expect. What are possible difficulties or challenges (topography or otherwise)? What types of terrain will you be walking on? Are you passing through public and/or private spaces? Are there steps? Are there places with obstacles, or areas where curb cuts are missing?

    b. Are you providing any printed materials, maps, or note-taking tools? Consider using cardstock to enhance durability and make note-taking easier than on lighter-weight paper. Consider contrast between paper and lines/text of any maps or readings.[11]

3. Where

    a. What are the start and end locations? What is the length of the route in miles/kilometers? What is the route between, or will participants be expected to develop their own route? Is parking needed/available? Are toilets and water/refreshment opportunities along the route?

4. When

    a. Duration in hours/minutes, and time of day—how will these choices affect who can participate? Are there seasonal or weather-specific considerations? Will there be breaks, or is it continuous walking?

5. Why

    a. Provide a rationale for why someone might like to participate.

6. How

    a. When and with whom will you rehearse? (you don't have to share this publicly) What obstacles might the walkers encounter? Should they be prepared for specific physical or emotional challenges?

    b. Any supplies/clothing/equipment needed? Any costs?

    c. Always ask about accessibility needs and accommodations (not all will apply every time) and be open and honest about what you can and cannot offer. Can you offer sign language interpretation, alternative language participation, audio descriptions, image captions for web accessibility, live streaming of events, alternative format texts, touch tours, or a real-time translation service? As needed, are you able to provide chemical sensitivity and air-quality awareness, childcare, mobility access, or content warnings? If needed, can you provide food/dietary restrictions accommodations, harm reduction and overdose preparedness, personal care assistants and service animals accommodations, restroom access, seating/rest options (and do people need special reservations), sliding scales for economic justice, transportation support, and more? If the walk is not accessible for some people, think critically about how you document and share the work in alternative formats. If you are unsure about accessibility, research local disability organizations or consultants, and pay for a consultation (never ask a disabled person to consult for free, unless they explicitly offer, as it is not fair or appropriate to request free labor in this way). Learn more by reading "Accessibility in the Arts: A Promise and a Practice" by **Carolyn Lazard** (1987–).

7. Imagery

   a. Can you provide a compelling image that will grab people's attention?

   b. Can you provide a map of any kind to give visual context?

Communication

Communicate with registrants before the walk. Send reminders with plenty of helpful information, and an easy way to contact you if they have questions. Remember that there isn't one correct way to communicate, as every group is different, and flexibility is key to supporting accessibility.

When you are leading a walk, don't forget to introduce both yourself and the walking experience, and encourage the group members to also introduce themselves. This simple act will help to begin building trust among the walkers. Also, you might consider sharing something about yourself to create a sense of connection, authenticity, and vulnerability. This could be a memory or dream that inspired the walk, or some sort of personal association with the site, and so on.

Assume participants haven't read anything or prepared in any way, even if you have sent information prior to the walk. This means refreshing people's awareness of any necessary directions and reminding them of any accessibility guidelines. For example, if anyone is participating with a service animal, remind people not to interact with it. Or, if anyone has low vision, encourage participants to verbally state their name before speaking, and so on. Give warning if you plan to ask participants to do, or not do, certain things during the walk, and remind them that they have the agency to opt in or out at any time.

During the walk, be clear and concise as you deliver directions. Make sure you are speaking at a volume that is accessible to your walkers. Consider telling the group you will be providing the walking prompts in printed form at the end of the experience, so they can enjoy the walk without worrying about taking a lot of notes. Carry one or two copies in case that is more accessible for some participants who have difficulty following the voiced directions. The printed directions also can be a good way to communicate estimated time spent on various elements. Be an active listener to help reduce misunderstanding and reference these active-listening tips.

Active-Listening Tips

Active listening is more than just hearing what someone says. It is being fully present, focused on the person who is communicating, and openly interpreting and applying information received.

As a listener:

1. Be quiet and make eye contact, while using body language to demonstrate understanding (nodding, etc.).

2. Avoid distractions, and don't interrupt the communicator.

3. Avoid completing someone else's sentences or rehearsing a response.

4. Ask questions or request rephrasing as necessary.

5. Repeat key points of what you heard, and/or convey how it relates to your own experiences.

6. Express gratitude.

As a communicator engaging others in listening:

1. Only speak when you have something relevant and of value to say. Keep it short.

2. Get to know the people you are hoping to engage.

3. Ask people to remove distractions from the space.

4. Provide important things in writing too.

5. Be aware of your body language as you communicate.

Collaborative Decision Making

When leading or following a group walk, there will possibly be some collaborative decision making at some point. When faced with one of these collaborative decisions, it can be helpful to frame the decision and its context, outline choices including pros and cons, and then decide the course of action. There are many benefits to collaborative decision making, including overriding individual biases, and helping to build individual investment in the experience everyone helped create together. Some of the disadvantages of collaborative decision making include increased time and effort, as understanding must be built and conflicts must be resolved.

When conflicts arise, it can be an opportunity to revisit the facts of the situation, note differing opinions, and call out misunderstandings, exaggerations, or other elements to help de-escalate. Oftentimes conflict arises from a difference between intent and impact, which can be identified and addressed. Similarly, issues of privilege and oppression might be at play, but have not been voiced (see chapter two discussion of privilege as an element of context). As a walking leader, it is your responsibility to be the facilitator of conflict resolution or enable others to do so.

EXERCISE: Practice Collaborative Decision Making

Like any activity, collaborative decision making gets easier with practice. Gather a group of five to ten people to decide where to go for lunch. Practice walking through the steps of collaborative decision making. Try applying the steps to other collaborative decisions of your own selection. Keep practicing.

1. Frame the decision and its context

2. Outline choices, including pros and cons

3. Decide a course of action

   If conflict arises, practice working through resolution:

1. Revisit the facts of the situation

2. Recognize differing opinions

3. Call out misunderstandings/exaggerations

4. Identify differences between intent and impact

5. Voice any issues of privilege or oppression

Group Walking Tips at the Event

Arrive to the walking experience early and plan to stay late. Participants tend towards both behaviors, and as the leader, you want to be prepared. If you have a coleader, be sure both of you arrive early so you can touch base before people arrive. Also consider the idea of warm-ups, both physical, like gentle stretching and movement, as well as social, such as brief introductions.

Leading the pace and spacing might be two of the more important elements of group walking. If someone is following too far behind, the group can become split. Similarly, if a participant is leading at a speed that doesn't match the group, it can cause confusion or frustration. Know that things will not always go as planned. Be okay with improvising and changing things in the moment.

Afterwards, you might consider a brief spoken reflection with the group before they leave. Simply asking each person to share a sentence summarizing their experience can result in exciting revelations and community building. Additionally, you might remind them of how to share their documentation of the experience, whether that's through sharing photos and videos on social media, sharing them in an online folder, or other relevant methods.

Lastly, don't forget to reflect on the experience yourself. Analyze what worked well and what didn't. Jot down thoughts on what you might do differently if you were to hold the walk again. How might you alter your processes? Did your intentions match the results? What are your next steps in organizing the documentation? Will you write about the walk? Make a plan to wrap up any loose ends.

EXERCISE: Leading and Following Practice

As a group, form a line. Each person will take a turn being the leader of the line for one minute (assign someone to be the timekeeper). The person at the front of the line can walk in any way they like (exaggerated movement, different paces, etc.) and choose the path. Those behind will follow and attempt to walk in the same manner. After everyone has had a chance at leading, pause and reflect as a group.

1. What was it like to be the leader and the follower?

2. What did you learn about pacing and spacing?

3. What did you observe about inclusion—did some struggle to follow? What did you do about it?

4. How did improvisation play a role?

Writing Scores and Directions

When developing a new walking score—sometimes also referred to as a set of directions, a protocol, scenario, instructions, or script—Shalom reminds us to think about what an artist can do with a score that they couldn't do by themselves. What are you trying to explore? What feels urgent?[12] Have a reason for each step in the score. The artist may or may not share that thinking with the walker, but it will improve the quality and cohesiveness of the walk. Remember that a score can also take the familiar form of a map, even a very simplified one, or a combination of visuals and written directions. Artists should think carefully about how they compose their scores and which senses to appeal to. This can also tie into issues of accessibility.

If you are writing a score for which you will be present to lead participants, pacing and timing can be an important element. Think about time of day, which can affect lighting and foot or vehicle traffic, as you develop the directions. Think about each task and how long it might take, which can help the walk to feel more or less focused. Include backup plans in case things move more quickly or slowly than anticipated. Also consider the scale of the walk. Does it work best for one person, a pair, a small group, or a large group? Indicating the intended scale of the walk will help people using the score.

Before sharing your score, review it for ethical concerns, safety concerns, and "how our work relates to the issues of power, privilege, appropriations, exploitations, etc."[13] Along these lines, know that some walks will attract attention. Shalom reminds us to consider what the walker's presence brings to a location and how it affects the community. Similarly, **Sheetal Prajapati** (1980–) makes good points in *The Questions We Ask Together* (Open Engagement, 2015), such as: Whose or what history (or histories) should be considered? Whose perspectives on a given history are acknowledged and available? Whose are not? Which discipline's historical narratives do you prioritize? How does the initiator understand their own history in relationship to their practice or community?

Another structure for analyzing walks is provided by **Animating Democracy**, a program of Americans for the Arts. It suggests evaluating projects based on eleven artistic attributes that address the potency of creative expression to embody and motivate change. While not all walking works aim to effect change, it is still useful to review a walking score by taking into consideration some of the following: risk-taking, openness (able to hold contradiction), sensory experience, emotional experience, commitment (to social justice underpinning if present), communal meaning, cultural integrity, disruption, coherence (strong clear ideas), resourcefulness, and stickiness (achieves sustained resonance, impact, or value).

EXERCISE: Write a Score

Take time to compose a walking score for someone else. This will be a score you give them, and you will not be present as they follow it. Try to be concise and simple to enhance clarity. Try to avoid being overly prescriptive so there is still room for the walker to improvise and bring their own knowledge and experience to the walk.

You can record the score in any way that makes sense: written instructions, audio or video instructions, a map, augmented reality, a series of signs in the environment, etc.

Recruit someone to follow your score. Ask them to reflect on the experience. Revise the score as needed. Repeat.

What did you learn about writing scores? Did any realizations or patterns occur?

Tourism

Walking tourism embodies both leading and following, and it is a format regularly adopted by walking artists due to its emphasis on concepts of localness and authenticity. Scholar Lucy Lippard has written at length on tourism as it intersects with art, and she states: "For the most part we see travel as escape, getting away, going to somewhere 'else'—often inhabited by 'others' whose dissimilarities will be exaggerated and exoticised, and whose similarities will be dismissed or hidden, although for them, 'somewhere else' is home.[14] . . . For some, travel simply proves the solidity or desirability of home base; for others, it provokes unsatisfied longings for the grass on the other side of the fence."[15] These facets of tourism provide ripe ground for artists hoping to appropriate the walking tour format for their own purposes. The 1921 Dada walking tour mentioned in chapter one parodied these ideas. More recently, *Miss Canadiana Heritage and Culture Walking Tour* (2011) by **Camille Turner** (1960–) also uses the format (see figure 4.1). In this walking tour, Turner dresses the part of a beauty queen, wearing a red evening gown, and acts as a tour

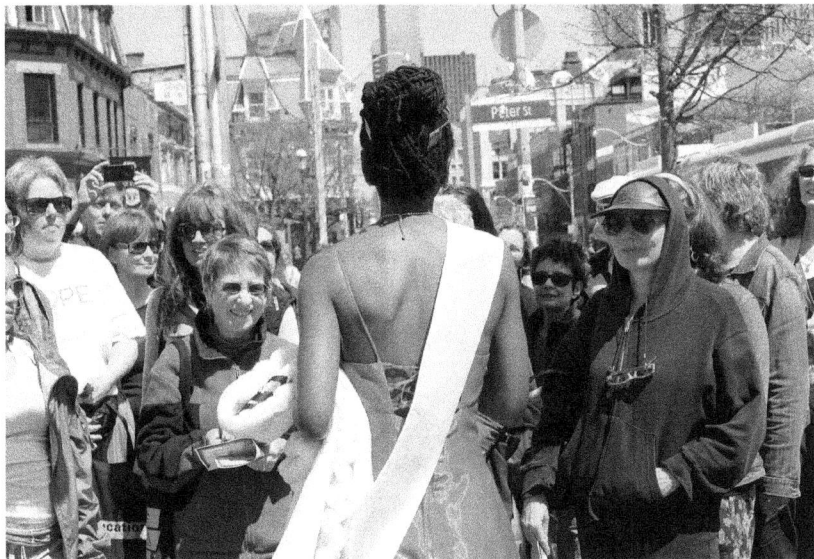

Figure 4.1. Camille Turner, *Miss Canadiana Heritage and Culture Walking Tour*, 2011, photograph, photo by Michele Pearson Clarke. *Source*: Courtesy of Michele Pearson Clarke.

guide to the hidden Black histories of Toronto's Grange neighborhood.[16] Using well-known aspects of walking tourism, including moving along a predetermined route, having a clearly visible guide person, using a distinct theme to spark interest, handing out printed materials, and slowing down to consider particular ideas or locations, participants feel a sense of familiarity as they take part in this walking piece.

Another example of artists adapting this tourism format is *Tourguide?* (1999) by **Christine Hill** (1968–), which used the storefront of Deitch Projects as a hub for improvisational walking tours focused on unexpected sites in New York City, providing a counterpoint to the well-recognized commercial walking tours in the city. By using this tourguide format to draw attention to the everyday and the humorous, such as a McDonald's with a doorman or a door to nowhere on Avenue A, Hill transformed tourism into an instrument of deeper looking. Both humor and familiar formats, like the walking tour, are ways to more easily engage participants into critical thinking and reflection.

EXERCISE: Group-Curated Tour

This is a group walking exercise. First, the group will identify a walkable area to work within (be sure to gauge everyone's ability and safety). Everyone will select a spot they feel is notable or important to them within the walkable area, and a route will be plotted to cover each of the destinations. From start to finish, walkers will take turns as the tour guide explaining what each notable spot is and why they wanted to take the cohort there.

A different facet of tourism is site-based walking tourism, where the destination, rather than a tour guide, draws people in and leads travelers on a ritualized walk. For example, the *Vietnam Veterans Memorial* (1982) by **Maya Lin** (1959–) is a well-known tourist destination that is specifically designed as a walking or rolling experience. The path to this engraved V-shaped granite wall slowly dips into the ground, revealing the 58,000 American service people's names in the order of their loss. The act of moving from one corner, descending to the vertex, and slowly emerging at the other corner, has become a ritualized walk for many people touring the Washington DC area. Similarly, the *Plaza de Cisneros* (2002–2005) in Medellín, Colombia, and designed by **Luis Fernando Peláez** (1945–), is a walking and rolling destination for tourists, with special nighttime enhancements. The plaza features 300 light poles, creating a forest-like illuminated walking or rolling experience. It is also the site of many walking-adjacent events, such as the Medellín marathon, which starts at the plaza.

Many pieces from the land art movement have this similar element of ritualized site-based tourism. Take for example, *Spiral Jetty* (1970) by Robert Smithson, which is located at Rozel Point peninsula on the northeastern shore of Great Salt Lake. This earthwork consists of six thousand tons of black basalt rocks and earth from the site piled and arranged into a coiled walking path. The path changes based on water levels, seasons, and human interaction. Despite its remote location, it draws thousands of visitors each year who make a ritualized trek to tour the site on foot. Chapter six goes into further detail of walking as ritual and pilgrimage.

Similarly, many national parks or other land preservation areas act as sites for walking and hiking tourism. Artists like Hamish Fulton will use these open spaces to create durational walking works that raise awareness of the environment. For example, he has taken several, seven-, fourteen-, and twenty-one-day walks through the Cairngorms National Park in Scotland, producing artist books, such as *Mountain Time Human Time* (2010), and large-scale graphically designed photographic works to encapsulate the walks and promote the park's preservation.

Some artists, such as Phil Smith, pay special attention to tourism and encourage tourist walkers to take a mischievous approach to heritage sites, as he details in *Counter-Tourism: The Handbook* (2012). Building on the legacy of the Situationists and the dérive, Smith recommends various tactics and infiltrations to see the world in new playful ways that questions established histories and places in favor of those least visited. He also points out in his book with Simon Persighetti, *A Sardine Street Box of Tricks* (2012), that there are several problematic elements associated with tourism, such as the singularity of the expert voice (which includes various prejudices and subjectivities), the passivity of those being guided, and the exclusion of elements from the route. It is important for any walking artist pursuing group walking to be aware of these challenges, and to consciously engage with them.

EXERCISE: Publish Your Own Tour Guide

This could be a group or an individual exercise. First, identify a walkable area to work within. Then, note all the important points of interest on a map—these might be points of general or personal interest (be mindful of safety).

You might create an online map or a physical map depending on where you would like to publish your tour guide and whom you would like the audience to be. For each point of interest, explain the who, what, why, where, and when for a future walker to enjoy. Consider how you illustrate the map, what markers you use, and how a future walker will access this tour guide.

Audio Tours

In a live tour, some guides will use a short-range audio-broadcasting system, and all the participants will listen via a special headset and receiver system. Others will simply speak loudly without added electronic amplification.

And still others will record their guidance as an audio file for walkers to listen to and follow on their own.

A notable example of artists using the audio tour as an art form is *Louisiana Walk* (1996) by **Janet Cardiff** (1957–) and **George Bures Miller** (1960–), which was first presented in the pivotal group exhibition *Walking and Thinking and Walking* (1996) curated by **Bruce Ferguson** (1946–2019) at the Louisiana Museum of Modern Art in Humlebaek, Denmark. This recorded walking tour guides followers through the landscape near the museum, citing particular visuals and adding a film-like soundtrack. The participant listens to a narrative between a man and woman looking back in time, trying to figure out when their relationship went wrong. By pointing out particular elements in the environment and using binaural audio optimized for headphones to recreate perception of distance and direction, the walker may feel like they are walking with the couple through memories, or as a voyeur. The piece also draws attention to walking tourism as it includes audio of a museum docent commenting on a sculpture on the grounds. This piece is just one of many guided audio walking tours Cardiff would go on to create.

A slightly different approach to the audio tour is a community-driven collection of audio tours. For example, *[murmur]* (2002–2013) was a documentary oral history project that recorded and hosted personal stories and memories about specific urban locations in Toronto, Canada. Distinctive signs were hung in specific locations with a phone number for people to call to hear the recordings related to the site. A walker could access a map of the sites online, and follow along with the recordings, learning more about how locals know and experience the location. Similarly, in *Hear Our Houston* (2012–2015) organized by Carrie Schneider, people were invited to record walking tours related to their personal knowledge, and anyone could download the audio tour online. Houston, Texas, is not known for its walkability, so this project helped reveal walkable neighborhoods, and invited people to walk in someone else's shoes or consider the familiar through a new point of view.

Yet another twist on the audio tour is the use of radio. In *Fracture Mob* (2016) by **Jennie Savage** (1975–), the artist collaborated with a Lisbon-based artist internet radio station to broadcast a non-site-specific audio guide for people to get lost in their own location, wherever that might be across the globe. This use of radio meant that people all over the world were experiencing the work at the same time. That sense of simultaneity lent a collective quality to the experience.

EXERCISE: Collaborative Audio Tours

Think of a location where you could collaborate with three or more people to create a collection of walking tours. Where are the boundaries of the location you've chosen? Who would you invite to lead these tours and why? Why would you highlight this area? When would you conduct the walks? Think about time of day, season, day of the week, safety, etc. What will you tell the collaborators to focus on and why?

Once you have answered these questions, invite your collaborators to record their audio walking tours. Collect their audio tour files and host them online. Invite others to listen to and follow their tours. Solicit feedback from the followers. What did the followers learn or reflect on? What have you learned from this experience?

Walking Tour as Social Critique

There are clear advantages to taking on the leadership role of a walking tour guide because participants see the guide as an authority on both the topic of the tour and a certain way of looking and experiencing a walking route. When an artist takes on this role, they can make specific choices to develop alternative narratives that disrupt well-known or institutionally-crafted narratives, draw powerful connections, or highlight little-known histories that might otherwise go unrecognized. For example, in Turner's tour of Toronto, she points out sites of Black history that might otherwise be overlooked. Similarly, in Hill's tours of New York City, she prompts critical examination of the walking tour itself in a city with a massive tourism industry.

Another example that is unique because it brings walking social critique inside a museum, is *Museum Highlights: A Gallery Talk* (1989) by **Andrea Fraser** (1965–). This satirical work, originally a live performance, now exists as a video of Fraser leading a tour of the Philadelphia Museum of Art using the fictional persona of a docent named Jane Castleton. Through her narrative choices, including conventional analysis of the museum's collection, but also the toilets, cloakroom, and gift shop, Fraser draws attention to the exaggerated praise and prescriptive aesthetic values museum docents sometimes employ. This work demonstrates how walking tours can be used as a form of social critique, specifically in relation to institutions' official and unofficial policies and assumptions.

EXERCISE: Tour for Critique

Think of local change you'd like to see take place. Develop a walking tour to address that social critique. This could be a serious and informational walking tour, or it could include humor and personas. Whatever you choose, be sure to provide actions that your walkers can take after the walk. Go on a practice run-through with someone else to get feedback before you announce your tour publicly.

Liveness and Participation

In chapter two a variety of documentation approaches were covered, and in chapter eight re-enactments and reprises will be discussed. Here we examine liveness, which in the case of walking as artistic practice, is the act of walking itself, rather than a representation or recording of it. A walking artwork can be live for those directly participating in the walk, or live for passersby who observe the event happening in real time. Specifically, when considering leading versus following, there is a question of liveness. In some scenarios, participants will engage with live in-person following, whereas in other circumstances, one might only have access to a score or archive to follow.

Many walks are documented by video, photo, or other media in order to share with the public, galleries, or educational institutions. Some argue that a live walking experience holds more room for individual interpretation, since photographs and videos are cropped and framed interpretations of the live experience; by being present oneself, the participant can choose what part(s) of the experience to pay attention to, rather than the prescribed viewpoint of the documentation. Other individuals believe the live walk itself is the artistic experience, not the documentation. Still others, like performance scholar **Andy Horwitz**, believe that a live work begins the moment a participant first hears about it and the idea of the work enters the participant's imagination.[17] All of these points serve to demonstrate there are a wide range of opinions about the nature of liveness and documentation, and when a work begins, ends, or whether it exists at all.

Actor, playwright, performance artist, and director **Laurie Carlos** (1946–2016) described the importance of liveness in her introduction to *Performance: Live Art Since the 60s* (2004): ". . . Live work by artists unites the psychological with the perceptual, the conceptual with the practical, thought with action. According to the current tenets of critical theory, the viewer of art, the reader of a text, the audience of a film or a theater production are all performers, since our *live*, immediate responses to an art work are essential to the completion of the work." It is important to note, Carlos's analysis is taken from a performance art text, which has very similar roots to walking as artistic practice. Both have early practitioners who were resisting capitalist economies of competition and profit (see chapters one and eight). The ephemerality of live art, or a live walk, resists traditional art collection, and values the live experience over all else.

Some might also believe that a live participant in a walk may have a greater sense of collective creation than a person later accessing the work through archival materials or a reprise experience. These hierarchical points of view ("better" versus "worse") might be useful and true in some scenarios; however, it can also be useful, and often more inclusive, to simply view the live versus archival experiences as *different* types of engagement, rather than "better" or "worse." Generally speaking, far more people will experience a walking artwork through its documentation than the live event itself. Performance studies scholar **Rebecca Schneider** (1959–) elaborates on this point when she notes, " 'gestic acts (re)enacted live' can be considered 'material traces' and provide access to radically different ways of accessing and creating new knowledge."[18] To this point, artist **Han Bing** (1974–) demonstrates the value of a walking archive with his project *Walking the Cabbage* (2000–2008), in which he walked with a cabbage tied to a string through various locations, such as Beijing's Tiananmen Square, Miami Beach (US), and the Champs-Élysées in Paris. His archive of photos distributed online reaches a far larger audience than the live events ever could.

Others might also highlight that giving outsized importance to the unique and singular live experience can stem from the norms of commercial art worlds, where irreproducibility, or being the first in something, is central to creating and inflating monetary value, leaning on a culture of exclusivity. In this way, ephemeral walking experiences can be commodified by selling tickets to limited-capacity live events, or by later selling the documentation of the event, thereby nullifying the argument that the liveness somehow is a rebellion against recognized institutions or capitalism.

The Artist's Absence

It's important to note that an artist does not need to be physically present to be a leader. For example, the development of maps, scores, and archives can lead a walking participant in the artist's absence. Yoko Ono's book, *Grapefruit* (1964), is a collection of instructions and drawings inviting participants on numerous walks, such as *City Piece* (1961), which states, "Walk all over the city with an empty baby carriage." Ono does not need to be present to lead any of these walks, and the outcomes could be wide-ranging.

Similarly, human interventions in the landscape or topography, such as desire lines (paths worn into the ground where people frequently walk, similar to Long's *A Line Made by Walking*), cairns (small piles of rocks) or trail markers, sometimes known as trail blaze, can be a form of leading without being physically present. Nancy Holt took a special interest in this type of guidance with her work *Trail Markers* (1969), which featured photographs of trail blaze (in the form of orange painted dots in the English countryside) during a trip in 1969. She thought of them as a type of found sculpture or ready-made, and later presented the work as a grid of twenty photographs in 2012.[19] The artist is absent from this work, aside from having selected the point of view for each photograph and arranging them on the wall. The collected orange dots do not require an artist to be present in order to lead a participant on the walk.

Other traces can be used to lead walkers, including those that are agricultural, industrial, natural, accidental, or intentional, such as tracks, fences, bollards, roads, etc. Artists **Heath Bunting** (1966–) and **Kayle Brandon** (1976–) paid special attention to fences in their work, *D'Fence Cuts* (2013) in which they pursued a walk following a circle traced on a map. As they encountered fences in the way of the circle, they trimmed holes in them to create passages. For a time afterwards, another walker could have followed their map and fence holes to recreate the same walk in their absence. Attention to absence can be a potent form of walking leadership, if handled thoughtfully.

EXERCISE: Accidental Path

Think about an accidental path you know of. Where is it? What marks it? Who might be able to walk there and when? If you cannot think of one, go outside and walk around looking for one. Look for those agricultural, industrial, or natural traces that could create a path, intentionally or not.

Archives

A walking artist might also use an archive as a means of leading a walk in their own absence. An archive is an organized accumulation of stored material (documents, recordings, images, files, and objects) that can be examined. Some archives might be quite simple and small, while others might be more complex and sprawling with several different types of material included for review. Art historian **Charles Merewether** suggests an archive ". . . provid(es) the last word in the account of what has come to pass."[20] In this way, archives can serve as a form of memory and historical knowledge, and they often highlight a particular point of view and/or site. For these reasons, archives can be appealing to walking artists who have specific viewpoints to convey and are often interested in specific places.

An example of this pointed use of archiving is *Circular Walk inside Arctic Circle, Around Inuvik, N.W.T.* (1969) by the collective **N. E. Thing Co.** (1966–1978, consisting of **Ingrid Baxter** [1938–] and **Iain Baxter** [1936–]). This walking work consisted of the two walkers wearing pedometers as they traversed the circumference of Inuvik, Canada. The archive of the work features a grid of black and white photographs mounted on a carefully designed sheet of paper that mimics the design of official records, complete with a foil seal, labels, date, and description boxes. The archival choices of N. E. Thing Co. affect how one reads this archive. Through their design choices, which included several markers of corporate structures, they affect how one might interpret and consider following this archive of a comparatively mundane walk.

Philosopher **Jacques Derrida** (1930–2004) pointed out, "There is no political power without control of the archive, if not of memory."[21] He went on to emphasize the importance of access to the archive, as well as participation in its development and interpretation. If a walking artist takes a particular interest in archiving as a means of leading future walkers, they should ask themselves, how might the archive be created and then function? This approach includes questions such as: What should be collected? How might the archive be arranged? How will the materials be made accessible to others? And where and when is it to be deployed? Even if walking documentation seems mundane at first glance, artists make political decisions when they decide to engage in archival practices. Writer **Hal Foster** (1955–) emphasized an artist's archival choices can also serve as a "gesture of alternative knowledge or counter-memory,"[22] especially when posed in contrast to existing societal understandings of a place or a history.

An example of this counter-memory is *Street with a View* (2008) by **Ben Kinsley** (1972–) and **Robin Hewlett** (1980–) (see figure 4.2). This work was a collaborative effort between the artists and the Google Street View team in Pittsburgh, Pennsylvania. The artists staged humorous action scenes along routes where the Google team was updating photographs for Google Maps with their 360-degree cameras. These entertaining tableaux photographs lived as an archive on Google Street view for a period of time until the street views were updated. Users of Google Maps could follow these artist-crafted views on a self-led walk. The humorous images were counter to the usual photographs on Google Maps, which are normally simply informative.

Merewether hints at the humorous elements of the archival impulse by emphasizing their "sense of the absurd, the futile, or the impossible, which ultimately haunts the logic of the archive."[23] In this way, the archive relates to the concept of chance, embraced by practitioners like the Dadaists, the Situationists, and Fluxus. Whenever a participant reactivates an archive, the particularities of the site, the identity of the participant, and the time at which it occurs, all affect how the walker follows the archive

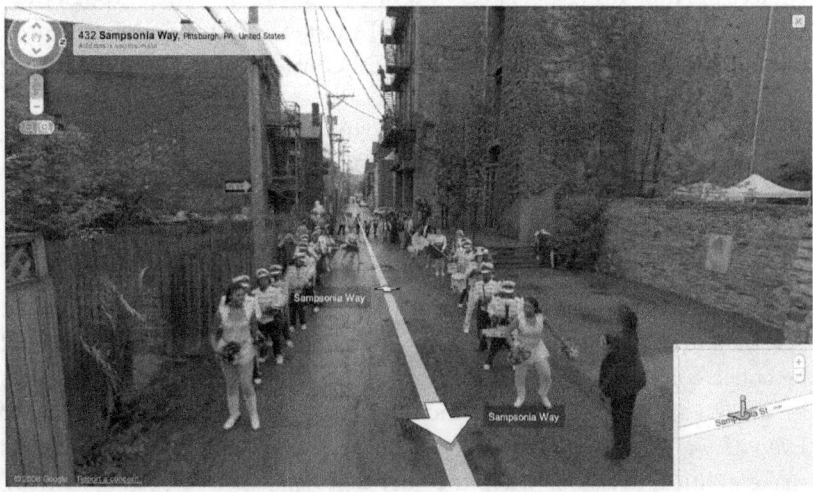

Figure 4.2. Ben Kinsley and Robin Hewlett, *Street with a View*, 2008, screen capture from Google Street View, © Google, Inc. *Source*: Courtesy of Ben Kinsley and Robin Hewlett.

on the walk. All of these archival choices are connected to modes of documentation, which can be reviewed in chapter two, as well as issues of accessibility, which are addressed in chapter five.

EXERCISE: Archive Walk

Think of a walk you'd like to take and that you'd like others to go on. Before you go on that walk, select three different modes of documentation that you will combine to create an archive of the experience, which will also compel people to follow your lead, even without you there. Try to select modes of documentation that are fitting for the site, and that complement each other. Ask yourself:

1. What will you collect?

2. What could be ethically or legally collected? Be mindful of consent and cultural misappropriation (when an individual from a powerful or dominant culture adopts elements from a culture systematically oppressed by the dominant culture[24]).

3. How might the archive be arranged?

4. How will the materials be made accessible to others?

5. Where and when is it to be deployed?

When you have answered these questions, go for your walk and use your three modes of documentation. Finally, assemble your archive and share with others as planned. Do you find that people are compelled to follow the archive you've assembled? What would you do differently if you did it again?

Summary

In this chapter leading and following as it relates to walking was the focus, shining a light on the diverse ways an artist might choose to lead. Issues of consent and group-walking dynamics were emphasized to assist in making future projects as productive and accessible as possible. Tourism was discussed with a focus on audio tours and social critique, which also highlighted the frequency with which artists rely on these formats.

Further topics included liveness and participation, the artist's absence, and archives, providing many examples and points of view to support an artist's decision-making on future walking projects. Several exercises help the reader explore more deeply.

Chapter 5

Who Gets to Walk and Where?

Artist and scholar Morag Rose points out the streets are free and belong to everyone.[1] These spaces have particular value because "the pavement is one of the few opportunities for casual, embodied encounters with difference."[2] This chapter examines a selection of the many different impediments to walking based on a person's identity or positionality, which lends itself to different privileges and forms of oppression. Determining who gets to walk and where intersects with systemic issues that are intertwined, such as colonialism, capitalism, classism, racism, sexism, ableism, xenophobia, and citizenship, among others. By surveying the work of artists such as SANTIAGO X (1982–, Coushatta/Chamoru), **Kubra Khademi** (1989–), **Amanda Heng** (1951–), **Christine Sun Kim** (1980–), and **Inua Ellams** (1984–), to name a few, readers will explore the intersection of walking-based projects with these systemic access issues.

Vocabulary: Systemic Oppression

Also see related vocabulary in chapter two.

1. **Colonialism:** "domination of a people or area by a foreign state or nation; the practice of extending and maintaining a nation's political and economic control over another people or area";[3] Specifically in the United States it refers to "removal of title from and removal of Indigenous peoples themselves. Treaties enacted dispossession of land as kin, and the material basis for culture. This settler colonial attitude towards land and other resources as things to be owned and used (up) manifests itself in all contemporary relations."[4]

89

2. **Capitalism:** "an economic system characterized by private or corporate ownership of capital goods, by investments that are determined by private decision, and by prices, production, and the distribution of goods that are determined mainly by competition in a free market."[5]

Note, the following can be both individualized (behavior and attitudes) or systemic (oppression via social, economic, and political systems).

1. **Classism:** discrimination against others based on their perceived status (social or economic).

2. **Racism:** discrimination against others based on their race.

3. **White Supremacy:** the harmful belief that white people are better than people of other races and therefore deserve extra privileges.

4. **Sexism:** discrimination against others based on their gender.

5. **Ableism:** discrimination against others with disabilities.

6. **Xenophobia:** fear, hatred, bias, or animosity towards strangers or foreigners, or of things perceived to be strange or foreign. It is often directed towards immigrants and is closely tied to racism.

7. **Citizenship:** status of being "a native or naturalized person who owes allegiance to a government and is entitled to protection from it."[6] This is different from **nationality**, which refers to where a person was born.

8. **Intersectionality**: understanding there are many overlapping embodied identity factors that impact a person's experience of systems of oppression and discrimination.

Public versus Private

In contemporary capitalist society, space is divided into public and private areas. Morag Rose points out that, in the context of the United Kingdom, "privatization and enclosure of common land has an impact on everyone, restricting where we go and how we act. Do you know who owns the pavement and whether you are at risk of trouble if you stop to chat? Who is absent from the pavement, park or cafe you use? How can it be made more accessible and open?"[7] This division of space can occasionally be confusing as private spaces will sometimes masquerade as public spaces—think of shopping malls, private parks and plazas, airports, waiting rooms and lobbies, etc. These spaces look open and invite people into them during specific time frames; however, behavior within those spaces is tightly controlled and often oriented around services, consumption, and profit. Artist, author, curator, and activist Lucy Lippard reminds us that "places that are merely accessible to citizens, rather than controlled by them through use, are not truly public places."[8]

Additionally, public spaces may look different in different parts of a city. Sidewalks might be wholly absent, tree canopies can be sparse or missing, and parks might be nonexistent. In the United States, many of these differences are affected by the practice of redlining, and its ongoing effects on contemporary space. Redlining was, and still is,[9] the discriminatory practice in which mortgages and housing sales were denied to people of color and minority populations based on color-coded affluence-based maps, which were developed by the federal government in the 1930s. These maps led to widespread racially segregated communities. Many of those same maps directly align to contemporary food deserts, reduced educational quality based on reduced property taxes, and missing parks and recreation investment, among other effects, leading to wide disparities in the quality and size of public space available.

Vocabulary: Public versus Private

1. **Accessibility:** the degree to which any given situation is available for use and access; this can include any elements that make a person feel they should or should not be in a particular place (welcomeness for people with disabilities, unhoused people, people who are neurodivergent, people of marginalized racial or ethnic identities, etc.).

2. **Privatization:** to change control or ownership from public to private.

3. **Surveillance:** watching, listening, or otherwise tracking people or things.

4. **Gentrification:** the process of new populations moving into a not affluent neighborhood (often wealthier people, artists and cultural workers, or other identity groups), which affects housing, social dynamics, and business to the detriment of the original inhabitants.

5. **Redlining**: a discriminatory practice in which mortgages and housing sales were denied to people of color and minority populations based on color-coded affluence-based maps developed by federal government in the 1930s.

6. **Right-to-Roam**: the idea that some public or privately owned land, lakes, and rivers should be accessible to the general public for recreation and exercise (also known as "the commons").

This organization of public and private space can result in conflict as it is a manifestation of classism, power, and discrimination, where a small number of wealthy people control large areas of land or space for specific extractive activities (shopping, sport hunting, mining, logging, etc.), and prevent access by the general public to a shared commons. These circumstances disadvantage those who are more heavily reliant on the walkability of public spaces, such as women, the elderly, children, people with disabilities, and other minority communities. The result of this hierarchical arrangement of public and private space can be trespassing, sit-ins, mass street actions, and occupations, which may involve walking processions, marches, or pilgrimages to start or end conflicts.

An example of one of these class-based conflicts is the Kinder Mass Trespass in 1932, in which over four hundred people trespassed onto Kinder Scout, a moorland plateau in England where a small group of wealthy people wanted exclusive use for hunting. The trespassers wanted to highlight how the public was denied access to areas of open country. The scale of this action and the context of this location were impactful, and five people were jailed. The action helped contribute to the creation of English National Parks in 1949, the development of long-distance footpaths across England, and the Countryside and Rights of Way (CROW) Act in 2000 securing walker's rights over open country and common land.[10]

Other parts of the world have enacted similar measures, such as the Right of Public Access ("Allemansträtten") in Sweden, which has existed informally for many centuries, but was formalized into the Swedish constitution in 1994. It states that people have "the right to walk, cycle, ride, ski and camp on any land with the exception of private gardens, near a dwelling house, or land under cultivation."[11] Similar formalizing laws have been passed elsewhere. For example, in 1967, a US motel owner attempted to wall off a section of Oregon's beach in front of his motel, despite the fact that the public had been using the beach for years under the assumption that it was public space. In response to extreme public pressure, the state government passed the Oregon Beach Bill of 1967, guaranteeing free, unrestricted, public access to all 362 miles of Oregon's coastline. Again, the specific context and location were vital to the success of this push for public space. This work to amplify the need for public access is ongoing worldwide, and collectives such as Jalan Gembira in Yogyakarta continue to push for walkable public infrastructure by holding walks, documenting their sensory experiences, and sharing that documentation widely.

Artist **Stuart McAdam** (1982–) highlights public versus private tension in his work *Lines Lost* (2013–2014) (see figure 5.1). This project featured walking the abandoned routes of Scottish railroad lines that were eliminated following the *Beeching Report* in 1963. These were performative group walks, drawing attention to transportation challenges in the rural north of Scotland, and the conflict between private property and right-to-roam,[12] which is the idea that some public or privately owned land, lakes, and rivers should be accessible to the general public for recreation and exercise (also known as "the commons"). As walkers followed the

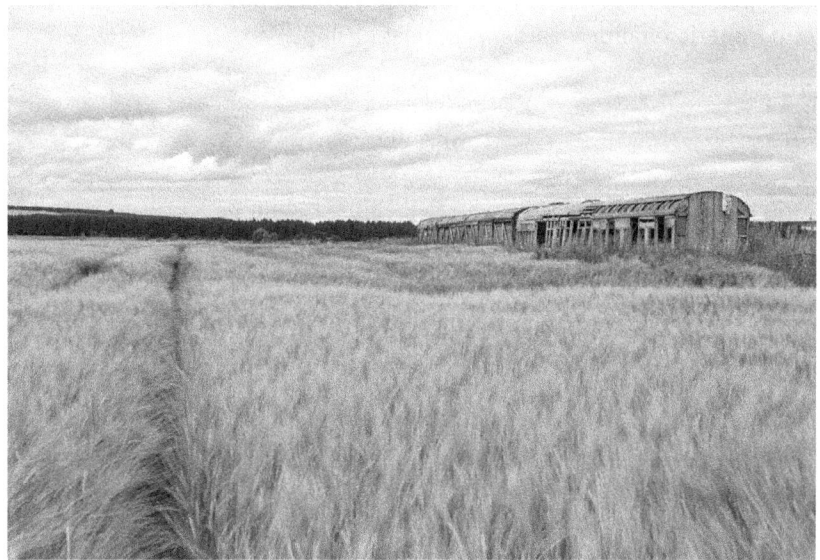

Figure 5.1. Stuart McAdam, *Lines Lost*, 2013–2014, photograph, © Stuart McAdam. *Source*: Courtesy of Stuart McAdam.

old railroad lines, they encountered physical obstacles along the lines and disgruntled private property owners who did not like having groups of people walking past their land or taking photographs. These energy dynamics and spatial relationships affected how local people understood the work. Issues of ownership and privacy continue to bubble to the surface, echoing Lippard's observation that "questions of access and multiple uses are important for city and borderland parks, as they are for the great national parks. Overregulated places become abstracted into mere spaces, but heavy use calls for much-debated policy decisions."[13]

Another example of combatting privatization, with focus on car-centric culture, is **Reclaim the Streets (RTS)**, a creative activist group from London that was founded in 1995 with carnival-protest tactics. "RTS saw the streets as the urban manifestation of the commons, in need of reclaiming from the enclosures of the car and commerce and transformed into truly public places to be enjoyed by all."[14] RTS planned these street parties in such a way that the police did not have time to prevent them from starting, and they used creative acts to block the roads for car traffic, but still allow people to walk through. In this way, RTS was answering a question posed by Lippard: "Can a public space escape its imposed character through use and through changing users?"[15] The answer in this case was clearly, yes, thanks to the use of energy dynamics, transitions, atmospheric qualities, and spatial relationships.

Surveillance

One of the main tools of control in both public and private spaces is surveillance. This can come in the form of video cameras, security officers, or even peer-surveillance such as the signs that remind people "If You See Something, Say Something." Often intertwined with surveillance is the phenomenon of gentrification, or the process of wealthier people moving into poorer neighborhoods and affecting housing, social dynamics, and business to the detriment of the original inhabitants. "Loitering, people hanging out in the street, and noise violations often get reported, especially in racially diverse neighborhoods."[16] Scholar **Simone Brown** (1973–), author of *Dark Matters: On the Surveillance of Blackness* (2015), reiterates this point, examining the history, practice of, and resistance to, surveillance of Black people in America. For these reasons, it is important for walking artists to be mindful of where they choose to walk and why, taking into consideration what their presence might contribute to gentrification, discrimination, or where they might be taking personal risks due to surveillance.

EXERCISE: Camera Awareness

Take a walk around the block and identify the placement of as many surveillance cameras as possible. Note their location on a map. Do you notice any areas you can walk without being surveilled? This walk is inspired by a walk from http://sharedwalks.com/.

To this point, walking artists have been interested in surveillance since the introduction of now well-recognized surveillance camera systems. For instance, Pat Naldi and Wendy Kirkup executed *Search* (1993) as an expression of concern when Newcastle-upon-Tyne became the first city center in the United Kingdom to install a closed-circuit television network. They took a synchronized walk in two separate locations in the city center and requested the surveillance footage from the police. The artists then edited the footage into twenty 10-second clips and transmitted the work during commercial breaks on Tyne Tees Television as a part of the 2nd Tyne International Exhibition of Contemporary Art. The artists' decision to create short duration clips that were shown intermittently on commercial-breaks for this large broadcast audience emphasized the experience of voyeurism introduced by the surveillance system, as the television viewers returned to watch the walkers again and again throughout the program.

Another example is **Bradley Davies**'s (1990–) *Echoing Movements* (2012), which features CCTV footage of the artist following various members of the public in George Square, Glasgow, Scotland, while wearing a high-visibility neon-yellow jacket. The work plays off Vito Acconci's work *Following Piece* (1969), also mentioned in chapter four. This walking work draws attention to potential high visibility of Davies's act of following, both in person, and from any location that has access to CCTV footage. This concept was especially pronounced considering that at the time, Britain had more CCTV cameras per person than any other nation. This work exists on the internet, available to a wide audience, and can also be shown in a gallery setting. These different contexts can affect awareness of spatial relationships, and how the viewer does or does not feel complicit in watching, following, and surveilling the people Davies follows in this walking work.

EXERCISE: Non-Commercial Walk

Locate a nearby shopping mall or plaza where you would feel safe walking. Note that safety will be different for each person depending on their positionality and identity. Devise a way to walk that is non-commercial, meaning you are walking without the intent to purchase anything. It might help to locate the rules for the mall, often available on the website. These can help spark your imagination, while still working within their code of conduct. What is allowed and not allowed? How might your walk help imagine different possibilities?

Colonialism and Indigenous Oppression

In chapter seven, place is addressed in depth, but here it is important to mention places are at least, in part, socially constructed, and as Marxist geographers point out, they are often founded by the powerful as acts of exclusion.[17] In many cases, that means Indigenous exclusion via oppressive colonialist actions and narratives that appeal to nationalist and bigoted points of view.[18]

Artists like **Renée Green** (1959–) have made walking works reflecting on these histories of division, colonialism, and their ongoing impacts, such as her film *Walking in NYL* (2016), which features footage of the artist walking in both New York City and Lisbon reflecting the complex multi-layered histories of these cities with multiple origins, identities, and relationships to imperialism. Green uses slowed pacing at times to draw focus to the details of each location, helping to emphasize the differences and similarities between the locations, past and present, as they relate to the Atlantic slave trade, post-industrialism, layered narratives, individual and collective experiences, crossings, oceans, and waterways.[19]

Vocabulary: Colonialism and Indigenous Oppression

1. **Indigenous:** originating or occurring naturally in "a particular place and having lived there for a long time before other people came there";[20] native; referring to people, plants, animals, and other elements of the environment.

2. **Imperialism:** "the policy, practice, or advocacy of extending the power and dominion of a nation especially by direct territorial acquisitions or by gaining indirect control over the political or economic life of other areas."[21]

3. **Nationalism:** a strong sense of loyalty to a specific nation; can be expressed individually or as a movement or government.

4. **Manifest Destiny:** the idea that the United States was destined by God (specifically referencing Christianity) to expand across the North American continent; the use of Christianity was one element of larger systematic attempts to remove Indigenous peoples through whatever means necessary, including genocide.

5. **Colonialism:** "domination of a people or area by a foreign state or nation; the practice of extending and maintaining a nation's political and economic control over another people or area."[22]

6. **Colonizer:** "a nation or state that takes control of a people or area as an extension of state power."[23]

7. **Settler:** a person who settles in a new region, most often as a member of a colonizing state power.

North American colonial history involves many events where walking is described through a nationalist lens, but it was displacement—a practice of walking into other people's places and assuming access to everything. This included events from forced Indigenous and enslaved African people's marches to invasive white-settler encroachment. Displacement is most commonly recognized as starting in 1492 with the arrival of Christopher Columbus, although there were also earlier explorers. Displacement continued with the idea of Manifest Destiny, a phrase first coined in 1845 to describe the idea that the United States was destined by a Christian God to expand across the North American continent. This place-based ideology was used to justify the forced removal of Indigenous people from their homes, including crimes against humanity such as genocide and forced marriage, while leading settlers on marches across the country to take their land.

Some of those westward expansion settler processions are now retold in US history books, such as the Oregon Trail or the California Trail. Other processions are less talked about, such as the 150-mile forced march of 1,700 Dakota women, children, and elders after the US Dakota War of 1862, or the 5,043-mile Trail of Tears that passes through nine US states and was used to displace approximately 100,000 Native Americans.[24] When these marches are mentioned, they often imply a false end or disappearance of the Indigenous population, a concept recognized by historian **Jean M. O'Brian** (1958–, White Earth Ojibwe) as "firsting" and "lasting."[25]

Since the origin of Manifest Destiny, US politicians have continued to suppress these narratives, minimizing emphasis on domestic death marches, and amplifying ideas of an empty frontier that was settled by a self-built, persevering people. For example, in the 1980 televised Reagan-Anderson presidential debate in Baltimore, Reagan referenced, ". . . a special kind of people—people who had a special love for freedom and who had the courage to uproot themselves and leave hearth and homeland and come to what in the beginning was the most undeveloped wilderness possible."[26] By endorsing the fantasy narrative of marching westward across "empty" lands of North America, politicians perpetuate harm against Indigenous people, denying them their history and humanity. To counter this harmful idea, one can start by asking, "Is this your ancestral land?" If not, readers can look up the native land one is currently occupying to learn about the Indigenous people who were there first, and who continue to work against oppressive systems.

EXERCISE: Research the Land and Language

Preserving Indigenous languages is important to countering forced assimilation of Indigenous societies. Take a moment to ask, "Is this your ancestral land?" Take a moment to research either your language as a native person, or the language of the native peoples of the land you are currently on. If you are not native to this land, you will need to do some research to learn about the language(s) of this region. For example, in southeastern Minnesota, a resource is the Bdote Memory Map: http://bdotememorymap.org/—similar resources may exist for the land you are on.

Start with regional place names, which are often named by people who walked to travel. This could include creeks, village sites, plants, and animals. Focus on seeing place names that are in the ancestral language and ask: What does it mean to travel through these places? If they are not currently named with their original name, can you find out what it is? How can you make moves to change place names back to their original names?

Try taking a walk to visit these sites and find examples of these regional plants or animals. Research pronunciation and speak the words aloud. Your approach will change according to your location and positionality/identity. Take time for inward reflection of what it means to walk through spaces that have been forced to assimilate. What does it mean to you and your ancestry?

Some contemporary groups of Native Americans have launched walking projects to highlight these oppressed histories, such as the *Dakota Commemorative Walk* (2002–2012). It was completed every other year for the ten years leading up to 2012, the one hundred fiftieth anniversary of the Minnesota-based US Dakota War. The walk retraced the footsteps of the Dakota women, children, and elders who were forced to march one hundred fifty miles from Morton, Minnesota, to Fort Snelling before being expelled from the state by the Dakota Removal Act of 1863. Professor and participant **Gwen Westerman** (1957–, Sisseton Wahpeton Dakota Oyate) emphasized that the walk was a spiritual ceremony honoring the women and children, not a protest or a reenactment.[27] Through their collective actions, this group demonstrated one of the ways walking can be used to honor and share history. For outside observers, the walk also highlights the fact that the Dakota Removal Act is still a federal law despite efforts as recent as 2019 to change it. Racist outdated laws are just one of the hurdles people face as they grapple with the question of who gets to walk and where. Other challenges include issues of housing, healthcare, access to land, and more. These many layers of accessibility issues come into play when considering questions of walking access affected by intersecting systems of oppression.

Artist Andrea Carlson took a slightly different approach when she presented a site-specific large-scale (15' × 266') installation along the Chicago Riverwalk entitled *You Are on Potawatomi Land* (2021). The sheer scale of the work requires walking to take in the full text: "Bodéwadmikik éthë yéyék—You are on Potawatomi land," and it is situated on a recognized public walking space. The site of the work is near the former sandbar in the Chicago River that lends its name to the Sandbar Decision, a US Supreme Court case that "denied the Pokagon Band of Potawatomi ownership of the unceded land that was built into the lake by settlers." In Carlson's words, this work is ". . . meant to reaffirm Native people where they live and where they seem invisible, which is often the case in urban environments."[28]

Indigenous Futurist artist ~~SANTIAGO~~ X, also located in Chicago and working large scale, used his background in architecture to pay homage to ancestral pre-colonization practices of mound building via "innovat[ing] on our own land again, which gets to the heart of what it means to be an Indigenous futurist."[29] With *Pokto Činto* (*Serpent Twin*) (2019), an earth-work installed at Schiller Park on the Des Plaines River, and nine miles away, *Fololokah Cin Cinto* (*Coiled Serpent*) (projected, 2023) at Horner Park on the Chicago River and meant to be walked on, X does just that. When interviewed by the *Chicago Tribune*, X stated,

> "For those who don't know, Cahokia is the largest mound civilization north of Mexico, and at its peak in the 1300s, it had a higher population than London," X said. "I'm trying to remind people of that presence and the grand nature of [I]ndigenous civilizations and their ability to create communities and trade networks and cultural epicenters. We had those things here pre-Columbus, preinvasion. I walk around these American cities, and I don't see the presence of the [I]ndigenous point of view, the [I]ndigenous architect. . . . I don't see the presence of [I]ndigenous place makers in any of these cities, so I would like to return to that or at least catalyze the movement to create [I]ndigenous spaces again."[30]

While many of the examples of walking projects above focus on Indigenous oppression in the United States, Indigenous people across the world have experienced similar violence and oppression at the hands of colonizers. It is important to continue studying and responding to these histories and the ongoing effects of colonialism on contemporary living, so oppressive systems can be dismantled, and walking practitioners can be responsive and thoughtful in their walking projects. Additionally, while there is a section below focused on race, it is important to note that racial profiling can be an important factor for Indigenous people walking in both public and private spaces. It is vital for walking artists to thoughtfully address racial profiling as they construct experiences, considering personal safety of all participants, while also advocating for policy change to improve systemic conditions.

Race

Writer **Garnette Cadogan** (1971–) wrote his well-known article "Black and Blue" (2015) in *Freeman's*, which was later republished in *Literary Hub* in 2016 with the title, "Walking While Black." This article shares his experiences of growing up and walking as a Black man in Kingston, Jamaica, then attending school and walking in New Orleans, Louisiana, and eventually moving to New York City. He details the difficulty of walking in areas of high crime, first in Jamaica as a majority Black country where he could blend into the crowd, and then in New Orleans, where he became a person of suspicion based on his race due to the United States' history as a country that previously enslaved people from Africa and demarcated their bodies as property that could not freely walk or circulate.

Cadogan outlines and analyzes different tactics he developed to avoid conflict with the cops in the United States, from thickening his accent and relying on college-affiliated clothing and ID cards, to avoiding holding objects—especially shiny ones. Cadogan notes that it was difficult to piece together these often unspoken rules, having not grown up within the US and not having received "The Talk" from his parents—explaining how to behave with extreme politeness and cooperation under all circumstances when stopped by the police. He notes, "For a black man, to assert your dignity before the police was to risk assault." He discusses the complicated ongoing heightened awareness of, and negotiations with, his surroundings as he walks, such as avoiding running or sudden movements, avoiding getting too close to people, avoiding salutations, and modifying how he dresses or whom he walks with. He points out, "Much of my walking is . . . a pantomime undertaken to avoid the choreography of criminality." Cadogan also points out, "Walking while black restricts the experience of walking, renders inaccessible the classic Romantic experience of walking alone. It forces me to be in constant relationship with others, unable to join the New York flâneurs I had read about and hoped to join." While Cadogan's essay focuses specifically on the experience of Black people walking in the United States (with its specific history of enslavement of Africans, segregationist Jim Crow laws, lynching, and redlining), nearly all people of color in colonial spaces encounter challenges and limitations to who gets to walk and where, due to the harm caused by imperialism across the globe.

This section focuses on the racial barrier in walking and moving through public space, which can be quite dangerous depending on the context, due to racialized stereotypes of people of color as dangerous or threatening in colonized or white-dominant societies. Artists must always consider those who are vulnerable to policing, violence, and incarceration, which authors like Simone Brown have pointed out in works such as *Dark Matters: On the Surveillance of Blackness*. There are, sadly, many examples in the United States of people of color suffering racially motivated attacks while walking.[31]

Walking-focused researcher Morag Rose points out the racialization of the trope of "the walking thinker" in psychogeographic practices, describing a physically mobile white man taking self-focused walks.[32] This stereotype is built on hundreds of years of literary works by white men, as well as seventeenth- and eighteenth-century practices like the Grand Tour, a trip through Europe undertaken by upper-class white European men as they came of age. Scholar **KangJae Lee** (1979–) has published a number of papers outlining how racial discrimination continues today in outdoor leisure and park participation.

Within art history, there are also examples of racial discrimination, as was mentioned in chapter one's examination of the Situationist Abdelhafid Khatib, whose 1958 attempt at psychogeographic walking in Les Halles, Paris, was foiled by two racially driven arrests. Similarly, critic Lori Waxman points out the racial difference between two 1963 Fluxus scores, Benjamin Patterson's *Man Who Runs* versus Robert Filliou's *One-Minute Scenario*, both of which reference men running in and out of city buildings. Patterson, a Black man, was to run into and up the stairs of the New York Public Library with the path marked on the ground, while Filliou, a white French Protestant man with a glass eye, was to run out the Chelsea Hotel, around the block on an unmarked path, and then back into the hotel. Certainly, both the locations, the running, and the racial identities of the performers would affect the audience's reading of these works.[33]

A more recent walking work that emphasizes race is a collection of twenty-five-mile walks along five of Detroit's major avenues in 2017–2018 by JeeYeun Lee, entitled *Walking Detroit* (see figure 5.2). These walks

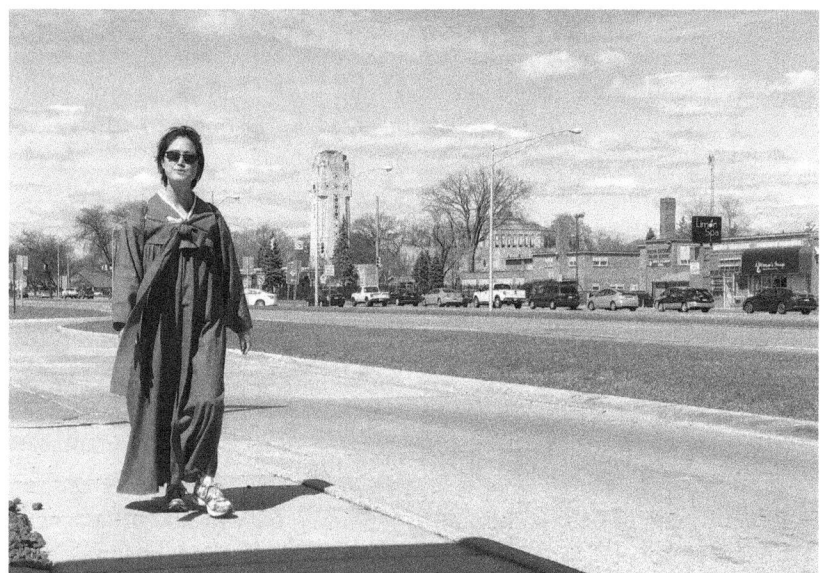

Figure 5.2. JeeYeun Lee, *Walking Detroit*, 2017–2018, photograph, photo by Brandon Bullard. *Source*: Courtesy of JeeYeun Lee.

passed through both the city and suburbs and were an effort to deeply explore the city of Detroit and its complex history. Lee does this from the positionality of a Korean immigrant studying at Cranbrook Academy of Art, and she acknowledges her status as an uninvited guest on Anishinaabe land. Lee traces the Indigenous roots of Detroit through early colonialism, to segregating practices that continue through present day, as gentrification moves forward. Lee states, "When I conducted these walks, I wore a traditional Korean Dress made from denim, an all-American fabric imbued with the history of slavery in cotton and indigo, and associated with frontier settler colonialism. I wanted to wear my identity on my sleeve, literally, and place myself in the landscape, to undermine any colonizing anthropological stance of neutrality or observation."[34] Lee uses photo documentation, mapping, statistical analysis, video, exhibition installation, and independent publications to showcase this walking archive, highlighting her observations and thorough research.

EXERCISE: Centering Data

Artist JeeYeun Lee uses data and statistical analysis in both her installations, and in her publication *Walking Detroit* (2020), which includes the five 25-mile walks mentioned above.

Take a moment to look up demographic statistics for the area or region you are currently occupying and pay attention to the racial breakdown. In the United States, the American Community Survey (ACS) five-year estimates can be helpful for locating demographic and racial statistics.

What do you notice? How have racial demographics changed or stayed the same in your region? How might this affect walking in your area?

Another example is the collaborative walking group, **Brooklyn League of Women Walkers (BLWW)**, which was founded by **Walis Johnson** (1960–) and **Amanda Gutiérrez** (1978–) in 2019 and focused on the intersection of race, gender, and walking. This "multigenerational collaborative art project [brought] together women of color (immigrant and native) from the communities of Sunset Park and Red Hook in a shared experience of walking and art-making." They aimed "to build solidarity and political consciousness among women walkers across different cultures and urban geographies of the gendered experience of walking."[35] Their walking events drew "women of Latinx, Black, Asian, and Middle Eastern descent who, because of ethnicity and geography, rarely cross paths in their neighborhoods, yet because of their gender are affected by the same feelings of vulnerability as they walk along city streets."[36] They walked individually, in pairs, and in groups, holding discussions, marking maps, taking photos, creating videos, and presenting their observations of their everyday walking experiences.

Gender

One element of identity that has a significant impact on one's ability to walk freely is gender, which is a social construct based on cultural norms, behaviors, and psychological traits or roles typically associated with one sex. Scholar Rebecca Solnit reflects on the history of walking and gender, with particular attention to women, when she notes,

> Legal measures, social mores subscribed to by both men and women, the threat implicit in sexual harassment, and rape itself

have all limited women's ability to walk where and when they wished. (Women's clothes and bodily confinements—high heels, tight or fragile shoes, corsets and girdles, very full or narrow skirts, easily damaged fabrics, veils that obscure vision—are part of the social mores that have handicapped women as effectively as laws and fears.) . . . Even the English language[37] is rife with words and phrases that sexualize women's walking.[38]

Author **Kerri Andrews** (1981–) adds that domestic and caretaking responsibilities traditionally assigned to women further restricted, and in some cases continue to restrict, access to walking and its benefits, in addition to the previously mentioned issues of safety and vulnerability.[39] These hurdles have shaped how women, trans, non-binary, or gender non-conforming people have walked, and continue to walk, in public.

Vocabulary: Gender

Note that there is a lot of vocabulary surrounding the idea of gender, and it is important to understand that sex is different from gender.

1. **Gender:** a social construct based on cultural norms, behaviors, and psychological traits or roles typically associated with one sex; gender varies and evolves across societies and over time, and is generally categorized as male, female, or nonbinary.

2. **Cis-:** a person whose gender identity aligns with the sex assigned to them at birth is called cisgender, or a cis-woman or cis-man.

3. **Trans-:** a transgender (trans-) person has a gender identity that differs from the cultural expectations of the sex they were assigned at birth.

4. **Sex:** a person's biological status, typically assigned at birth, usually on the basis of reproductive anatomy, and is generally categorized as male, female, or intersex.

5. **Sexuality or sexual orientation:** "refers to the enduring physical, romantic and/or emotional attraction to members of the same and/or other genders, including lesbian, gay, bisexual and straight orientations."[40]

Walking with any gender identity other than a straight cis-man has historically, and continues to be, varying levels of challenging, dangerous, and sometimes life threatening.

An example of a walking work that foregrounds these gender-based challenges is *The Sissy's Progress* (2014) by queer academic **Nando Messias** (see figure 5.3). This flamboyant procession piece was a reaction to Messias's experience of an urban homophobic attack years earlier near their home in East London. In this performative participatory walk, Messias defied gender norms and wore a red gown with balloons, and led a live marching band along city streets, pausing at the site of the attack, and performing various symbolic rituals from start to end. Through this act of spectacle, featuring varied energy dynamics, musicality, juxtaposition, and atmospheric qualities, they highlighted the contradictions of gender, celebration, vulnerability, and city violence.

Gender is closely linked to feminism, the belief in equal rights and opportunities across genders. Several books have been written about women and LGBTQ people struggling to walk freely in public with their bodies, needs, and desires accommodated, such as *Feminist City: Claiming Space in a Man-Made World* (2020) by **Leslie Kern** (1975–) or *Flâneuse: Women Walk the City* (2016) by Lauren Elkin. Combine gender with any other oppressed identities (sexuality, race, class, religion, age, ability, etc.), and walking freely becomes even more difficult. For example, Human Rights

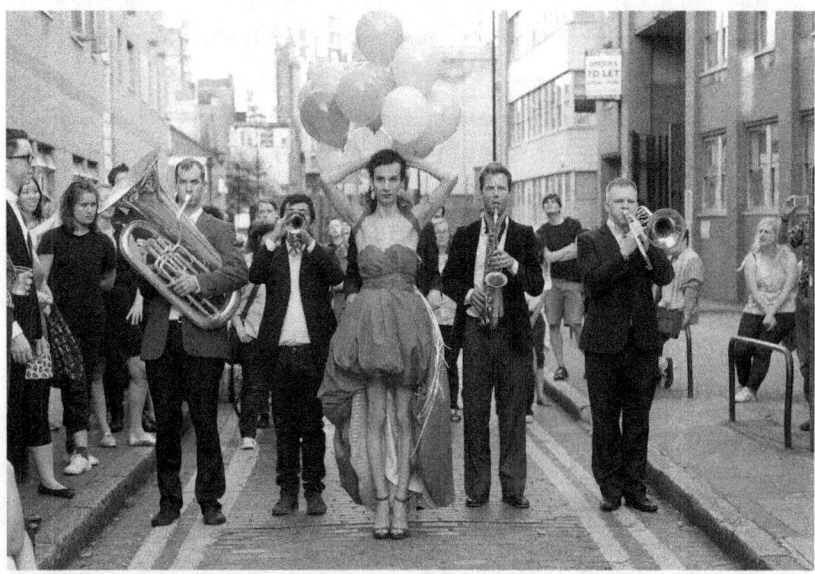

Figure 5.3. Nando Messias, *The Sissy's Progress*, 2014, public performance, photo by Loredana Denicola. *Source*: Courtesy of Nando Messias.

Campaign recorded fifty-one (2021) and forty-four (2020) known murders of trans, non-binary, or gender non-conforming people throughout the United States, and most of those murders were of transgender women of color.[41] This understanding of many overlapping embodied identity factors and the impact that has on their experiences of systems of oppression and discrimination is called intersectionality.

We see intersectionality at play in works like *Armor* (2015) by Kubra Khademi, which is an eight-minute walk by Khademi down a busy street in central Kabul, Afghanistan, wearing custom-made armor that emphasized her breasts, stomach, and buttocks. This work has a specific impact due to the intersections of gender, religion, and citizenship, and how those systems of oppression are at work in the specific context of Afghanistan. The work went viral gaining enthusiasm from Western outsiders, and messages of hate from Afghan people who interpreted the work as a project of the United States against Islamic values and encouraging female prostitution.[42] The work resulted in a fatwa and her exile from Kabul to Paris, France, for her safety. In this walking piece, it was clear that multiple facets of identity were at play and disrupted the intersecting systems of oppression.

While these walking works and texts have all occurred in the last decade or so, the history of gender discrimination and walking goes back as far as the first patriarchal power structures, or those societies in which men hold more power, either officially or unofficially. For example, Rebecca Solnit in *Wanderlust: A History of Walking* points out how as far back as Middle Assyria (1700–1100 BCE), women marked their legal and societal status by either walking publicly with their heads covered (wives and widows) or uncovered (sex workers and enslaved women), thereby prioritizing and empowering the male gaze and unavoidably sexualizing women. This significantly limited who could walk and where.

This close observation of women walking in public continues with various complex courting rituals across cultures and times. Solnit cites one such ritual, the paseo in El Salvador, in which a teenage couple could walk around the plaza at the center of town, allowing them privacy for conversation but little else under the public watch of the townspeople. This is just one example of how women entering public space, walking or otherwise, can imply sexual availability, and explains various chaperone customs across cultures. These systems further bolster ideas of walking in public as a performance of being seen, rather than a free act of individual movement through space with the purpose of seeing and doing things for oneself.

Let's Walk (1999) by Amanda Heng built on these concepts of walking, the male gaze, and performing gendered beauty by asking participants to hold high-heeled shoes in their mouths and walk backward using handheld mirrors or their phone cameras to guide themselves. This walking work was developed in response to the 1997 Asian financial crisis in which working women in Singapore turned to beauty and cosmetic treatments, even plastic surgery, to keep their jobs, emphasizing how in many contexts "a woman's looks are still worth more than her abilities."[43] Heng aimed to highlight the absurdity of this situation by changing the direction of her walk (backwards), creating unexpected contrast (shoes in mouths), requiring interactivity to participate, and using repetition of objects (both mirrors and shoes).

Early surrealist and situationist artistic walking practitioners demonstrate these gender biases via their own acts of following women sex workers through city streets in the name of drifting or deambulating. Later practitioners continued problematic, non-consensual gender-based following, as in the works discussed in chapter four. It is important to counter these biases in contemporary practice, by acknowledging gender differences in various walking projects, scores, books, and articles.

EXERCISE: Considering Gender

Reflecting on the gender-related walking examples mentioned above, develop a walking score that takes into consideration gender. Start by narrowing your focus. Are you going to home in on safety, the male gaze, societal traditions, attire, language, or something else? How will you craft this walk to emphasize gender? Who will walk? What will they do? Where and when will they do it? Be ready to explain why you created this score and made the choices you did.

Disability

More than one billion people live with disabilities across the globe.[44] A dictionary-definition of disability is "a physical, mental, cognitive, or developmental condition that impairs, interferes with, or limits a person's ability to engage in certain tasks or actions or participate in typical daily activities and interactions."[45] However, disabled people have adapted, added onto, or otherwise defined the term to suit their lived experiences. For example, **Ellen Ladau** (1964–) emphasizes that disability isn't static and evolves both physically and emotionally, while historian **Jaipreet Virdi**

(1982–) points out disability "is an oppression of difference rather than an impairment."[46] It's also important to note that all people will move in and out of disability throughout their lives through injury, illness, or simply the aging process, which reduces walking speed and reaction times.[47]

Vocabulary: Disability

In discussing disability, it's important to know about two categories of language:

1. **People First Language [PFL]:** puts the word "person" first before any mention of disability, which emphasizes the person's humanity and that the disability is something they have, rather than who they are. With PFL, you might say "person with a disability."

2. **Identity First Language [IFL]:** acknowledges the disability as part of what makes that person who they are. With IFL, you might say "disabled person."

Neither category is wrong, however people have strong preferences, and it is important to respect their choices. When in doubt, default to PFL, and be open to shifting if someone asks you to.

1. **Apparent / visible disability:** the disability is noticeable to others via appearance or communication, such as a visibly uneven gait, rolling in a wheelchair, using a prosthetic, or walking with a white cane in front of themselves.

2. **Non apparent / invisible disabilities:** the disability is not noticeable from looking at or communicating with a person, such as a chronic pain, a learning disability, or mental illness.

3. **Temporary disabilities:** broken bones, or other events that pass over time.

4. **Acquired disabilities:** non-reversible disabilities that are acquired, such as hearing loss, paralysis, brain injuries, complications due to aging, etc.

And some disabilities will only be apparent in certain scenarios, such as partial hearing loss, which might only be noticeable in noisy environments like restaurants or on a noisy street. Activist and author Emily Ladau further explains, "In fact, some people with disabilities like to refer to non-disabled people as **temporarily able-bodied**, meaning that disability is something we'll most likely all experience at some point in our lives."[48]

There are a variety of disabilities that intersect with walking as artistic practice, and often these have been historically overlooked. Take for example, the dérive or psychogeography, which prescribe wandering, but without a caveat for those who are prevented from wandering past various physical barriers, such as missing sidewalks and curb cuts. Consideration of disability is frequently overlooked in group-walking practices, or when artists are writing walking scores, although with careful attention and thoughtful planning, adjustments and accommodations can be made.

For example, in *Art, Access and Urban Walking* (2017) by **Mindy Goose** (1975–), the artist led a walk built around examining accessibility in urban and green spaces. She drew attention to ways the built environment neglected the needs of disabled people in terms of both mobility and the need for frequent resting options, especially for those with chronic illnesses. Using photography, writing, sketching, and spoken word, the group used slow-looking practices and noted elements like missing signage, uneven topography, extra distances to use ramps or special access points, and so on. This type of careful examination of the physical world helps highlight how "physical access leads to social access."[49]

Similarly, in her work *A Crash Course in Cloudspotting* (2020–), **Raquel Meseguer Zafe** (1976–) brings attention to stillness and horizontality, both of which might at first seem counter to the act of walking. This piece invites people to engage in rest by lying down and listening to an audio journey inspired by the collected stories of over 250 people living with invisible disabilities and chronic illnesses and how they navigate the city in creative and artful ways.[50] While participants aren't walking during the piece, it highlights the need for walking artists and city planners to include rest options to enhance accessibility.

EXERCISE: Observing Accessibility

Select a local walk that you are familiar with. From start to finish, take note of ways the path is and is not accessible, photographing obstacles. Feel free to also take notes, or audio/ video recording, or other means of recording your thoughts.

After your walk, make a list of the actions you would have to take to improve the points of inaccessibility. Some might be simple, like letting a shop-owner know that their sidewalk seating is blocking wheelchair accessibility, while others might entail contacting the local government to request a curb cut where one is missing.

Once your list is complete, select at least one item to take action on. When the obstacle has been fixed or removed, display the before and after photos as an exhibition.

Walking artists and authors **Alyson Hallett** (1963–) and Phil Smith wrote a short book reflecting on this idea of moving in and out of disability as seasoned walkers: *Walking, Stumbling, Limping, Falling: A Conversation* (2017). They focused on two temporary disabilities, Hallet's hip replacement and Smith's recovery from an infection, and relied on anecdotal recollections of healing and slowly returning to walking. By highlighting this often-overlooked idea of temporary disability, these walkers remind artists to keep this common occurrence in mind when planning walking works. Further, due to the unpredictable and ever-changing nature of temporary disability, it's important to always ask how you can support accessibility and accommodations for people participating in walking projects. See suggestions in chapter four.

One example of centering a physically disabled experience is *Walk This Way* (2010) by **Norma D. Hunter** (1958–), in which the artist collaborated with disabled community members to create a choreographed wheelchair walk exploring the town square of Huntly, Scotland. Participants were asked to cross the square twice before executing a specific trip, such as going to the post office.[51] Through this immersive and repetitive experience, Hunter highlights the need for inclusive thinking in walking discussions. Similarly, in *Fissures, Holes, Limbs* (2019) by **moira williams** (1962–, disabled Secatogue, Lenape, cross disability cultural activist), the artist prompts walkers to consider the use of walking sticks for mobility, and to be mindful of the width of pathways via the brim of her hat, which was the width of a wheelchair and marked with bright yellow dangling ribbons. This use of color and contrast was an innovative way of drawing attention to often-overlooked walking challenges. Another example is the score *Perambulator* (2012) by **Clare Qualmann** (1977–), which asks the participant to walk through a city (any city) with a wheeled device, such as a pram, stroller, wheelchair, or walker, and explore inequalities perpetuated by the everyday construction of pathways, such as the lack of curb cuts or the narrowness (or total lack of) certain sidewalks. Where these accommodations have been overlooked, participants will quickly notice how the built everyday environment perpetuates inequality, overlooking caretakers (an often-gendered role), and people with different mobility needs.

An example of centering deaf experience or hard of hearing (HoH) experiences is *(LISTEN)* (2016) a group walk led by Christine Sun Kim. For this walking tour, Kim led about a dozen participants to various sites in New York's Lower East Side, pausing at each one to share a personal memory via American Sign Language, which was interpreted aloud. Each stop also included sharing a written composition on a tablet, suggesting various understandings, visualizations, and feelings of sound to ponder. The tour was inspired by an earlier work, *LISTEN* (1966) by **Max Neuhaus** (1939–2009), in which he brought traditional concertgoers out into the streets to walk and listen to everyday sounds, building on the work of John Cage who first introduced everyday sounds to the concert hall.

Artist and disability activist Carmen Papalia regularly addresses ableism, and specifically visual impairment, in combination with walking. Take for instance *Mobility Device* (2019) in which he replaced his white cane with the **Hungry March Band** (1997–), an eighteen-piece ensemble, collaborating and walking together along the High Line elevated linear park in New York City. The band played a site-reactive score to help guide Papalia along the walkway, paying attention to spatial relationships between Papalia and the group, while soloist musicians used music to lead in challenging spots as they walked. This work brings up ideas of care, collaboration, choice, institutions, and hierarchical understandings of sensory experience. Other participants were encouraged to experience this public space through their non-visual senses.[52]

Citizenship and Legal Status

> . . . and it strikes her, as she walks, that borders, like hatred, are exaggerated precisely because otherwise they would cease to exist altogether.
>
> —Colum McCann

Citizenship and legal status affect who can walk and where based on borders, whether those are city, state, country, or other legal borders. Scholar **Kate Morris** (1966–) points out some of the key questions that arise in relation to borders are ". . . who exercises the right of passage into these spaces and who has the authority to control that access?"[53]

The arbitrary nature of borders is highlighted in *Walk the Line* (2016) by **Lauren Brincat** (1980–), a durational video work featuring the artist slowly walking into the ocean along the imaginary line that separates the Southern Ocean and the Indian Ocean until fully immersed. The contrast between the artist being visible in the landscape, and then not, helps create conceptual impact of this simple gesture, as does the speed and the atmospheric qualities of the scene. Many artists combine walking and poetic interpretations such as this one to examine borders, citizenship, and legal status.

Vocabulary: Citizenship and Legal Status

One's citizenship and/or legal status can have a profound effect on where and when a person can walk. Citizenship can limit individuals to travel only to select countries. Various legal statuses can also severely limit the freedom of one's mobility.

1. **Refugee:** a person who has been forced to flee due to war, violence, or persecution, often without warning, and is protected under international laws.

2. **Asylum seeker:** a person seeking international protection from danger in their home country, but their claim to be a refugee hasn't yet been legally recognized, so they must apply at a border crossing. Asylum seekers are sometimes incorrectly referred to as "illegal immigrants," especially at the southern US border.

3. **Immigrant:** a person who decides to leave their home to move to a foreign country with the intention of settling there. Immigrants are free to return home and might spend time exploring employment opportunities or study in the new country.

4. **Migrant:** a person who chooses to move from place to place (either within their country or across borders) for economic reasons such as seasonal work or other opportunities.[54]

Many artists reflect on citizenship and these legal statuses through the medium of walking.

Another example of combining walking and poetic interpretation is *Slow Marathon* (2012) by Ethiopian artist **Mihret Kebede** (1978–), which she made in collaboration with the Walking Institute in Huntly, Scotland. Initially, Kebede had hoped to walk from her home in Addis, Ethiopia, to Huntly, Scotland, but had to adapt the idea when she ran into visa restrictions, border controls, and the desert. Instead, she decided on a metaphorical walk in collaboration with people all over the world who would walk and donate their miles to the joint 5,850-mile effort. There was also a shoelace exchange between the walkers in Addis and Huntly. The entire experience shed light on how movement can be frustrated in various locations, especially borders.[55]

An echo of Kebede's walk was a collaborative reenactment of the slow marathon by **May Murad** (1984–) of Gaza, Palestine, and **Rachel Ashton** (1976–) of Huntly, Scotland, entitled *Walking without Walls*. Over the course of 2017–2018, they planned their own slow marathons in their respective countries, exchanging videos, drawings, and texts electronically. Each artist dealt with issues of access, whether restricted by occupation, or by issues of public versus private land ownership. The scale, duration, and repetition of completing this work simultaneously in two separate and politically charged locations helps to create the conceptual impact of this walking work.

Iman Tajik (1982–), a Glasgow, Scotland-based artist and photographer originally from Iran, took a similar collective approach in his project *Under One Sky* (2020). He engaged people across the globe in a collaborative walk that added up to equal one time around the planet earth. Participants were asked to photograph the sky while they were walking and submit the image for a composite photograph by Tajik. Walkers were asked to consider freedom of movement, immigration, borders, and the global refugee crisis during a time when many borders were closed due to the COVID-19 pandemic.[56] The finished work helped to convey the interactivity and scale of the effort needed to complete it.

A different approach to framing the immigrant experience is Inua Ellams's *Midnight Run* (2005–). This project seeks to combat loneliness and connect people in cities. It was inspired by Ellams's own experience as a Nigerian immigrant to London and Dublin. Finding it difficult to connect with others in the bustling city of London, he was inspired by a nighttime walk with his friend, in which they walked and talked late into the night. Building off this experience, he has since developed several nighttime group walks with artistic activities to enhance group communication, making different art forms accessible, supporting local artists, and exploring cultural dynamics within urban environments.[57] *Midnight Run* events have been commissioned in Manchester, London, Leeds, Milan, Firenze, Barcelona, Madrid, and Auckland. Ellams's work is successful in part because he has taken advantage of the interactive nature of walking.

In North America, artist **David Taylor** (1965–) engaged with citizenship and legal status as he considered the US–Mexico border via a photographic journey to visit the 276 obelisks that mark the international boundary west of the Rio Grande. This work was entitled *Working the Line* (2007) and "inevitably led to encounters with migrants, smugglers, the Border Patrol, minutemen, and residents of the borderlands."[58] This type of photographic work shines a light on locations and situations that most people do not have access to and brings up complex social and political questions related to borders, citizenship, class, xenophobia, and the human and environmental toll border maintenance exacts.

EXERCISE: Photography and Borders

Where do borders exist near you or in your region? Take a walk to photograph that border (consider your personal safety and take any necessary precautions, knowing that some people might need to skip this exercise if it is unsafe).

Is there anything that clearly marks the border? Who is being separated by this particular border and why? Where does the border begin and end, and are you able to photograph the start and finish? When did this border first appear? What is this border's relationship to citizenship or legal status?

Summary

In this chapter the question of who gets to walk and where is the focus. Issues of public and private space, as well as surveillance take center stage. Additionally, topics included colonialism and Indigenous oppression, race, gender, disability, and citizenship or legal status. Several vocabulary boxes help readers understand the words used to discuss these systemic issues. Selected exercises open up space for further exploration.

Chapter 6

Rituals

Rituals are repetitive activities that mark a set amount of time (daily, weekly, yearly, once-per-lifetime, etc.) and are linked to particular actions, events, objects, locations, people, or other elements. They can be personal or communal, and participation can be private, limited to a certain membership group (families, clubs, schools, religious groups, etc.), or public. Rituals can also help build and maintain relationships, with oneself or others. Their tone can be solemn, mysterious, celebratory, humorous, mournful, or any other combination of emotions. Rituals sometimes highlight important moments and remind people of meaning throughout life. Finally, they often have a narrative quality with an emphasis on beginning, middle, and end, or simply before the ritual, and after.[1]

EXERCISE: Design Your Own Walking Ritual

Start by brainstorming something that you might want to acknowledge or celebrate. Many rituals mark transitions or regular occurrences. Determine the scale of the walking ritual, including who will be invited to participate. Is this a ritual for yourself or others? How will you emphasize interaction if it is communal? Consider the narrative of the ritual. How does it start, proceed, and conclude?

This exercise is inspired by *Design for Belonging* (2022) by **Susie Wise** (1968–), 104.

Walking has many connections to ritual through pilgrimages, rites of passage, protests, celebrations, sporting events, and more. For example, graduation ceremonies often include walking across a stage, marriage ceremonies can involve walking down an aisle, and some organizations will use walking as a fundraising event. Once one starts noticing it, walking pops up in many long-standing rituals. Walking together for a ritualistic purpose provides a psychological high and sets humans apart from other species.[2] Through repetition, walking rituals involve emotions and anticipation as one considers not only themselves but perhaps also their community and others in the past who have walked in the same way. The repetitive nature of rituals allows people to notice if there are any small changes over time, or inversely find comfort or boredom with the repetition and predictability.

EXERCISE: Change the Ritual

Think of a walk you take that has a ritualistic feeling, whether that's a daily walk or a walk you take when you're visiting a special place, etc. Reflect on what makes this walk ritualistic and list out those qualities. Next, select just one element of the walk to change. Take the walk with the changed element. Afterwards, reflect on how the change affected your experience. Did the walk retain its ritualistic qualities? Why or why not?

Contemplation

I have walked myself into my best thoughts.[3]

—**Søren Kierkegaard** (1813–1855)

I like walking because it is slow, and I suspect that the mind, like the feet, works at about three miles an hour. If this is so, then modern life is moving faster than the speed of thought, or thoughtfulness.

—Rebecca Solnit (1961–)

As mentioned in chapter one, walking has a long history of being paired with thinking. Scientific studies demonstrate that just standing up enhances cognition,[4] while walking enhances learning and memory.[5] Humans have created all sorts of paths, cloisters, ambulatories, gardens, trails, and labyrinths to formalize these paired practices of walking and thinking. One might trace some of the first recorded contemplative walking back to Aristotle's Peripatetic School of Philosophy, where scholars and cultural producers used walking as a means of contributing to society through thoughtful reflection. Later, monasteries and universities formalized the practice with the architectural addition of cloisters, which are characterized as covered walkways surrounding a central garden or gathering space, to allow scholars to walk outdoors with overhead shielding from the elements.[6]

Some walking artists who specifically address contemplation include **Bas Jan Ader** (1942–1975) in the piece *In Search of the Miraculous (One Night in Los Angeles)* (1973), which consisted of fourteen photographs the artist took while walking alone at night, presumably in search of the miraculous, and to which he added handwritten lyrics from pop songs. His work references ideas of romanticism and the sublime, as well as formal references to German Romantic paintings like *Wanderer Above the Sea of Fog* (ca. 1818) by **Caspar David Friedrich** (1774–1840), which features a lone walker in a broad open landscape (see figure 6.1). This work was the first of three pieces, which was meant to be followed by an Atlantic Ocean crossing in a very small boat in 1975, and then a nighttime

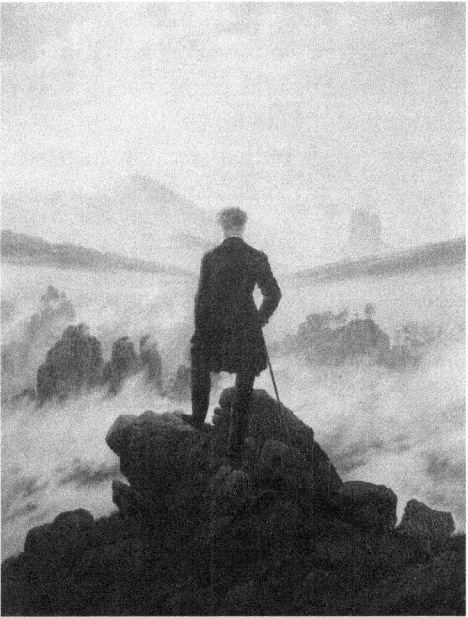

Figure 6.1. Caspar David Friedrich, *Wanderer above the Sea of Fog*, 1817, oil on canvas, 38.5" × 29.1". *Source*: Wikimedia Commons, public domain.

walk in Amsterdam (similar to the one in Los Angeles). However, Ader perished at sea, and the series was never fully realized with the second contemplative walk in Amsterdam.

Another artist highlighting walking and contemplation is **Tehching Hsieh** (1950–) who walked and existed fully outdoors in *One Year Performance* (1981–1982). Hsieh is known for these endurance-based works, and in the directions for this piece, he stated he would not be going into "a building, subway, train, car, airplane, ship, cave, tent." In this way, there was very little else to do other than walk and contemplate.

François Morelli (1953–) similarly took a durational walk for contemplation in *Transatlantic Walk 1945–1985* (1985). This thirty-day walk from the Berlin Wall to Philadelphia was a means of commemorating the fortieth anniversary of the bombing of Hiroshima. Morelli carried a hollow fiberglass sculpture resembling a charred human figure on his back, engaging in many conversations and creating photos, drawings, and writings. He also regularly filled the figure with water, almost as if it were a ritual to keep his walking companion nourished. This walking project has a sense of pilgrimage, which is a sub-category discussed in more depth below, as well as activism, discussed further in chapter eight.

In contrast to the previous works, *Narcotourism* (1996) by **Francis Alÿs** (1959–) is a walking work that examines contemplation, but over a shorter period of time—seven days—and each day under the influence of a different drug. Alÿs documented the process of his walking contemplation via photographs, notes, and any other media that became relevant. A photo of his feet walking and a page of diaristic written reflections were all the artist used as the gallery-ready representation of the work.

Daily Walks

Daily walks involve relatively frequent repetition in comparison with other ritualistic, contemplative walks. The walker observes certain routes repeatedly, often at the same time of day, which can bring about either a sense of monotony, or pique one's interest as the smallest changes. Changes in light, temperature, wind direction, and humidity can draw one's attention during a daily walk. The presence or absence of other daily walkers also becomes apparent. Two commonly recognized forms of daily walking include commuting to and from work, and walking with an animal, such as a dog.

EXERCISE: Daily Walk List

If you don't already walk once a day, plan a route and walk it for five days in a row. Each day, list three things that stood out to you on the walk. After five days have lapsed, look back on your daily lists. Did anything stand out to you? Why or why not? What might happen to your lists if you did five more days?

Commuting

Commuting might be the one of the most common of daily walks. Artists have considered these walks from several points of view and through varied media. For instance, **Gwen MacGregor** (1961–) tracked her movements for three months in New York and Toronto using GPS in *3 Months New York/Toronto* (2004). The data is used to create a two-minute animation in which each day's movements are drawn on screen and then partially fade away as the next day's path is drawn on top. With this pattern, the saturation of the most-traveled paths is enhanced, showing a data visualization of the daily movements.

Artist **Michael x. Ryan** (1956–) took a slightly different approach to documenting his commuting walks by tracing spilled drinks he encountered in the street. He transferred the tracings to a wood carving, which was painted white and displayed in a gallery setting. The work was entitled *Roadstains* (2007). While this archive of a daily commute is much more abstract, it also communicates some of the atmosphere of the everyday encounters that is unavailable within a GPS map. His use of scale, directionality, and color, in addition to changed context (street versus gallery), all add visual interest to this collection of often overlooked shapes in the urban environment.

Yet another approach to walking and commuting as a daily practice is *Check It Out* (1998) by **Matthew McCaslin** (1957–), which is a sculpture featuring four televisions strapped to a rolling cart and showing footage of urban commuters in various locations. In this case, the work encourages contemplation of the everyday ritual of walking commutes using the juxtaposition of multiple moving images. The contrast between the gallery setting and the hustling figures on screen heightens awareness of the movement in different contexts.

Taking a slightly different, critical approach to walking commutes is Amanda Heng in *I Walk from the South to the North* (2017) in which she spent two months taking daily walks in Singapore, contemplating the speed and architecture of this bustling developing urban setting. While walking, she asked for directions and depended on chance encounters with strangers. People generously provided drawn or written directions and maps, which later became documentation for the project. While Heng mourned the reduction in walking in the city and the accompanying chance encounters (as well as an overreliance on Google Maps as a mode of navigation), the people she encountered were surprised by her requests and often asked why she didn't just take the rapid transit nearby for a trip of such distance.[7] In this way, the project showcased opposing points of view on urban development and commuting.

Similar to Heng's work, the collective Jalan Gembira based out of Yogyakarta, Indonesia, has an ongoing practice of walking together since 2016, with the aim of questioning the condition of motorbike cities. In a space where walking infrastructure has not been prioritized, this group is trying to question hierarchies and highlight the challenges that not prioritizing walking infrastructure poses to women, adults at risk, minority communities, and children. The group documents their walks through photography and writing, which is archived on their website.[8] By bringing a critical eye to the lack of walking infrastructure and amplifying these challenges, the group is raising awareness that there is a desire to make walking commutes more available. Often these initial gestures can be instrumental to effecting larger systemic change.

This selection of works showcases how artists have observed, documented, and questioned the act of walking commutes over time and used maps, animation, video, sculpture, and online archives to amplify these experiences.

Walking with Animals

Walking with animals is a part of some people's daily rituals and routines. In rural spaces that might include walking with horses, cows, sheep, or other livestock as they move across farmland. In urban spaces, it may consist of a few daily walks with a dog, or other household pet, depending on the context in which an individual finds themself.

Artist Ernesto Pujol highlights, "Dogs have been some of the most revealing teachers, teaching me how non-humans move across terrain. We need more movement perspectives than the anthropocentric."[9] Artist **Lee Deigaard** (1969–), who works predominantly with horses, seems to have connected with this perspective and points out, "Animals walk through the world without carrying anything, their bodies as vehicles of motion and expression; in the Anthropocene each of them, predator or prey, feels and is utterly vulnerable."[10] It is perhaps via this heightened sense of vulnerability and awareness that humans connect with both their animals, and the places they walk with them on a daily basis.

For example, Deigaard has made multiple series focused on dog walking, including *Quarantine Drawings (March 17–May 19, 2020).* This body of work started as an effort to create twelve drawings each day, early in the pandemic quarantine, using black ink on index cards, featuring her canine walking companion. The project continued for nine weeks, resulting in six hundred drawings that showcased a loving and devoted relationship between dog and human, as well as a specific walking perspective in the US city of New Orleans. Elements of the pandemic affected walking with the dog, which affected the drawings, evident through subject, form, content, and context. Deigaard elaborates, "The movements of my hand and pen could not be separated from our circumstances, our feelings, and our grappling," referencing to her joint experience with her dog. The work was later displayed as a wall installation, and also as a 160-page artist book containing all the drawings.[11]

When artist **Rebecca Gallo** (1985–) adopted a dog in 2014, she started creating *One Walk Sculptures* (2016), which consisted of collected trash and discarded material that she and her dog came upon through chance during their daily walks, particularly potentially harmful items her vulnerable dog might sniff out and try to eat or chew on. The found materials were reassembled as a type of sculptural archive of each walk and were displayed in a gallery setting. These intimately sized assemblages demonstrated a playfulness, as well as a snapshot of everyday human waste encountered through the experience of a dog.

Another artist who has worked with dog-walking and chance encounters as a way to reconsider places, is **Roz Crews** (1990–) in *Dérive and Psychogeography Walk: Dog Days* (2018), which was a sub-project of her *Center for Undisciplined Research* (2017–2018), a nine-month, decentralized, and student-focused "center," which questioned how learning and research are, and can be, structured. This work was hosted by the New Bedford Art Museum and invited participants to show up with their dogs and travel mugs,[12] allowing their pets to lead the way on a dérive via their curiosity and sense of smell. Two dog-walking professionals attended, providing tips for dog walking. Participants split into two packs for the walk, and followed where their dogs led them, opening themselves to the chance encounters the dogs pursued, and experiencing a familiar place with a new awareness.[13]

Keith Arnatt (1930–2008) also takes dog walking as his subject in *Walking the Dog* (1976–1979), which features a collection of over two hundred portraits of people with their dogs. Both the person and their dog are fully within the frame of the image, and they are looking directly at the camera as they pose on the street. Through the repetition of the series, the everyday nature of these daily dog walks is emphasized, and viewers may look for relationships between the dogs and their owners. Chapter four takes a deeper look at archives.

Whether through sculpture, photography, or simply the experience of path discovery, daily walking with animals clearly heightens contemplation and spatial awareness.

Gardens

Walking in nature holds a certain appeal across history and cultures. In some cases, the practice has been formalized, as in Japanese forest bathing (*shinrin-yoku*), "the practice of absorptive, enveloping walking in deep forests for the soothing properties of being connected to, and fully immersed in, the sights, sounds and feel of nature."[14] A variation of this practice would be walking through gardens. Artist and author Lucy Lippard speaks about gardens in her seminal text *Lure of the Local*, when she states,

> Mediators between nature and culture, gardens are, paradoxically, communal places that encourage solitude and self reliance. There is something impersonal (public, perhaps) about the notion of a park, whereas even a public garden evokes a more intimate (private) landscape. Canadian artist Glenn Lewis has pointed out that gardens are metaphors for both the center, or home, and for the four directions they symbolically "look out on." The communal gardens flourishing in urban vacant lots and their funkier independent siblings bridge the gap and establish a comforting sense of place, transitory though it may be.[15]

There are particular styles of gardens that lend themselves to walking. For example, Japanese-style gardens, first recorded at the imperial palace by the fifth century CE, have a recognized style—simple, restrained, and minimalist—with particular elements to stimulate contemplation, such as a pond with an islet connected to shore by bridges, artificial hills, a waterfall, specific rock arrangements, bonsai trees, or little pavilions or rooms built for tea ceremonies, among other possibilities. "A studied irregularity in the arrangement of stepping stones is a noteworthy feature of the *chanoyu* (tea ceremony) garden, where beauty and use are combined. . . . The aim is to bring humanity close to nature and every conceivable means may be employed to realize it." [16] This attention to creating space for contemplative ritualistic walking is noteworthy.

Similarly, hedge-maze gardens, first noted in Renaissance- and Baroque-era Europe, aimed to facilitate walking, but also provide privacy for all sorts of activities and affairs. These designs spread, with artists like **Giuseppe Castiglione** (1688–1766) who designed *Wanhua Zhen (10,000-Flower Maze)* (1756–1759) for the Summer Palace in Beijing, China (it was later rebuilt in 1977–1992). The maze featured a European-style elevated circular pavilion at its center, where the Qianlong Emperor would sit and watch people compete during the Mid-Autumn Festival, attempting to escape while under moonlight and yellow lanterns, almost as a form of walking performance.[17]

Labyrinths and Mazes

Unless a person is closely studying the topic, the terms labyrinth and maze are often used interchangeably, however each does have a unique definition. A labyrinth has a single path to the center, known as a unicursal model, with no false turns or choices. The walker starts on the outside, follows a single winding path to the center, and then turns around to retrace their steps back to the entrance. A labyrinth also fills the entirety of its external shape with its pathway, repeatedly leading the visitor past its center before arriving there.[18] Mazes, on the other hand, are multicursal and contain dead ends, branching paths, and lack a clear center, promoting a sense of confusion through their complexity. Some mazes can even elicit fear or a sense of punishment or torture due to their complexity, and this harrowing element is often referenced in literature.

The labyrinth is an old concept, with the oldest known mention of it on a Mycenaean clay tablet from Knossos ca. 1400 BCE.[19] There are many interpretive meanings associated with labyrinths, such as embodied contemplation through the path's repetitive twists and turns, as in church labyrinths. These were often located in northern French churches and were made of flagstone pavement, measured ten–twelve meters in diameter, and were located near the entrance of the church to encourage people to walk through the labyrinth on their way to the altar (this was before pews or seating were a common element). The idea was that the labyrinth stood in as a ritualized path of repentance, or a substitution for pilgrimage to the Holy Land.[20] While they were not originally viewed as art, these labyrinths are now a regular part of art history studies. For example, the Chartres Cathedral (~1220 CE), which is the largest existing church labyrinth, or the Amiens Cathedral Labyrinth (1288 CE) designed by **Renaud de Cormont**, are both well-known art historical works.

Some interpret the labyrinth's abrupt changes in direction as symbolic acts of death and rebirth or reincarnation. This explains why some scholars believe that turf labyrinths (predominantly English) may have been tied to ancient pagan traditions or celebrations surrounding the rites of spring. Turf labyrinths consist of lines cut into the turf, guiding walkers along grass paths towards the center. Some examples, like the Saffron Walden Turf Maze (Labyrinth) in Essex, England (unknown date of origin, was re-cut in 1699), have had bricks laid around the path. Similar labyrinthine patterns can be found scratched into the ground on the Nazca Plain in Peru, although these do not have all the attributes of a labyrinth as outlined above.

Similar to the turf labyrinths, the predominantly Scandinavian "Troy Towns" are labyrinths with a comparable design, but were built by arranging stones on the surface of open fields. The name references the Troy Game, ". . . a solemn ritual performed at irregular intervals by the ancient Romans to signalize their alleged descent from the Trojans: notable for the interweaving labyrinthine maneuvers executed by youths on horseback,"[21] although scholars cannot confirm the true meaning of these sites, some of which date back 2500 years.[22] There are also labyrinths made of rock arrangements in India, such as the example *Lakshmana-mandal* in the village of Sitimani (now submerged in a lake after the installation of a dam in 1996).[23]

Regardless of their intended meaning, both turf labyrinths and Troy Towns can now be walked with the same spirit of ritualized self-reflection and meditation, and both models have frequently been adopted by artists across the globe due to their relatively easy installation and low environmental impact (rocks can easily be removed, and grass can grow back). Take for example, Richard Long's *Connemara Sculpture* (1971, now dispersed), which was a simple recreation of a Troy Town labyrinth.

Several contemporary books have been written on labyrinth walking as a mode of meditation, healing, and spiritual growth. One might walk to clear the mind or use visualizations of transformation. Walkers can set whatever intentions suit their labyrinth walk, such as expressing gratitude, deepening compassion, letting go of judgment or expectations, increasing patience, or simply quieting the mind.

EXERCISE: Make Your Own Labyrinth

Create your own labyrinth (see figures 6.2 A, B, C). It could be outside or indoors, temporary or long-term, and made of whatever materials you have accessible. Some people will paint or draw their labyrinth on canvas or a series of blankets (which makes it portable and reusable), while others might use stones or sticks like the Troy Towns. Think creatively—there are many materials you could use (masking tape, rope, flags, rocks, bricks, mown grass, drawings in the sand, reusable canvas tarp, etc.).

Once you have created your labyrinth, set an intention or thought to focus on as you walk from the entrance to the center and back. Afterwards, reflect on how the walk felt—what was different from one of your daily walks?

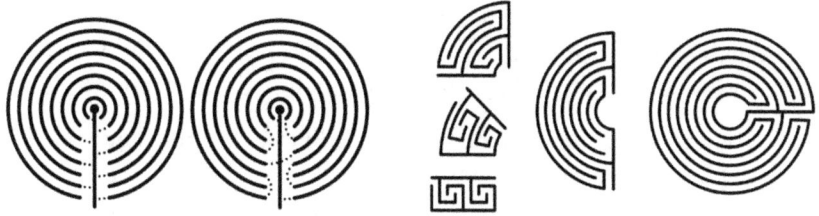

Figure 6.2a. Explanation for constructing cup-and-rings marks (left) and labyrinth (right), © Phil McCollam. *Source*: Courtesy of Phil McCollam.

Figure 6.2b. Explanation for constructing double meander, © Phil McCollam. *Source*: Courtesy of Phil McCollam.

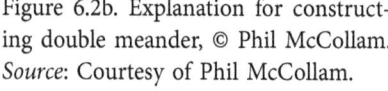

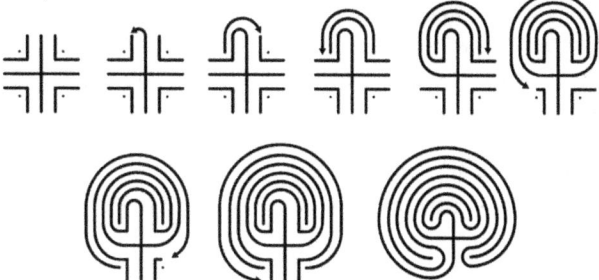

Figure 6.2c. Explanation for constructing Cretan labyrinths, © Phil McCollam. *Source*: Courtesy of Phil McCollam.

128 | Walking as Artistic Practice

Others associate labyrinths with concepts of either refuge or prison, as mentioned above in relationship to mazes where a person can become lost,[24] or rites of initiation, as discussed in the next section. Still, other labyrinths and mazes may focus on spatial perception by emphasizing materiality and optical effects. For example, *Chain Link Maze* (1978–1979) installed by **Richard Fleischner** (1944–) at the University of Massachusetts, included maze walls created from chain link fencing eight feet tall and covering 60' × 60'. Depending on how many layers of fencing a participant gazed through, from one to eleven, the environment and other walkers became more or less visible, sometimes creating moiré-like surfaces.[25] Similarly, *Two-Way Mirror Punched Steel Hedge Labyrinth* (1996) by **Dan Graham** (1942–2022) has a fairly self-explanatory title and elicits a visual playfulness from walkers through the use of two-way mirrored glass. Both of these maze-like installations focus on a visual sensory experience.

EXERCISE: Historical Labyrinth Meditation Themes

If you have a labyrinth at your disposal, use it. If you don't, you can set up a simple labyrinth with temporary materials. Then select a historical meditation theme of your choice from below. See if any of the prompts resonate with you for enhancing creativity or calming a busy mind. As you walk the labyrinth, focus on your selected meditation theme.

1. **Good fortune and protection**: In Scandinavia, fishing, hunting and shepherding people would walk or run a labyrinth near the edge of the sea to generate good luck and lure bad omens into the labyrinth where they would get stuck.

2. **Hero's journey:** This theme references the Greek myth of Theseus and Ariadne. As part of a sacrificial ceremony, Theseus was sent into King Minos's labyrinth to be eaten by a Minotaur. However, he planned ahead and used Ariadne's magic thread to find his way out after defeating the Minotaur at the center. Afterward, they celebrated with a dance that mimicked the turns of the labyrinth.

3. **Cycles of life**: Labyrinths have been used to symbolize both birth and death across several cultures and can be found near burial sites in multiple countries.

4. **The feminine center:** In addition to the symbolism of life and rebirth, and the potential relationship to goddess-worshiping, in many cultures, a woman would stand in the center of the labyrinth and young men would race to get to the center as part of festivities.

5. **Initiation:** Walking into a challenge (going into the labyrinth) and then returning from it to join a group of others who have faced the same challenge, is symbolically represented by walking to the labyrinth's center and back.

These themes were drawn from *The Way of the Labyrinth* (2000) by **Helen Curry** (1948–) and *Exploring the Labyrinth* (2000) by **Melissa Gayle West** (1954–).

Memory, Community, Initiation

Walking can bring together groups of people through shared memories, as noted by authors like **Anaïs Nin** (1903–1977) or Dorothy Wordsworth, who referenced the idea of walks as repositories for shared memories.[26] Author Kerri Andrews reminds, ". . . going over the same ground brings into being a connection between past and present selves, and between these selves and the future."[27]

EXERCISE: Memory Walk in Pairs

This is a pair walk. It is also a walk for a place you are familiar with. With a partner, walk and share memories related to the places you walk through. The memories might be specific to past experiences in the place, or simply related to things the place reminds you of. Afterwards, what did you notice about this memory walk? How was it similar or different from other walks you've taken recently?

Similarly, those shared memories can also be instrumentalized as initiation walks, a concept mentioned with labyrinths in the previous section. As a walker follows the path of a labyrinth, they are symbolically moving towards an interior space isolated from its surroundings, which implies a conscious choice and maturity to decide to venture inwards. "The experience of repeatedly approaching the goal, only to be led away from it again, causes psychological strain." The labyrinth requires one to overcome that strain, embodying a certain physical ability and social or mental adaptability,[28] much like other rites of initiation. Each person's memory of ritualistic labyrinth walking adds to the shared experience and creates community cohesion.

An example of engaging memory, community, and initiation is *The Coyote Walks* (2009–2017) by **Dillon de Give** (1978–). These annual group walks were initially in response to the story of Hal, the coyote who was captured in New York City and died when being released into the forest (he had eaten a poisoned rat in the city). However, the walks evolved into a group reflection on the walking transition between urban and rural nature spaces.[29] The walks centered on a shared memory and initiated individuals into a group via a shared walking experience, thereby building a community.

Another memory-based walk is *¿Quién puede borrar las huellas? (Who Can Erase the Traces?)* (2003) by **Regina José Galindo** (1974–). In this work, the artist walked through the streets of Guatemala City, from the Palacio Nacional de la Cultura (National Palace of Culture) to the Corte de Constitucionalidad (Constitutional Court of Guatemala), carrying a basin filled with blood, which she dipped her feet into, leaving a trail of footprints. This work was in response to learning a former military dictator would be allowed to run for president despite constitutional prohibitions. By physicalizing this memory of the dictator's war victims in public space via the bloody footprints, José Galindo drew together community awareness with her ritualized walk.

Other walking projects also focus on community building. For example, Nin ". . . saw [walking as] an opportunity to create an imaginative community connected not only by their shared ideas, but by pedestrianism"; she noted, ". . . walking had the power to transform isolation into fellowship."[30] These ideas are put into practice by various individual artists and collectives, such as the *Walking Institute*, hosted by Deveron Projects out of Huntly, Scotland. Bringing in a range of visiting walking practitioners, the *Walking Institute* fosters community-building through walking projects, with special focus on fifty percent support for the local rural communities and fifty percent support of global communities.

Other artists may stand still and focus on the memory and emotion of others who are walking by. For example, in *I March in the Parade of*

Liberty but As Long As I Love You I'm Not Free (2007–2008) by **Sharon Hayes** (1970–), the artist stood on the street with a bullhorn and read a love letter to an anonymous "you," thereby implicating each passerby as the "you" she was speaking to. By presenting the work publicly, the community was engaged, voluntarily or not. Volume and location played a central role in this walking work.

EXERCISE: Talking Along a Mile

This is a group activity, starting with discussion of where the group could draw a one-mile-long line with chalk. Once the path is determined, the group will divide up the line into sections, working in pairs. Each pair should travel to their starting point, and begin drawing the line until they reach the start of the next section, connecting each one into a single one-mile-long line. As one person in the pair is drawing, the other should document any conversations with passersby as chalk captions next to the line.

After completion, return to a group meeting point to share and reflect on the experience. The group will document the line and the captions with photo and video afterwards. This is a socially engaged project. Walkers will learn about the element of chance, as one cannot control or predict who one will encounter.

This exercise is inspired by an exercise developed by **Geoffrey Hendricks** (1931–2018), as shared in Lori Waxman's book, *Keep Walking Intently* (2017).

Pilgrimages and Questing

Mentioned early in chapter one, a pilgrimage is a ritualized, prolonged physical and philosophical journey towards a specific destination that removes the participant from their home environment and identity,[31] while a quest is a journey of seeking existential change. There have been, and continue to be, many well-known pilgrimages throughout the world including Mount Kailash Pilgrimage in Tibet (a 32.2-mile trek around the mountain's base), the Inca Trail in Machu Picchu, Peru (a 26.7-mile walk to view the Lost City of the Incas), or the Char Dham in India (four pilgrimage sites in the state of Uttarakhand (formerly Uttaranchal).

Scholars note that pilgrimages are often religious, but not always, and "the physical and emotional and spiritual challenges the individual encounters whilst on the journey offer time for reflection and renewal, and recognition of both the immanent and the transcendent in the course of the journey."[32] Author **Dean MacCannell** (1940–) notes that "contemporary tourists are sometimes similar to pilgrims in their quest for authentic experiences, as well as prized photos or videos of the journey, although directionality has been inverted. . . . pilgrims used to come from the peripheries to the centers, whereas today many of us go from the centers to the margins to find what is missing."[33]

Sometimes pilgrimages are oriented around visiting sites of remembrance for painful or shameful histories, such as the sites of Nazi concentration camps in Europe, or the National Memorial for Peace and Justice in Alabama, US, which honors Black victims of lynching and racial terrorism. Scholar Lucy Lippard reminds, "At these tragic sites, these vast memento mori, we can contemplate mortality and evil. We can pay homage to those less fortunate than we have been (so far), enjoying vicarious restitution for our relatively good luck . . ."[34]

In contrast to pilgrimages for reflection on history, scholars **Warwick Frost** (1959–) and **Jennifer Laing** reflect on pilgrimages for personal reasons, noting that research has suggested ". . . long-distance walking can 'facilitate processes of relief and disengagement from common stresses and problems in life and can help people find ways to resolve their issues.' It allows time to mull over problems or reflect on the past, as well as looking ahead to a potentially brighter future. It may also boost self-esteem and help to instill a sense of meaning or purpose in one's life, which assists with dealing with change."[35]

This concept of long-distance walks as a means of self-transformation or rite of passage is so prevalent that popular literature and film also regularly feature this trope, such as **Cheryl Strayed**'s (1968–) memoir, *Wild* (2012)—and its 2014 film adaptation—reflecting on her time on the US Pacific Crest Trail; or *The Way*, a 2010 film about pilgrims on the Camino Way in Spain. Some of the land art pieces mentioned in earlier chapters, such as Robert Smithson's *Spiral Jetty*, can also act as pilgrimage sites for some individuals.

In this vein of reflection, artist Anthony Schrag's *A Contemporary Pilgrimage: Walking from Huntly to Venice* (2015) was a 2657 km, eighty-eight-day reflection on the prestige and international draw of the Venice Biennale, regarded as the largest and most significant art festival in the world. In this case, the act of walking to the festival helped underscore questions about the event's prestige and meaning, posing questions about artists' general desire to be accepted there. Along the walk, Schrag collected relics to deliver to Venice, echoing acts from religious pilgrimages. The duration of the work in combination with its interactivity (the artist walked with over one hundred people and stayed in eighty different beds, encountering many different events along the way) ended up providing the most compelling elements of the project.

Similar in its element of self-reflection, **Marina Abromović** (1946–) and **Ulay**'s (1943–2020) epic walk, *The Lovers* (1988), consisted of a ninety-day pilgrimage along the entire length of the Great Wall of China. They each started at opposite ends of the wall to meet in the middle, where they ended their twelve-year relationship. The poignancy of ending the relationship after such a difficult, long-duration journey enhanced the emotional impact of this walking project and mirrored the larger journey of their relationship up to that point in time.

EXERCISE: Epic Walking Story

Take a walk, and as you go, develop an epic imagined walking story about the route. Include themes of pilgrimage or questing. Record the story as you go in a mode that suits you. Share the story with others.

Laboring and Tests of Character

While laboring and tests of character may seem implicit in all pilgrimages or quests, some walking works foreground this idea more prominently. For example, in *Effugio c, you're always only half a day away* (2011) by artist **Guido van der Werve** (1977–), he spent twelve hours running around his house (sixty-five miles in total), an extreme exercise in exertion and self-reflection with attention to the concepts of running in circles, running addiction, emotional poverty, and the fact that people "can theoretically fly almost anywhere in the world within twelve hours or less."[36] The extreme nature of the duration is a testament to the artist's commitment, much in the same way that pilgrimages or circumambulation are for religious walkers. Circumambulation is the act of walking in a circle around sacred objects, places, or deity images, and could take the form of a solitary or group practice with a more serious tone.

Ana Mendieta's (1948–1985) work, specifically the *Silueta Series* (1973–1978), in which she travels to various sites across Mexico and Iowa creating these ephemeral silhouette-shaped earthworks, is a many-years-long labor, as she travels from site to site. The effort required to create each work in combination with the act of pilgrimage, lends meaning to Mendieta's reflection on diaspora, gender, and connection to the earth. Each piece was documented via photography or video, and their accumulated presence helps convey the breadth of the pilgrimage and the passage of time, both of which acted as a test of character or conviction.

Francis Alÿs has also made work that centers around labor and ephemeral materials. For example, in *Sometimes Making Something Leads to Nothing* (1997), he spent nine hours walking through the streets of Mexico City, pushing a block of ice until it completely melted. The work was documented via video, and as the block shrank, the labor became less rigorous until he was simply kicking along a pebble of ice.

Wandering and Journeying

Here, wandering and journeying are a subset of pilgrimages and questing because the goal is not a specific endpoint or destination, but instead focuses on the process and experience of walking a significant distance or duration. Art historian **Lexi Lee Sullivan** (1982–) points out that in ancient Greece, there were nomadic Cynics who searched for truth outside of the norms of society, meaning they gave up their possessions and resisted the status quo, using walking as a countercultural activity.[37] Unlike the ancient Greek nomads, current-day nomadism—which is the ever-declining practice of moving to and from various areas without a fixed habitation—involves ongoing travel for the purpose of following food sources, raising livestock, or trading to make a living. These nomadic practices grow more and more difficult as the privatization of space and militarization of borders continues to expand.

Architect Carlos Pérez Marín studies present-day Saharan caravans through the ongoing collaborative group research, *Project Qafila* (caravan). These journeys include nomadic residencies for widely varying researchers and artists, who study ideas ranging across geography, nomadism, history, architectural heritage (the oases, the ksor or fortified cities, the fortifications made to control caravan routes), and sociology (with the tribes that occupy a territory or pass through it). They travel with and interview current-day families living nomadically, and produce writing, audio, and visual documentation.[38] *Project Qafila* has had several stages consisting of caravans of different lengths and participants. The second stage is discussed in more detail in chapter three.

An artist reflecting on the nomadic lifestyle is **Zig Jackson**, also named **Rising Buffalo** (1957–, Mandan/Hidatsa/Arikara), who created the photographic series, *Entering Zig's Indian Reservation* (1997), which consists of self-portraits situated in a variety of locations, standing or seated next to a custom road sign emblazoned with the title of the series, as well as a sub-sign that states, "Private Property; Open Range Cattle on Highway; No Picture Taking; No Hunting; No Air Traffic; New Agers Prohibited; Without Permission from Tribal Council" (see figure 6.3). When creating this work, the artist asked himself, "Why can't I be my own Indian?; Why can't I be my own medicine man?; Why can't I have my own reservation?"[39] Scholar Kate Morris points out that "the series affirms the artist's modern nomadism; he, his sign, and his territory are itinerant but not ungrounded."[40]

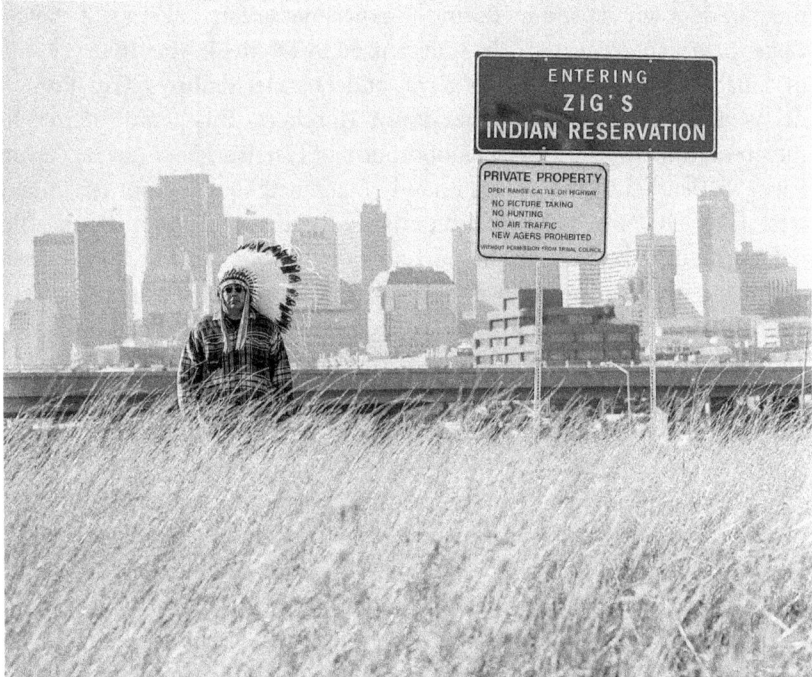

Figure 6.3. Zig Jackson, *Entering Zig's Indian Reservation*, 1997, photograph, © Zig Jackson. *Source*: Courtesy of Zig Jackson.

Parades and Processions

A procession is a group of people moving forward in an orderly fashion, often as part of a ceremony or festival. Artist Phil Smith adds, processions are "a disruption of the everyday, characterized by a key dramatic quality: there is always something at stake."[41] Readers may recognize this quality in various processions in religious processional practices, including Hindu and Buddhist circumambulation. Similarly, a march, protest, or demonstration could be characterized as a procession, but each of these has an activist tone (discussed further in chapter eight).

In comparison, a parade is a procession with a specific celebratory quality, and might also include marching bands, floats, and other performers. These qualities are present in some notable religious parades including Sri Lanka's ten-day Buddhist celebration, Kandy Esala Perahera, featuring many different performers and floats that increase in lavishness as the days progress, or Semana Santa, Catholic Holy Week in Spain, where crowds gather to view penance processions.[42]

In terms of artistic walking practice, several artists have embraced the parade as an artistic medium for experimentation. Take, for instance, *Consequences of a Gesture* (1993) organized by **Daniel J. Martinez** (1957–) in collaboration with **VinZula Kara**, and **Los Desfiladores Tres Puntos del West Side / West Side Three-Point Marchers**. This parade started in the predominantly Mexican neighborhood of Harrison Park (a.k.a. Zapata Park) and ended in the predominantly Black neighborhood of north and west Garfield Park.[43] The inhabitants of these two neighborhoods did not normally mix, but for the purposes of this parade, which was open to anyone who wanted to join, plus thirty-five community organizations, an estimated one thousand total participants from both neighborhoods joined in.[44] This work specifically took advantage of the socially engaged elements of a parade and walking together in public. The scale and duration of the work helped drive home the conceptual goal of bringing together these groups.

Dave McKenzie's (1977–) has also produced parade-based work, such as *Dave* (2010), in which he commissioned a parade balloon of a caricature of himself for a Fourth-of-July parade in the predominantly white-populated city of Aspen, Colorado. Parade-goers struggled to understand the balloon and guessed that it was depicting any number of different famous Black men (President Obama, Lebron James, etc.), which highlighted issues of Blackness, celebrity, and the occupation of public space by Black bodies. Through the medium of walking a balloon along a parade route, McKenzie was able to broach many of these ideas in a unique and compelling way with a large group of people.

A project that contains both the processional quality and the celebratory parade quality is an annual march across the US-Canada border, which artist **Jolene Rickard** (1956–, Tuscarora) has helped maintain as an annual tradition (originated in 1928) of the **Indian Defense League of America** (IDLA). The procession celebrates the basic right of Indigenous people to walk without passports across the border at Niagara Falls, demonstrating their rights guaranteed by Great Britain's Jay Treaty of 1794, and reaffirmed by the Treaty of Ghent in 1814. Rickard shares that the march alternates each year, entering from either the US or Canada, and "when it enters the US," she said, "it is called a 'celebration' because the US government still honors the Jay Treaty. When it enters Canada, it is called a 'commemoration' because the Ottawa government does not consider itself bound by a treaty made between the US and Great Britain in its colonial era."[45] This example helps illustrate the difference in energy dynamics and atmospheric quality between different types of processions.

EXERCISE: Your Parade

This is a group activity with at least three people. You will create a parade based on an idea of your choosing. Remember that parades have a celebratory quality. Create costumes, floats, and/or invite instrument players to join you. Include some sort of signage to signal the theme of your parade to passersby. Be open to others joining you. Talk along your walking route with those who join you. Afterwards reflect on the experience. What was best, and what would you do differently if you did it again?

Summary

In this chapter, walking rituals are the focus. Contemplation is a significant topic, with attention to daily walks, commuting, walking with animals, gardens, labyrinths, and mazes. Additionally, issues of memory, community, and initiation are discussed. Pilgrimages, questing, laboring, wandering, journeying, parades, and processions are also examined. Selected exercises open up space for further exploration.

Chapter 7

Place

The concept of place is often defined in relation to the idea of space. A place is a space people have made meaningful. Places can also change or shift over time due to changes in people and the environment. Place comes in many different scales, from the corner of a park (think *The Coyote Walks* [2009–2017] in Central Park, NYC), to the perimeter of a city (think *Hear Our Houston* [2012–2015] and the city specificity), to the earth itself within our galaxy (think of the Apollo 11 moonwalk [1969] and the importance of the moon in relationship to Earth), as these are all locations and spaces made meaningful by people.[1] Geographer **Yi-Fu Tuan** (1930–) goes deeper into this definition, "what begins as undifferentiated space becomes place as we get to know it better and endow it with value. . . . The ideas "space" and "place" require each other for definition. From the security and stability of place we are aware of the openness, freedom, and threat of space, and vice versa. Furthermore, if we think of space as that which allows movement, then place is pause; each pause in movement makes it possible for location to be transformed into place."[2]

If a place equals space plus meaning, it is important to state that meaning is created by a place's inhabitants and their cultural values, media representations, political commentary, and economic forces. Place is also shaped by the materiality found there, such as the proximity to water, land formations, other species, architecture, transportation systems, and so on.[3] Additionally, geographer **Jeff Malpas** (1958–) points out, "No place exists except in relation to other places, and every place contains other places that are related within it. The distinctive character of places is thus something that emerges through the interplay of places . . ."[4] Geographer

Tim Cresswell (1965–) also explains that one should note that "places are constructed by people doing things and in this sense are never 'finished' but are constantly being performed."[5]

Some might also reference the idea of "landscape" when discussing a place. While the two are related, landscape is a visual idea related to the material topography of a portion of the land, and the viewer is outside of it looking in, whereas a place is something a person enters or exists within.[6] This distinction might feel like a small detail as it relates to walking; however, with art history's long engagement with landscape via painting, drawing, and photography, it is important to call out, especially as it relates to walking artists' documentation choices. To illustrate the use of landscape in a walking work, one can look at *Pasajes IV* (2013) by **Sebastián Díaz Morales** (1975-), a video work featuring a single character crossing a wide range of landscapes throughout Patagonia. By showcasing these seemingly disconnected landscapes, connected by a lone walking figure, the artist tries to understand the region's present.[7]

Similarly, the term *site-specific* is sometimes used to describe selected socially engaged works, land art, some sculptures, and the like. This simply means the artwork is in response to a specific place. A walk could be site-specific, or not, but either way, it is the artist's responsibility to consider a place, or consciously choose not to, and to be able to discuss that choice.

EXERCISE: Weather Walk

The local weather is inextricably tied to place. For this walk, you will respond to the weather.

1. First, observe the current weather. Is it sunny or cloudy? Dry or humid? Windy or still? (Do not walk in dangerous weather.)

2. Next, alter your walk in response to your weather observations. For example, is it so hot that you need to walk more slowly to avoid overheating? Or is there so much snow that you need to take exaggerated steps to clear drifts? Do you need to wear any special attire to walk in this weather? Do you need water to avoid dehydration?

3. On the walk, observe your sensory experience. Record observations.

4. Adjust your destination based on the weather. For example, if it's raining, you might aim for a sheltered area, or if it's hot, you might want to end at a water fountain, and so on.

Seeing, knowing, and understanding place helps people empathize with other experiences, attachments, and connections. Tuan called the human affective bond between people and place "topophilia." [8] A clear example of topophilia intersecting with walking as artistic practice is *Folding Landscapes* (1984–2020), a specialist publishing house and information resource center focused on Galway Bay in Ireland, which was run by **Máiréad Robinson** (1934–2020) and **Tim Robinson** (1935–2020). With a place, culture, and landscape focus, *Folding Landscapes* has produced maps and books inspired by walks through the Aran Islands, the Burren, and Connemara, "nourish[ing] community spirit by identifying the irreplaceable uniqueness of local environment and history."[9]

Place also brings up ideas of value and belonging,[10] which is why understanding place can also help people to better understand, and counter, reactionary views aligned with xenophobia, racism, bigotry, and bias.[11] For example, *Wordsworth Heritage* (1992) was a billboard series of photographs by **Ingrid Pollard** (1953–) that focused on a specific place, the Lake District in England, as well as its well-established racial bias towards retelling narratives of white people walking through the area. These narratives are built on the famous literary works of Romantic writers like Dorothy and William Wordsworth, Samuel Coleridge, **Thomas de Quincey** (1785–1859), and **John Ruskin** (1819–1900), who wrote some of their famous works in the Lake District. Pollard had noticed that tourist postcard stands featured white people situated in the Lake District, but never Black people. To counter that visual narrative, Pollard shot images featuring Black people in the landscapes, and adopted some of the popular design layouts of Lake District tourist postcards, before displaying them on twenty-five urban billboard sites around the United Kingdom. By highlighting the absence of Black people in this particular place, Pollard helps viewers recognize and better understand racial bias connected to the Lake District, tourism, as well as systems and narratives elsewhere. Systemic racial bias and walking are covered in further detail in chapter five.

Indigenous Perspectives

In chapter five, Indigenous and colonialist perspectives were discussed in terms of who gets to walk and where. Ernesto Pujol summarizes, "The history of walking is contaminated by the pale, masculine virus of colonialism: by the fever of 'discovery,' of being 'the first man' to arrive and step into an 'unknown' territory."[12] This chapter looks further into Indigenous and colonial walking connections to place.

Around the world, various Indigenous groups have developed a breadth of rituals and narratives to describe walking, caretaking, and relationships with the natural environment to support a shared moral history. For example, anthropologist **Miriam Kahn** (1948–) describes landscape-related stories passed down through the generations of Wamiran people in Papua New Guinea. Of specific interest is a cautionary story about sharing food, which has been a scarce resource in this area. The tale describes a husband who goes to a garden every day, but only brings back firewood, forcing his wife to boil stones to create a broth each evening. Finally, the wife becomes frustrated and fashions wings to fly away. As she departs, the husband throws stones at her, which now line a walking path leading from the village to the mountain. As people walk the path they are reminded of this story and the Wamiran shared history, identity, and morality, as well as their "social obligations to feed and care for one another."[13] Incorporating the place-specific landscape features into moral lessons is a common feature of many Indigenous groups across the globe, and one that contemporary walking artists have also embraced.

Continuing with examples from North America, diverse Native-American traditions also focus on the importance of place and the natural environment, and those traditions were disrupted with the arrival of colonizing settlers who were focused on landownership. As discussed in chapter five, when the United States pursued westward expansion, Indigenous people were often sent on forced walks to new reservations far from their original homes. Later, the US government's Indian Removal policies displaced even more Native-American people from their homelands in an effort to separate children from traditional place-specific environmentally based knowledge and understanding by sending them to American Indian Residential Schools[14] where administrators aimed to "kill the Indian, save the man," as stated by **Richard Henry Pratt** (1840–1924), the developer of these schools.[15] These residential schools were also used in Canada. This deeply harmful approach highlights how both the US and Canada recognized the importance of place as it applies to power and control, and how it contributes to one's development of identity. Walking can be a means of familiarizing oneself with the foods, medicines, climate, harvesting practices, place-specific travel practices, particular artistic inspirations, and specific relationship-building practices that can form the foundation of one's identity. When colonizers used forced walking as a weapon to separate families and sever the cord of generational knowledge of the land, they disrupted people's freedom to walk, their sense of sovereignty, and their sense of belonging to a particular place.[16]

Many Native-American children attempted to escape the residential schools, and some successful individuals were able to walk back home. In fact, artist **Lisa Myers** (Beausoleil First Nation) has created multiple works inspired by her grandfather's escape from Shingwauk Residential School in Sault Ste. Marie, Ontario. He walked approximately 250 kilometers along the Northern Ontario railroad tracks, eating wild blueberries to survive. Myers retraced this walk herself and went on to create video works, abstract and map-like prints using blueberry pigments, and social practice activities with spoons and blueberries, all reflecting on this history, the walk, and the environment. One work in particular, *and from then on we lived on blueberries for about a week* (2013), a stop-motion animation, showcases the journey as Myers animates blueberries moving across wooden spoons accompanied by environmental sounds. The work pays homage to the walking journey her grandfather undertook in a visually poignant way, using repetition and movement to share this important story.[17]

Another example of a place-focused Indigenous walking project, also from Canada, is *The Journey of Nishiyuu [Journey of the People]* (2013) led by six James Bay Cree youths[18] who initiated a 1,600-kilometer trek in support of the **Idle No More Movement**, also known as the **Broken Treaty Movement**, from Whapmagoostui, Quebec, to Parliament Hill in Ottawa. As they walked, people joined their journey, eventually ending with four hundred people in the final hours of the walk, resulting in a meeting with the Aboriginal Affairs Minister to voice their concerns.[19] The *Idle No More Movement*, initiated in November of 2012 in response to the Canadian government's dismantling of environmental protection laws, aimed to build a movement for Indigenous rights and the protection of land, water, and sky, all of which form important material elements of human understanding of place.[20]

Urban Versus Rural

Differentiating between urban and rural walking is a long-standing place-based comparison. Writer Rebecca Solnit differentiates between the two stating, "the rural walking measures the body and the earth against each other, the way urban walking elicits unpredictable social encounters."[21] Some would add further classifications to create a spectrum instead of a dichotomy: the city, the suburb, the countryside, the wilderness, etc.[22]

The urban-rural comparison also brings up complex questions about nature, and what defines it, as well as issues of colonization and immigration. Writer **Jeffrey Kastner** (1963–) points out nature is ". . . a system we are fundamentally native to, but unavoidably separate from; one that produces us, even as we (physically, conceptually, discursively) produce it . . ."[23] Other scholars, such as **Karen Malone** (1963–), have highlighted how nature has been characterized as distinctly separate from urban settings, furthering the idea that one must travel to designated rural sites free of pollution or culture, like state and national parks, to experience nature, when in fact rivers, trees, parks, gardens, and other nature-based elements are found in many urban environments alongside all the elements of urbanization.[24]

EXERCISE: Think about Categories

Considering the difference between urban and rural categories, what other categories of space can you identify or create? How does history and the passage of time affect our understanding of spatial categories? Particularly consider colonization and human presence (the act of categorization is common in settler ideology). What categories are currently in use, and which have faded away? How do categories of space change over time? What categories might you like to see in the future? You can develop your own categories for space according to your interests and observations (sensory, absurdist, mathematical, narrative, use-based, historically informed, etc.). How do categories of space help shape and define a space?

1. For this exercise, start by thinking of an everyday walk you take.

2. Then, write down the different categories of space you encounter along the walk. It can help to consider who uses which spaces, where they are located, what they are used for, and so on.

3. Take time to also address where the edges of various spatial categories are blurry and consider their impacts and histories.

4. Afterwards, create a map of the walk with the categories and the blurry edges indicated.

This exercise is influenced by the discussion of taxonomies in Phil Smith and Simon Persighetti's book, *A Sardine Street Box of Tricks* (2012), and conversation with Wakáŋyaŋkéwíŋ/Liz Cates.

Regardless of the complications of the urban-rural comparison, and whether it is a dichotomy or a spectrum, there are famous walkers with strong preferences for one end of the spectrum or the other, and some theorists specifically address the difference between the two. Take for instance, writer **bell hooks** (1952–2021), who notes, "Nature was the place where one could escape the world of manmade constructions of race and identity," referring to her childhood home in the Kentucky hills.[25] Others embrace walking in rural spaces due to their connections to identity, such as photographer **Nici Cumpston** (1963–, Kaurna Country, Barkandji people, western New South Wales) who uses medium-format photography on her walks around the backwaters and inland lake systems in the Riverland of South Australia and the rocky ridges on Barkandji Country, to connect with her ancestry. In her work, *Shelter I & II, quartzite ridge* (2011), Cumpston states, "Using a medium format film camera slows my pace. Spending as much time as I can in the environment, and speaking with cultural custodians to get a true sense of place are significant steps in my process."[26]

Artist **Sarah Rodigari** (1976–) also combines walking and rural settings in her developing work, *This Must Be the Place* (2020). Through a series of walking interviews with rural residents in remote Western Australia, she pieced together a performance piece responding to place, and connecting narratives of rural utopia (open spaces, no rules, anything is possible, and anything goes)[27] with information from the interviews. Themes of social, economic, cultural, historical, and environmental sustainability surfaced, with particular attention to climate change and settler-colonialism in Australia. The performance was characterized as humorous, poetic, and insightful.[28]

This theme of environmental awareness seems to naturally connect with rural walking, as **Kate Green** (1973–) addressed in *Watershed Line* (2021) (see figure 7.1). This walking work consisted of the artist following the concrete post markers that outline the watershed of the Elan and Claerwen rivers, as determined by the Birmingham Corporation in England in 1892. These seventy square miles were intended to provide water to fuel the city's industrial growth, and because of that economic value, the site has been protected from pesticides and other chemicals. While this particular site now houses rare flora and fauna thanks to those protections, it came at the cost of accelerated Victorian industrialization, which has contributed to current global climate change. Green's walk is meant to highlight this complex narrative of preservation and destruction bound up in human interactions with the rural environment.[29]

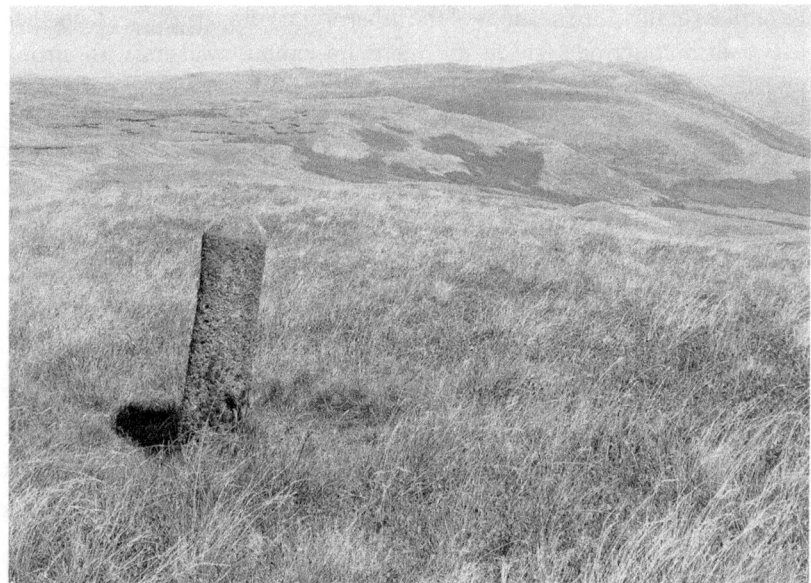

Figure 7.1 Kate Green, *Watershed Line*, 2021, photograph of concrete post marker, © Kate Green. *Source*: Courtesy of Kate Green.

In contrast to these walkers who embrace and examine the rural, writer Lauren Elkin points out the unique value of urban walking in her book *Flâneuse* (2016), "I found her [the flâneuse] using cities as performance spaces or as hiding places; as places to seek fame and fortune or anonymity; as places to liberate herself from oppression or to help those who are oppressed; as places to declare her independence; as places to change the world or be changed by it."[30] Elkin was particularly influenced by Paris, the city that popularized the sidewalk in the 1800s via the urban design choices of **Georges-Eugène Haussmann** (1809–1891).[31]

EXERCISE: Conceptualizing the City

The Surrealists often played games, as described in *A Book of Surrealist Games* (1995). In 1933, this game was played: "Certain Possibilities Relating to the Irrational Embellishment of a City." Participants were prompted to state "whether they would conserve, displace, modify, transform, or suppress certain aspects of a city."[32]

For this exercise, get two or more people together and start by making a list of objects, systems, or concepts related to a city of your choice. Write them down on slips of paper and put them in a container for randomly selecting one at a time.

For each item drawn out of the container, take turns stating whether you would conserve, displace, modify, transform, or suppress it. Take note of what the group comes up with.

In the spirit of possibility outlined by Elkin, artist **Hui-min Tsen** (1975–) highlighted an urban novelty of Chicago in her place-specific work *The Pedway* (2009–2013). The pedway is a series of underground corridors spanning forty blocks of downtown Chicago that protect walkers from the intense midwestern weather. Tsen created a tour showcasing thirty-six points of interest along these tunnels and walkways, and eventually published a book so participants could take a self-guided tour. This project highlights issues of "urban development, utopian impulses, and fears of the city from the Renaissance until now."[33]

While Tsen's work focuses on a walk within the core of the city, **JJ Tiziou** (1979–) focuses on the perimeter of the city of Philadelphia in *Walk around Philadelphia* (2016–). This ongoing work, which developed from a four-person artist residency to a biannual event, invites people to sign up to walk around the city's oddly-shaped 104-mile boundary, moving along highways and waterways, new housing and decaying factories—from shipyards and scrapyards to graveyards and farmyards. The multi-day walk highlights similarities and differences on either side of the city's border, drawing attention to social and environmental justice, infrastructure and ecosystems, commerce and incarceration, Indigenous history and colonization, privilege and access, and a sense of scale.[34]

Artist **Catherine D'Ignazio** (1975–) takes a critical eye towards urban walking, or in this case running, with her work *It Takes 154,000 Breaths To Evacuate Boston* (2007–2009). For this audio piece, D'Ignazio recorded her breaths along Boston's twenty-six evacuation routes, and accompanied the recording with a drawing of the routes. The work was intended to critique urban insecurities post-9/11, and measure fear. This work is particularly interesting because its context has shifted with world events, in this case with the Boston Marathon bombing in 2013, which was the type of terrorist attack the evacuation system was meant to address.

In this way, the work demonstrates the importance of context and intent in analyzing walking works.

Taking a similarly critical stance, **Rozalinda Borcilă** established the *Center for Getting Ugly* (2004–2008), a counter-institution focused on experimental artistic and political work. The center collaborated with "Walk, Talk, Eat, Talk Some More" (2006), via *Walk to the Beach* (2006) led by **Kara Clark** (1975–), in which the group attempted to walk to Tampa, Florida's last remaining public beach, relying only on instructions from passersby who struggled to adapt their understanding of the automobile-centric roads to a walkable route. The group agreed to hold a picnic at the beach or when they could no longer travel by foot.[35] Documentation from the event features images of the walkers parading along the side of a highway and treading in the grassy dividers between roads. The project highlighted the challenges that urban sprawl poses when walking is not considered for access to public spaces, especially for those who might not have access to a car.

Other artists concern themselves with the non-human inhabitants of urban spaces, such as plants. For instance, **Lucia Monge** (1983–) has an ongoing project, *Plantón Móvil* (2010–), which invites participants to march plants through city streets, ending with the creation of a public green space (see figure 7.2). Conceptually, the work highlights the dual

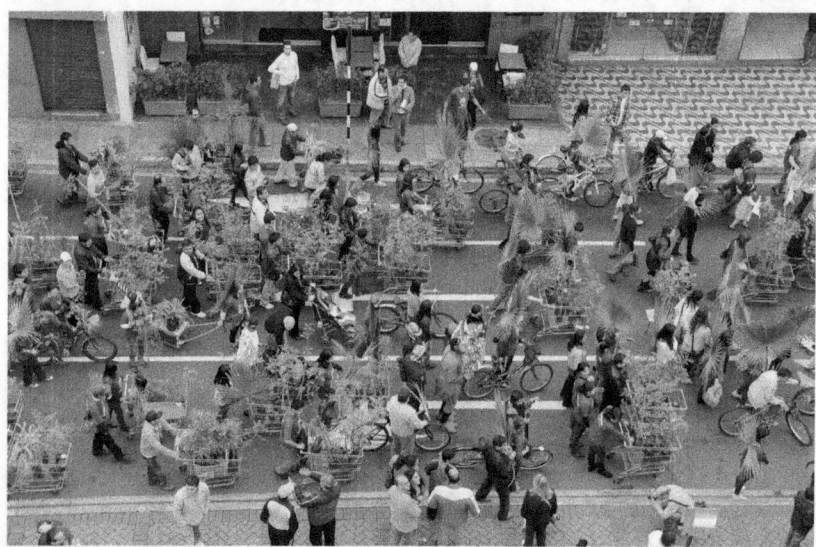

Figure 7.2. Lucia Monge, *Plantón Móvil*, 2011, people walking together with plants at Miraflores, Lima, Peru, photo by Jorge Ochoa, © Lucia Monge. *Source*: Courtesy of Lucia Monge.

meaning of *plantón*, which can mean a young tree ready to be planted in the ground, or it can mean sit-in. Some might even see the marching plants as humorous, which is a recognized tactic for inviting participation in socially engaged works. Formally, the visual impact of a group of people walking with plants helps draw attention to both collective action and environmental concerns in urban spaces. Additionally, the artist's use of speed is critical to the work: the human participants lend their speed via walking the normally stationary plants, while the plants lend their slowness via the act of planting and caretaking.[36]

Both the rural and urban artists and writers make excellent points, illustrating the range of opinions on the value of rural versus urban spaces, and the value walking artists might find in each.

EXERCISE: Signage

Signage changes and shifts according to where you are walking. Take a fifteen-minute walk and snap a photograph of every sign you encounter. Afterwards, create a photo collage of the signs. What do you notice when these images are collected together? What does it say about this place? How is it similar or different from other places?

Home and the Local

Home is a specific place that is different for each person. Some might define it as where people feel a sense of attachment and rootedness, or as a center of meaning or a site of care. Others might say it is an intimate space of rest where you can be yourself. Artist and author Lucy Lippard points out, "Home changes. Illusions change. People change. Time moves on. A place can be peopled by ghosts more real than living inhabitants."[37] Philosopher **Gaston Bachelard** (1884–1962) suggested home is a first-space that frames later understanding of all spaces outside, while containing memories, imaginings, and dreams.[38] Feminist geographer **Gillian Rose** (1947–1995) counters, pointing out that homes can be sites of stifling drudgery, abuse, and neglect for some.[39] Writer bell hooks describes home as a place of resistance against imperialist, white supremacist, capitalist, patriarchal oppression outside, further emphasizing the point that there is no universal definition of home.[40] Tuan suggests, "Home obviously means more than a natural or physical setting. Especially, the term cannot be limited to a built place. A useful point of departure for understanding home may be not its material manifestation but rather a concept: home is a unit of space organized mentally and materially to satisfy a people's real and perceived basic biosocial needs and, beyond that, their higher aesthetic-political aspirations."[41]

Artist **Mary Mattingly** (1978–) reflects on the definition of home in her multifaceted project *House and Universe* (2011–2013), in which she bundled most of her possessions into a series of boulder-sized collections. She photographed them and displayed them in galleries, and also pulled them through the streets of New York City in sub-project *Pull* (2013), as an absurd walking performance to emphasize the weight of the objects, both in her life, and as an eventual contribution to a landfill. The exchanges and memories associated with each possession contribute to an understanding of home, and their physical weight on the walk makes visible the emotional importance of one's home.

Other artists have used walking to examine the political- and identity-based facets of home. For example, the duo **Mwangi Hutter** (Ingrid Mwangi [1975–] and Robert Hutter [1964–]) examined violence experienced in Kenya after the 2007 election through a performance entitled *Human Walk* (2007–2008). In this work, documented in a fourteen-minute video, Mwangi walked in Nairobi with two signs hanging on either side of her torso reading "I am human" and "I am Kenyan." The intention of the work was to invite dialogue, a first step towards forgiveness,[42] while also raising questions about nationality, diasporic peoples of African descent, mixed race identities (Mwangi is of Kenyan-German descent), and ideas of home.[43]

Home, as a specific place, is also related to the concept of "the local," which focuses on belonging to a particular area or neighborhood via nature, culture, history or ideology.[44] Lippard describes localness as "a layered location replete with human histories and memories, place has width as well as depth. It is about connections, what surrounds it, what formed it, what happened there, what will happen there."[45] A walking piece that centers the local is *Night Walk* (2005) by the collective walkwalkwalk. The artists invited locals to participate in a nighttime walk through possibly unfamiliar places, with no purpose other than walking. They then repeated the walk annually for several years, with some repeat walkers each year. On each iteration, they accumulated a list of things that had changed or disappeared since the last walk, creating a type of local history and archive through their collective memories.

EXERCISE: Evidence of Absence

Take a walk and look for evidence of things that were once there but are now gone. Look for outlines, silhouettes, gaps, holes, etc. Document the absences and present the documentation. Reflect on what these absences could say about the place.

This exercise is influenced by the discussion of missing things in Phil Smith and Simon Persighetti's book, *A Sardine Street Box of Tricks* (2012).

Another example of exploring the local is *Long Trace of Minneapolis* (2016–2018) by **Larsen Husby** (1990–), which involved walking every street in Minneapolis, a total of 1,315 miles, through this city of 422,331 people. Husby set up guidelines for himself that involved walking the entire length of each street, as legally allowed, and recording each route. Through the walking, Husby noted chance encounters with other pedestrians when they were present, changes in architecture and landscape, and the car-centric nature of the city. This exercise was in part an effort to get to know his local city better, and this literal trace of the street grid was his means of reflection.[46]

EXERCISE: All the Affordances

People use spaces for many different things, which in turn can affect our understanding of particular places. All the possible uses for a space are called *affordances*. In this exercise, select a space in a place you are familiar with. List all the affordances (uses) of the space. Next, develop a walking score related to the place and inspired by your list. Think broadly about affordances. Don't be afraid to be playful.

Both home and localness tie into concepts of memory and nostalgia, which are simultaneously personal and social, created through a combination of materiality, meaning, and practice.[47] Lippard elaborates when she states, "Nostalgia is a way of denying the present as well as keeping some people and places in the past, where we can visit them when we feel like taking a leave of absence from modernity."[48] Some physical manifestations of memory and nostalgia are museums and monuments, both of which intersect with tourism and walking mentioned in chapter four. These physical manifestations of memory and nostalgia solidify particular interpretations of the past as defined by their powerful founders, often suppressing some memories in favor of others. Walking artists will sometimes work against these canonized narratives through their projects. Take for example *[murmur]* (2002–2013) or *Hear Our Houston* (2012–2015), both of which were audio walking tours discussed in chapter four, foregrounding everyday people who would not normally have input into the official nostalgic narratives recorded for institutions like museums or monuments.

In discussing home, it's also important to touch on those who do not have housing. Previously, the term *homeless* was used, and terminology is now evolving towards "unhoused" or "people without housing."[49] Vocabulary continues to shift and change. Historians highlight Elizabethan times as a moment when contemporary ideas of living without housing started to develop. At this time feudal ties were being broken and large numbers of people were freed to wander the land.[50] Sociologist **Zygmunt Bauman** (1925–2017) describes "what made the vagabond so terrifying was his apparent freedom to move and so to escape the net of the previously locally based control. Worse than that, the movements of the vagabond were unpredictable; unlike the pilgrim or, for that matter, a nomad, the vagabond has no set destination."[51] It is much the same in contemporary society with frequent attempts to criminalize the unhoused. A walking work responding to this topic is *Homeless Vehicle* (1988–1989) by Krzysztof Wodiczko. It consists of a multifunctional tool that assists the user to wash, cook, rest, and sleep, as well as safely storing collected bottles and cans. The mobile device can be collapsed and pushed through the streets, similar to a shopping cart. Wodiczko stressed that the work was not meant to solve individual's challenges with lack of housing, but more so to highlight the social need that exists, and push people to make the walking device unnecessary.[52]

EXERCISE: Walk Your Block or Perimeter

If you live in an urban setting, walk around your block. If you live in a rural setting, walk around the perimeter of the land area you consider your home. As you walk, try to slow down and engage with each of your senses one at a time, recording your observations (sight, sound, smell, taste, and touch). Do you know your neighbors? How do you define your neighborhood, and what is its perimeter on a map? Consider making a one-page zine (fold in quarters) explaining your block/home area and neighborhood to someone who has never been there before.

Getting Lost

Getting lost can lead to a sense of confusion, panic, and chaos, as was described in chapter six in the discussion of mazes. For others, being lost can elicit a sense of freedom, fortitude, and discovery as they experience a place with all their attention turned to the current moment. Writer Rebecca Solnit has written an entire book on the topic of getting lost, entitled, *A Field Guide to Getting Lost* (2005). She references the well-known act of not finding the location you're seeking or of losing track of familiar surroundings. She also references the idea of losing oneself in the current moment or of seeking out the unfamiliar in an effort to enlarge one's world experience.[53] Walter Benjamin describes the difference between these two types of getting lost when he states, "Not to find one's way in a city may well be uninteresting and banal. It requires ignorance—nothing more. But to lose oneself in a city—as one loses oneself in a forest—that calls for quite a different schooling."[54]

EXERCISE: Defying Direction

This walk is inspired by *Direction* (1962) by George Brecht, in which he tells the participant to first move in the direction indicated by a sign, and then travel in another direction.

Start by looking up directions on a mobile device to a location you can walk to. Next, take the opposite direction, step by step. For example, if the directions tell you to turn right and travel .2 miles, instead turn left and travel .2 miles. Be safe and don't endanger yourself. Are you able to complete the directions?

Various art historical practitioners have sought after getting lost as a desirable experience. For example, the Situationists' aim of drifting in the city is very similar to striving to get lost in a familiar place. Some Fluxus scores explicitly instructed participants to get lost, such as Yoko Ono's *Map Piece* (1964) that simply stated, "Draw a map to get lost." These approaches to getting lost help the walker attempt to encounter the unknown, which can be difficult in the media- and technology-saturated contemporary moment. Solnit and Benjamin imply that getting lost is more of a state of mind, or a state of discovery.

More recently, Jennie Savage recorded *The Guide to Getting Lost* (2014), a thirty-minute audio guide for getting lost in a familiar location. Later in *Fracture Mob* (2016), the instructions were broadcast on a radio station worldwide, providing the same instructions for everyone regardless of location, which means participants had to make improvisational decisions on the fly based on the specifics of their own geography, almost as if they were using a map from a different city to navigate their own. This piece is still available online for those who might like to try it out.

EXERCISE: Wayfinding

This is a walk for an urban area the walker is unfamiliar with. It is a good walking exercise for travel-based studies or walking while on vacation, although it could also work when simply visiting an unfamiliar part of the city or town you are already acquainted with. This exercise references wayfinding, which is the use of signage or other design elements to help people navigate a space.

1. Upon arriving at the new walking location, look around. What do you notice in terms of wayfinding? Record your observations.

2. Select a wayfinding sign and try to use it to find the indicated location. Did it work? Did you need more information? What would have helped you find your way more quickly or easily?

Summary

In this chapter, walking and place are the focus, helping to draw attention to sometimes overlooked spatial and cultural elements. Indigenous perspectives are a significant topic, followed by discussions of urban versus rural, home and local, and the idea of getting lost. These are popular themes in contemporary walking-based works, and conceptual connections can be made to nearly any reader's context. Selected exercises open up space for further exploration.

Chapter 8

Activism

Walking has been a form of resistance for a very long time, as referenced in chapter one with the Egyptians and Romans. However, there is a noticeable uptick in walking activism after the Industrial Revolution, when countries in Europe and the Americas started shifting from a farming economy to a manufacturing economy in the late 1700s and early 1800s. This period is when walking started to become a slower transportation choice for some, although certainly not all. For those who had access to alternative modes of transportation, to choose the relative slowness and deliberateness of walking was to make a statement, or act against the alienation of new technologies.[1] This aligns with many of the Romantic writers.

Moving forward in time, as mentioned in chapter four on leading and following, walking projects can be a way of sharing alternative narratives. By highlighting different ways of understanding current situations and potential futures, walking can become a tool of activism. While several projects mentioned in previous chapters fit this description, this chapter goes into further depth and with more focus on protests, demonstrations, performances, attire, props, reenactments, environmentalism, and moving beyond commercial art worlds.

Protests and Demonstrations

In chapter one there is a brief introduction of walking and activism. This chapter picks up the thread starting in the 1900s with examples such as **Mohandas Gandhi** (1869–1949) leading the 240-mile Salt March in 1930 to protest British salt policies as an act of mass civil disobedience against colonial rule (see figure 8.1). Also well-known are the various civil rights marches of the 1950s and 1960s, including the March on Washington in 1963, where **Martin Luther King Jr.** (1929–1968) delivered his famous "I Have a Dream" speech, or the 1965 Selma to Montgomery March, also known as "Bloody Sunday," in which six hundred peaceful protesters were attacked by law enforcement on the Edmund Pettus Bridge. While these events might not be categorized as art events, they have certainly had a heavy influence on future walking artists.

The 1960s and 1970s also brought marches protesting the Vietnam War, LGBTQ+ rights, and immigrant workers' rights. For example, **Cesar Chavez's** (1927–1993) famous March for Justice took place in 1966 as a group of nearly one hundred striking farmworkers, most of them Mexican American and Filipino, marched from Delano to Sacramento, CA (280 miles), helping to earn the National Farm Workers Association's first union contract.[2] Perhaps the most influential anti-Vietnam War protest was the 1971 May Day Protest in Washington, DC, where tens of thousands gathered, and police arrested more than seven thousand people, with a further five thousand in the days following (the largest mass arrests in

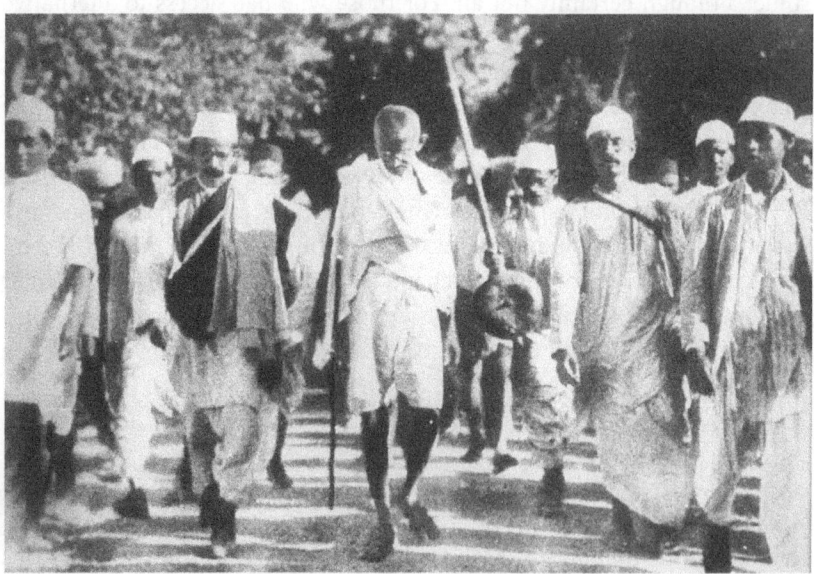

Figure 8.1. Gandhi leading the famous 1930 nonviolent resistance Salt March. *Source*: Wikimedia Commons, public domain.

US history).[3] 1970 was also the very first Pride parade, marking the first anniversary of the Stonewall uprising in New York City. This first parade was officially known as the Christopher Street Liberation Day March. It was spearheaded by a group of activists and the march covered roughly fifty blocks.[4]

Of particular interest for walkers are some of the major milestones in disability activism, such as the 1968 Architectural Barriers Act, which mandated accessibility of US federal buildings. Similarly, in the summer 1978, the **Gang of 19** in Denver, Colorado, blocked an intersection chanting "We will ride!" to force a meeting about the lack of wheelchair-accessible buses in the city. And perhaps one of the most iconic moments in disability activism is the 1990 Capitol Crawl, which involved people leaving their mobility aids to haul themselves up the US Capitol steps in a demonstration of the need to pass the Americans with Disabilities Act (ADA).

Another notable walking protest is the Crash the Market March (1997) led by **AIDS Coalition to Unleash Power (ACT UP)** (1987–). It marked the ten-year anniversary of ACT UP's first demonstration and brought together chapters from across the United States. While not all ACT UP actions included marching together, this demonstration did. Protesters gathered at City Hall Park in New York City and marched to the Stock Exchange, demanding congressional hearings on the price of AIDS drugs, calling out the profiteering of pharmaceutical companies, and protesting cutbacks to Medicaid funding. ACT UP was also known for its striking visuals developed by the activist art collective, **Gran Fury** (1988–1995), which developed the iconic "Silence = Death" motto. Combining this important graphic material with the large-scale march helped to amplify the importance of the demonstration.[5] Observers can see how walking combined with graphic design continues to be influential through the works of Hui-min Tsen (chapter seven), Andrea Carlson (chapters two and five), any of Hamish Fulton's works (chapters two, four, and ten), and more.

Indigenous groups have also had a long history of using walking as a form of protest or consciousness raising. Take for instance the Mother Earth Water Walks (2003–2017), founded by two Anishinaabe grandmothers and continued by many people over the years, which drew attention to water-protection issues by walking the perimeters of the Great Lakes.[6] Another example is the *Mirror Shield Project: Water Serpent Action* (2016), organized by **Cannupa Hanska Luger** (1979–) (Mandan, Hidatsa, Arikara, Lakota) and **Rory Wakemup** (1976–) (Ojibwe) in response to the Dakota Access Pipeline construction, a pipeline that poses a threat to the Standing

Rock Reservation's water supply. The performance was an act of resistance and was recorded by a drone camera. It consisted of over 150 Water Protectors outfitted with reflective shields held overhead as they moved through loose formations, referencing the sky via reflection and the nearby river via shape.[7] Additional projects have been mentioned, such as *The Journey of Nishiyuu* (2013) in chapter seven, or *Dakota Commemorative Walk* (2002–2012) in chapter five.

Slowalk (In Support of Ai Weiwei) (2011) by Hamish Fulton was a performative collective artistic action to protest the disappearance of Chinese artist **Ai Weiwei** (1957–), who was later returned to his home. For this walk, a group of people meditatively walked together very slowly and silently for two hours in a particular formation in the Tate Modern Turbine Hall. This silent walking activism drew media attention and added to the public outcry over the suppression of Ai Weiwei's free speech.

Not all walking protests involve large groups of people. Take for instance **Alex Villar's** (1962–) *Temporary Occupations* (2001). This work consists of the artist running throughout New York City and inserting his body into awkward small negative spaces that have been fenced off or marked as private through other means. The work is recorded on video, allowing viewers to ponder ideas of the everyday, public versus private space, various architectural tools and devices employed across urban areas, and subverting boundaries. As a solo running performance, it encourages activism by exposing subtle daily acts of dissent against spatial codes.[8]

Performances, Attire, and Props

Walking projects that integrate activism sometimes include performances, specific attire, or props to heighten the impact or enhance storytelling, which can be a vital part of prompting people to take action. Below are a series of examples that engage performance, attire, and props as part of walking activism.

Artist **Adrian Piper** (1948–) focused on the idea of racial and gender discrimination while performing a walk in public as her work *I Am the Locus #2* (1975), in which she put on an Afro wig, pasted a mustache on her face, and wore large wire-rimmed sunglasses, embodying her alter-ego Mythic Being. She dressed and acted like a man in the streets of Harvard Square in Cambridge, Massachusetts, muttering memorized passages from her journal, and was followed by a film crew. This work challenged passersby with an encounter that posed questions about race, gender, and class as they either brushed shoulders with her or looked the other way. Later, photographs from the walk were enhanced with oil crayon and text in preparation for creating posters.[9] The text included phrases such as "Surrounded and Constrained," "I Am the Locus of Consciousness," and "Get Out of My Way, Asshole," among others.[10] While the photographs of the walking performance weren't originally intended for display on their own, they have since entered museum collections.

EXERCISE: Attire for Impact

Pause for a moment to think about the impact of attire on an activist walk. Next, taking inspiration for Phil Smith and Simon Persighetti's *A Sardine Street Box of Tricks* (2012) select a uniform to wear on a research walk of one block (or equivalent length). Think about how your uniform attire can relate (or not) to the site you are walking. Revisit the walk several days in a row, wearing the same uniform.

How does the attire shift your interactions with passersby? How does it shift your attitude and behavior? What would you change about the uniform after this experience, if anything? Why or why not?

For *Cultural Graffiti: A Tahltan Indian Declares War on the British Monarchy* (2013) by **Peter Morin** (1977–, Tahltan), the artist walked across London and assumed a facedown position, lying on the ground, and sang to the bases of various buildings and monuments related to the history of British colonialism. Through songs performed at sites related to the support of colonialism, he informed the British ancestors that they had failed to eradicate Indigenous people. At sites of Indigenous presence in London, like Pocahontas's grave, he sang songs to commemorate those who were taken from their homelands.[11] The performative nature of this multistop walk demonstrates how performance and walking can be used to heighten an activist message through thoughtful conceptual and formal choices.

Artist **Barbara Lounder** (1955–) used props for a subtler form of activism in *Pedestrian Detour* (2010), a work that centered on walking with props like blindfolds, walking sticks, and stilts to draw attention to the political, social, and poetic significance of everyday objects, images, and sensory experiences of the topography. By modifying participants' normal sensory experiences and changing the way they move through space, awareness is heightened during these observational walks (more available on observational walking in chapter three). The project had two phases: first the walking experience, and later the display of the props in a gallery. The props were all carefully crafted with attention to material, color, and surface quality.[12]

In *Ayum-ee-aawach Oomama-mowan, Speaking to Their Mother* (1991–1996), **Rebecca Belmore** (1960–, Anishinaabe) created a giant portable wooden amplifier, six-foot high and twelve-foot long, in response to a seventy-eight-day standoff between a Mohawk community near Oka, Quebec, and the Royal Canadian Mounted Police in an effort to block the development of a golf course on sacred land. The scale of this work caused it to operate similarly to some of the land art or monuments discussed in earlier chapters because the scale invokes walking, as the work itself is a destination. The amplifier was moved to sites of environmental conflict over five years, becoming a mobile monument or pilgrimage path, attracting many people for the purpose of speaking to the land, although the temptation to use the work to speak to humans in powerful positions was overwhelming. The work was utilized in public parks opposite government buildings, in front of the Canadian prime minister's residence, and on Parliament Hill in Ottawa.[13] The scale of this prop created visual impact on site, and its mobile nature drew attention to the breadth of environmental crises. Additionally, its engagement with sound helped to empower people, as their voices were amplified speaking to the land.

Another politically engaged work that relied on a large prop is *Walk the Walk* (2010) by **Kate Gilmore** (1975–) (see cover image). This walking performance featured a bright yellow simple architectural box with doors and a flat roof featuring a railway. The eight-foot-tall box was placed in Bryant Park in New York City. On the one-hundred-square-foot roof, groups of seven women working in shifts walked around in matching yellow dresses and beige-heeled shoes, improvising with shuffling, stomping, and walking. These women remind the viewer of office workers moving through the mandated repetitive movements of contemporary life, situated in capitalist and patriarchal systems.[14]

An earlier, protest-based walking work that combined both feminism and a large prop is *Gates of Troy* (1969) by **Rosemarie Castoro** (1939–2015), in which she pulled a large roll of unraveling aluminum through the streets of SoHo in New York City. The awkwardness of pulling the unwieldy roll in a public street is a physicalization of the difficulty of being a woman creating works in an art world dominated by men.[15] This protest echoes *The Iliad* (800 BCE), in which Achilles pulls Hector's corpse behind his chariot as an act of revenge. The scale, noise, pace, and spectacle of this work all add to its impact as a performative walking protest.

Content warning in the following paragraph: Sexual Assault.

Using a similar carrying and dragging action to Castoro, but with a much longer duration and a mattress instead of a roll of aluminum, **Emma Sulkowicz** (1992–) staged a walking protest against Columbia University in *Carry That Weight* (2014). In this work, Sulkowicz vowed to carry a mattress with her on campus everywhere she went until the institution dismissed the man whom she said sexually assaulted her, or until she graduated. In the rules of engagement she developed for the performance, she could not ask for help carrying the mattress, but could accept help if it was offered. Sulkowicz ended up carrying the mattress for the remainder of her time at the institution and at the 2015 graduation ceremony. In collaboration with other campuses, a national day of action was held with organizers at over 130 schools in acknowledgment of survivors of sexual and domestic violence on campuses.[16] Again, the physicalization of a normally unseen emotional burden, paired with the spectacle of walking in public with a prop, help to enhance the impact of this performative walking protest.

A final example, also engaging gender issues, is *Walk a Mile in Her Veil* (2016) by **Yasmeen Sabri** (1992–). In this work, the artist uses hijabs, niqabs, and burqas as props to invite participants to explore wearing these various pieces of clothing. There are many different associations with the experience of wearing these items, from feminist critique to feminist celebration, and sometimes religious discrimination. This project asked the participants to walk *as* or *for* the artist, rather than *with* the artist, which is different than many other walking projects.[17] Each person had a unique experience of the work, as they each brought their own point of view and history to the moment. The work also provoked a strong response when an intoxicated person attempted to destroy the work, and later pleaded guilty to religiously aggravated criminal damage.[18] Sabri also made a video work as part of this piece, and it showcased various participants putting on the veils and walking through the city.

Altogether, these diverse examples demonstrate the impact of performative walking, and the use of attire and props to engage activism.

> **EXERCISE: Your Prop**
>
> Considering the examples of walking artworks that utilize a prop, select a prop of your own to walk with. Why are you choosing this object? Go for your walk, and record in any way that feels appropriate. Display the walking archive next to your prop. Observe how people take in the work.

Reenactment

A reenactment, sometimes also called a reprise, can be a powerful exercise for developing deeper understanding of historic events or past artworks. For example, *Slave Rebellion Reenactment* (2019) by Dread Scott was a participatory reimagining of the German Coast Uprising of 1811 just outside New Orleans (see also: contextual analysis in chapter two). This extensive event was documented on film by **John Akomfrah** (1957–) and included hundreds of reenactors in period-specific attire marching for two days over twenty-six miles. The work examined this historic event in which the enslaved people planned to seize Orleans Territory and end slavery.[19] In a very tangible way, it also brought this often-overlooked history to people living along the procession route.

Another well-known walking and running political reenactment is *Battle of Orgreave* (2001) staged by **Jeremy Deller** (1966–), in which a combination of eight hundred reenactors and two hundred former miners from the original 1984 strike collaborated on a restaging of the striking miners being chased up a hill and pursued through a village.[20] This historical event was a key moment of activism in the conflict between the British government and the Union movements. Deller was posing questions about the relationship between reenactors and their events, and stated he wanted "to openly acknowledge that any history is inevitably impure, highly mediated, and in need of being re-written."[21]

Similar to Scott's and Deller's reenactments, but with a more single-protagonist focus, *Cistemaw inyiniw* (2001) presented by **Cheryl L'Hirondelle** (1958–, Cree/Métis, German/Polish) restaged the running of Cistemaw inyiniw (Cree for *tobacco being*), who delivered tobacco to communities to request their attendance and support at ceremonies. Cistemaw inyiniw was known for his speed and distances covered. In L'Hirondelle's reenactment, she ran approximately twenty-five kilometers across the Makwa Sahgaiehcan Reserve in northern Saskatchewan. She wore a racing jersey with a number and sent collaborators ahead to interact with the community and mark Cree syllabics in chalk outside the houses of welcoming people. L'Hirondelle was able to stop and visit with these members of the community. Additionally, during the running performance, three radio stations broadcast the story of Cistemaw inyiniw in Cree, interrupting the Top 40 hits, a subversive addition to the event.[22]

Another type of reprise is presented by **Alan Michelson** (1953–, Mohawk) who created a type of sculptural reenactment when he installed *Earth's Eye* (1990) in lower Manhattan's Collect Pond Park, outlining the now absent pond, a freshwater source that sustained Manhattan residents until tanneries polluted it and it had to be filled in during 1803. Forty cast concrete markers (22" × 14" × 6" each) referenced the lost natural and social history of the pond with low-relief imagery of plants and animals. These markers were arranged in the outline of the pond, and passersby walked around and within the installation, "bringing previous states of the locale into the here and now."[23] The work highlighted environmental destruction to walk to and within, acting as a reenactment of a lost site and helping participants to embody the harm to the land and water.

EXERCISE: Reprise of Slowalk

Organize a reenactment of Fulton's *Slowalk* in a space with similar properties. Over the two hours, consider the social justice concepts underlying this slow silent walk. Afterwards, talk with the group to hear what others were thinking.

Environmentalism

Many walking artists have connections to environmentalism, or a general concern for protecting the earth and preserving natural resources. Some of those projects are dramatically long, such as the twenty-two years of walking by **John H. Francis III** (1946–), also known as "the Planetwalker," who was named a United Nations Environmental Program Goodwill Ambassador in 1991. While his walking wasn't specifically artistic, it was definitely concerned with the environment: Francis witnessed an oil spill in 1971, and later vowed not to ride in a motorized vehicle, a vow he kept until 1994.

Meanwhile, other walking works are much shorter in both scale and duration, such as *Goldenrod Transect* (2021), in which **Christy Gast** (1976–) presented a performative walk reflecting on a place-specific native plant, goldenrod, found throughout the High Line Park in New York City. She wore a mesh eye covering attached to her microphone and inspired by insect eyes, as well as golden-colored clothes, accompanied by interactive props. The walk was both entertaining and educational, helping participants to understand the many insects that call goldenrod home.[24] This type of performative walk with accompanying attire and props is a common approach for artist-educators hoping to increase environmental awareness and heighten engagement with a particular place.

Another example of an environmentally focused walking project is *Yamuna Walk* (2007) by **Atul Bhalla** (1964–), which lasted five days and took place along fifty-three kilometers of the banks of the Yamuna River, passing through New Delhi, India. This walk, recorded through photo and video, showcased the contrast between the river as a beautiful primary symbol of the divine and also as a tool of refuse disposal. After completing the walk, Bhalla produced a photo book to continue engagement, which is another popular approach for raising environmental place-based awareness. The photo book allows a larger audience to access the work, due to the book's portable and intimate handheld nature.

EXERCISE: Body of Water

First, research where the nearest body of water is located. Is it a nearby pond, a river, lake, ocean, bog, or something else?

Next, walk along the edge of that body of water.

Reflect on what you observe and what water-related questions arise as you walk.

A slightly different approach is used in *Longitudinal Installation* (2007–2008) by **Xavier Cortada** (1964–). This interactive installation engages ritualized walking around an installation at both the North and South poles. Each installation has twenty-four quotes on a sign and a circle of twenty-four shoes arranged around a pole. Each quote is from a person in a different time zone describing how they have been personally affected by climate change. Participants are directed to take a photo of the sign, and then move from shoe to shoe around the circle reading aloud the corresponding quote. The walking piece can be performed alone or in groups. The close proximity of the shoes, arranged according to the longitudinal lines of each time zone, helps the participant to understand the interconnectedness of people across the globe.[25]

Hamish Fulton is also well-known for his focus on environmental conservation. Many of his works consist of graphically arranged words, such as one design from his walking artwork, *21 Days in the Cairngorms* (2010) in which he highlights "CLIMATE CHANGES," numbering each letter in both words, one through seven. Many of Fulton's works are structured by multiples of seven, such as seven-, fourteen-, or twenty-one-day walks. The long duration and meditative qualities of Fulton's works lend themselves to environmental contemplation. In his book *Mountain Time Human Time,* Fulton notes, "As I write this, the UK government is planning to sell off nature reserves, rivers, forests. Perhaps David Cameron should read Wallace Stegner's 1960 *Wilderness Letter.* At the top of the 2010 list, the most important is wild nature."[26]

In discussing environmentalism, it is important to point out traditional ecological knowledge or Native knowledge of the ecosystem. Counter to Western conceptions of ecology that divides material into living and non-living elements, professor **David Begay** (Navajo) reminds us that ". . . water, air, sunlight, soil, and minerals are considered living in the Diné definition of ecology. Rather than referring to these as 'non-living resources' as explained by the Western definition, Diné would refer to them not only as resources, but *bitsisiléí,* translated as 'that which precedes all life,' including human life. If you eliminate or cut off the air or water, for example, humans will cease to exist. Everything is interrelated and therefore everything is considered living."[27] Similarly, scholar **Bonnie Freeman** (1962–, Algonquin/Mohawk, member of the Six Nations of the Grand River) shares, "place-based knowledge is knowledge that we receive from and with the Land, and that this knowledge is also collective and relational . . . Indigenous guardianship of Land comes in the form of interaction with Land . . ."[28] Walking can be an important form of interaction with the Land. Scholar **Kaitlin Debicki** (1985–, Kanien'keha:ka) builds on these ideas when she contends that "trees don't simply grow *out of* or *on* the land, they *are* Land. Walking, then, happens *with* rather than *on* Land."[29]

It is also important to note there is a long tradition of colonizers and their descendants advocating for spaces to remain undeveloped or return to a deindustrialized state by commercial interests, so people can walk and do recreational activities in those spaces, preserving them for future generations. This approach, often referred to as *landscape urbanism*, has similarities to gentrifying urban spaces, although it often takes place in more rural areas. It can take the form of national and state parks or redesigning former rail lines or hydro corridors into public spaces.[30] This type of environmentalism has strong ties to tourism, as described in chapter four, and implies a generally untouched or pristine idea of nature, as described in chapter five, which was not the case when colonizers arrived in North America. Native Americans were active in managing the land through ceremonial fires to clear out underbrush and encourage new plant growth,[31] as well as careful planting and pruning. In the present day, without these traditional land-management techniques, there have been unintended consequences including wildfire challenges in western North America. Additionally, while an increase in walking paths is beneficial to some populations and is certainly better than an industrial waste site, it is also "a normalizing process based on racialized, classed, ableist and heteronormative ideologies that co-opt conservation in order to 'clean-up' and 'push out' different populations, and maintain settler colonial heteronormative elite spaces."[32]

A walking work that reflects on this exact phenomenon is *Times Beach* (2017), a sound walk recorded by artist **Teri Rueb** (1968–). This recording is available freely as a downloadable app, sharing traces of the various histories of, and field recordings at, Times Beach Nature Preserve located in the Buffalo Outer Harbor, near the mouth of the Buffalo River. Before colonial times, Native Americans lived along the shores of Lake Erie and the Niagara River for thousands of years, until European settlers arrived and built up an urban beach that later became industrialized, then turned into a park, then back to a disposal facility for dredging, and finally to its present state as a nature preserve. Sonic traces of this densely layered history are combined for walking participants.[33] The site has since changed significantly due to a major storm in 2019, and the walkways were damaged beyond repair, so people can still follow along with the app, but with the understanding of the altered space.

EXERCISE: Walking to Clean Up the Environment

Supplies needed: a bag to collect trash; gloves recommended; GPS mapping optional

Using chance encounters with trash as your guide, walk until you encounter a piece of trash. Pick up the trash and retain it in your bag. Walk on until you encounter another piece of trash. Continue collecting the trash, letting each piece guide you to the next. Walk for a predetermined length of time. Consider mapping this trash walk on GPS. Compare maps with other walkers also on a trash walk. Do you see any patterns? Where are the greatest concentrations of trash?

Beyond the Commercial Art World

As mentioned in chapter one, walking as artistic practice is connected to many happenings in the 1950s aimed at protesting and departing the formal commercial art world of studios, stages, galleries, and museums. For example, the group **Action Against Cultural Imperialism** targeted the Museum of Modern Art (MoMA), the Metropolitan Museum of Art, and the Philharmonic Hall with picketing in 1963. Signs read "Demolish Serious Culture!," "Destroy Art!," and "Demolish Art Museums!"[34]

As scholar **Miwon Kwon** (1961–) states, "The seemingly benign architectural features of a gallery/museum . . . were deemed to be coded mechanisms that actively disassociated the space of art from the outer world, furthering the institution's idealist imperative of rendering itself and its hierarchization of values 'objective,' 'disinterested,' and 'true.'"[35] Artists used many activist tactics to try to work outside these institutional systems, including focusing on ephemeral events and elements of the everyday, as discussed in chapter three. French philosopher Michel de Certeau, famous for his book *The Practice of Everyday Life* (1980), was particularly interested in ". . . the ingenious and devious ways by which the weak, the marginalized majority, make use of the strong. These tactical responses are necessary," he argues, "since the individual is increasingly situated in a position where the social structures are unstable, boundaries are shifting, and the context is too vast and complex either to control or to escape."[36]

Walking artists are still using the ephemerality of the walk and everyday elements to create meaning and activist statements. For instance, Kubra Khademi's *Kubra & Pedestrian Sign* (2016) was a performative intervention on the streets of Paris, deliberately outside the gallery system. The artist walked around at night with a pedestrian crossing lightbox on her head featuring a glowing walking figure with a skirt, drawing attention to both the everyday traffic-light infrastructure and concepts of gender. Like many socially engaged works, the ephemeral encounters and conversations on the streets were an integral part of the work.

David Hammons (1943–) was similarly concerned with happenings on the street in his video recording of a walk, *Phat Free* (1995–1999). This work is a short color video of Hammons kicking a metal bucket through the streets of a city at night. In 1986, Hammons explained that he preferred the audiences he found in the street to those that attend galleries, stating that "the art audience is the worst audience in the world. It's overly educated, it's conservative, it's out to criticize, not to understand, and it never has any fun. Why should I spend my time playing to that audience? The street audience is much more human, and their opinion is from the heart. They don't have any reason to play games; there's nothing gained or lost."[37]

Another example of working outside of commercial art spaces is Carmen Papalia's *White Cane Amplified* (2015), in which the artist replaced his white detection cane with a megaphone. He stated phrases like "I can't see you, I can't see you," identifying himself and requesting support from others on the street. This work poses questions about accessibility, disclosure, and community engagement, which are common themes in Papalia's ongoing work. The volume and spatial relationships of this work helped elevate the impact of the walking work.

EXERCISE: Walking Exhibition

Inspired by an exercise from *Learning to Love You More* (2007) by **Miranda July** (1974–) and **Harrell Fletcher** (1967–), create a walkable exhibition in outdoor space with an activist theme.

You might staple copies of the art (or the art itself) to telephone poles, or place sculptures in locations where they won't blow away. Perhaps you project video-based work on the side of a wall, and so on. Create a map for walkers to follow and take in the exhibition, along with a brief statement explaining your curatorial choices and your activist theme.

Sites and Monuments

There is a long history of developing sites and monuments that honor activism and incorporate walking, such as *Mantle* (2018) by Alan Michelson, which sits at Richmond's Capitol Square Park in Virginia.[38] The spiral-shaped walking path honors the original inhabitants of the region, especially seventeenth-century **Chief Powhatan** (d. 1618) who united thirty-four Algonquian tribes. The site incorporates cast images of corn, squash, and bean plants around the edge of a reflecting pool, surrounded by groves of trees native to the area. The site requires active participation, unlike a statue on a plinth. It becomes a reflective activation of the space of reintroduced Native life and cultural memory.[39]

In a less permanent monument, **Hock E Aye Vi Edgar Heap of Birds** (Cheyenne/Arapaho, 1954–) developed a temporary signage-based memorial at the Venice Biennale in 2007 for Pine Ridge Sioux warriors who died in Europe, performing as part of Buffalo Bill Cody's Wild West Show in the late nineteenth century. These warriors were imprisoned in the US before they were given the choice to remain in prison or go perform in Europe. The installation consisted of a series of sixteen outdoor signs to remember and honor their loss, and eight outdoor signs that serve as commentary, which visitors to Venice would encounter while walking through the city. There were also several signs in the water taxis encouraging repatriation of the Native people's remains from Europe to the US, as well as a large billboard at the Venice airport that stated in Italian, "welcome to the spectacle, welcome to the show," as a faux welcoming sign. This billboard was visible as people slowly walked through the airport checkpoint.[40] This temporary monument scattered on signs throughout the city provided many opportunities for walking encounters with the work, helping to amplify a history many people may not have been aware of.

Without constructing any permanent structures, **Pope.L** (1955–) similarly honored a specific politically charged site using walking, or in this case, walking's cousin—crawling—in *The Great White Way: 22 miles, 9 years, 1 street, Broadway, New York* (2001–2009). In this case, the site is the street of Broadway in New York City, and the artist chose to crawl the full length of the thoroughfare over the course of nine years. The street has a great deal of symbolism embedded, from the Statue of Liberty at its start, to crossing the Financial District, to the theatrical associations and dreams of making it big. Pope.L crawled on elbows and knees the entire length of Broadway wearing a superman outfit. He strapped a skateboard to his back to cross streets more quickly, but otherwise crawled the entire distance. Through this lengthy and arduous performance, he raised questions of race, class, gender, labor, and absurdity.[41] The crawl was recorded and later turned into a video piece.

EXERCISE: Monument Walk

First, take a moment to research some of the monuments, memorials, and site markers in your walkable region. Develop a walk to visit a selection of them. When you arrive at each place, take note of the site including who it celebrates, what it looks like and says (is there written material?), where it is located, and when it was established and why.

As you move along your walk, start to notice if any trends emerge. After the walk is complete, take a moment to reflect on what you would have liked to have seen added to the walk. Who would you like to see honored with a monument, memorial, or site marker, and why?

Education and Pedagogy

While not as flashy or eye-catching as a march or parade, activism can also often take the form of education and pedagogy. Further, if that pedagogy and education takes place outside of established institutions, it can also be a form of activism by critiquing recognized educational systems. Scholar **Jack Halberstam** (1961–) elaborates on and endorses "embrac[ing] the absurd, the silly and the hopelessly goofy,"[42] in contrast with long-held educational concepts of success, mastery, and heteronormativity in educational settings.[43] These alternative pedagogies can also include exploratory exercises, and the slowness of walking as a means of slowing down thought processes, and more carefully critiquing oppressive systems.

For example, *Foxfire Magazine* (1967–), was an alternative learning tool devised by an English teacher at Rabun Gap-Nacoochee School in Northeast Georgia, who was struggling to engage his students. They collectively decided to interview their neighbors and family members about Appalachian traditions and publish a magazine together. In 1974, the Foxfire group used funds from sales to purchase the land for the current Foxfire Museum site, made of over twenty historic log structures showcasing artifacts of mountain living along a half-mile walking trail. This alternative pedagogy organically led to the activism of preserving a way of life from which future generations can learn and creating a walking site for living history and ongoing education.

Another example is the walk that **Amish Morrell** (1974–), OCAD University students, and participants from OCAD University Indigenous and Decolonial Reading and Learning Group took along the Humber River entitled *On the Land, in the City: Snowshoe on Niwa'ah Onega'gaih'ih (The Humber River)* (2019) (see figure 8.2). As they walked on the frozen river, they discussed the river's role as a traditional Indigenous travel route and had tea along the marshes.[44] This type of outdoor walking education is a common form of alternative pedagogy, allowing for the spread of alternative histories and narratives, beyond those shared by recognized institutions.

Somewhat similar is the course on experimental composition John Cage taught with botanist **Guy Nearing** (1890–1986) in 1959 for the New School for Social Research in New York. The course embraced radical pedagogy and mainly focused on slow looking as they took groups of thirty students mushroom foraging on the weekends in the woods of upstate New York.[45]

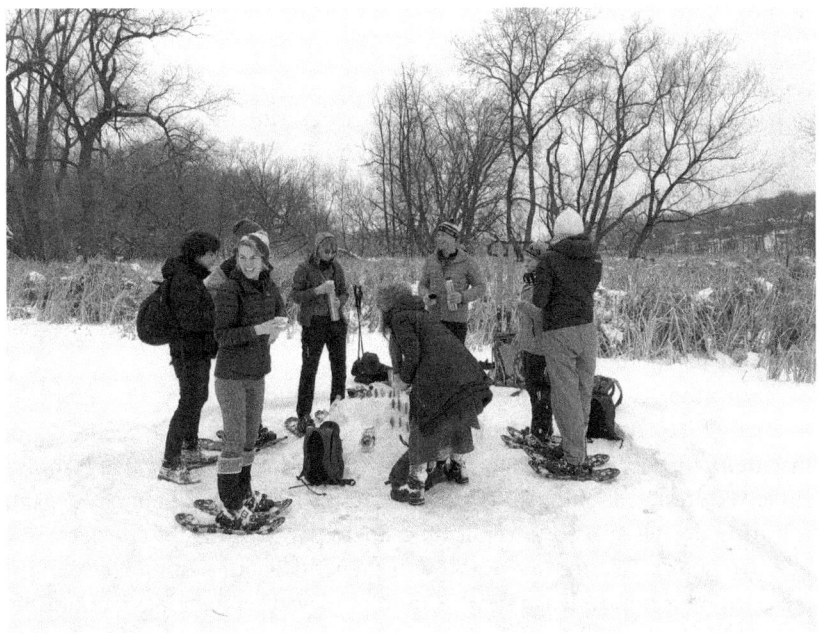

Figure 8.2. Amish Morrell, *On the Land, in the City: Snowshoe on Niwa'ah Onega'gaih'ih (The Humber River)*, 2019, photograph, © Amish Morrell. *Source*: Courtesy of Amish Morrell.

EXERCISE: Walking School

If you were to create a free school of walking, what would it be like? Who would you like to learn with? Where might it be located? What would you do, and how? When might you hold "classes," activities, or other modes of learning? Why might you include walking in this free school?

Humor

Another common tool used to draw participants into activist work is humor, and several walking works engage with this device. For example, in *Street with a View* (2008) by Robin Hewlett and Ben Kinsley, mentioned in chapter four, the artists used humorous situations to draw attention to the surveillance the Google Maps car brought to their neighborhoods. By sprinkling humor into their project, more people were likely to pay attention, engage, and consider the larger conceptual ideas of the project.

Let's Walk (1999) by Amanda Heng, described in chapter five, also uses humor and absurdity to engage more people. In this case, Heng's request that participants hold high-heeled shoes in their mouth and walk backward, helped create a large group of humorous-looking people along public streets. This public, group, absurdist act helped amplify her conceptual message about how difficult it is to operate in a patriarchal society where a wide range of expectations and responsibilities are put on women's shoulders.

In other cases, humor can be used to build empathy. For example, in *Stoat* (1999) by **Marcus Coates** (1968–), he creates a video recording of his attempt to become a stoat, a member of the weasel family. He fashions some very rough-looking stilts strapped to his feet with rubber bands, and featuring dowels spaced to replicate a stoat's paw spacing and dimensions. His struggle to balance and walk with the stilts is quite humorous, and it takes time for him to learn how to shuffle sideways, much like a bounding stoat.[46] While it might not be the work's primary intention, it illustrates the clumsy nature of humans trying to empathize with and understand ecosystems and their nonhuman inhabitants. The humor creates a point of access, and the space to consider an activist message more deeply.

Summary

In this chapter, walking and activism are the focus. Some forms of activism are more pronounced, while others are more subtle. Topics included protests and demonstrations, performance, attire, props, and reenactments. Environmentalism, humor, and moving beyond commercial art worlds were also a focus, including sites, monuments, education, and pedagogy. Selected exercises open up space for further exploration.

Chapter 9

Connections to Drawing

As mentioned in chapters one and eight, in the post-World War II era, artists across the globe moved towards performance and other ephemeral art forms as they wrestled with the unprecedented loss of human life during the world wars. Art historian **Kristine Stiles** (1947–) elaborates, "Emphasizing the body as art, these artists amplified the role of process over product and shifted from representational objects to presentational modes of action."[1] This shift led to many of the walking works discussed in this chapter, which emphasize using the body as a drawing instrument.

When considering the body as a drawing instrument, one might think very directly of walking actions that cause drawings, such as *Making Painting with His Feet* (1956) by **Kazuo Shiraga** (1924–2008), which consists of the artist moving around a painting surface (unrolled on the floor) with paint on his feet. Indeed, there is an entire vein of drawing and painting artists who use full-body engagement and walking across or around the drawing or painting substrate.

For example, **Fabienne Verdier** (1962–) creates large-scale paintings by walking with a giant ceiling-mounted paintbrush outfitted with handlebars, traversing canvases arranged on the floor. Or there is *Ashiato (Footprints)* (1956) by **Akira Kanayama** (1924–2006), which consists of footprints along a long strip of vinyl sheeting laid throughout an outdoor park area. Similarly, **Rudolf Stingel** (1956–) walks across sheets of Styrofoam wearing boots that have been dipped in acetone, leaving shallow footprints where the chemical eats away at the material. The footprinted sheets are then hung on the wall in a gallery setting. In 1968, **Atsuko Tanaka** (1932–2005) created a large-scale drawing on the beach of Awaji

Island entitled *Round on Sand*. This work could only have been made by walking and was washed away by the waves soon after.

There are also artists like **Gerhard Richter** (1932–), who walk along their work, which is mounted on the wall, and pull or scrape drawing implements as they go, as in *Cage 5* (2006). In *Walking Drawing* (2000) by **Tom Marioni** (1967–), he walked along paper mounted on the wall, with colored pencils tracing along at his waist height. Alternatively, **Helen Frankenthaler** (1928–2011) developed a soak-stain method of pouring highly diluted paint onto large-scale canvases arranged on the floor, walking around the picture plane, and sometimes lifting and tilting the canvas to control the flow. Frankenthaler was mentored by another artist who walked around his canvases while dribbling paint, **Jackson Pollock** (1912–1956). Pollock influenced many, and as fellow artist Allan Kaprow pointed out, "Pollock's near destruction of this [painting] tradition may well be a return to the point where art was more actively involved in ritual, magic, and life than we have known it in our recent past."[2] (More about ritual in chapter six.)

In contrast, there are also artists who use a slightly less direct approach to making walking-based drawings, such as the backpack-generated works in *The City as Written by the City* (2004–) by Sarah Cullen (see chapter two), or *Untitled (Pocket Drawings)* (1969) by **William Anastasi** (1933–). In these works, the artist would fold a sheet of 11" × 14" paper into eight squares, creating a small rectangle he placed in his pocket with a soft pencil. The mark-making would occur in his pocket as a result of his walking, without him looking at it, and was captured on each of the eight surfaces. He would switch to a different rectangle whenever he felt a particular drawing was complete. Anastasi also created similar drawings, without looking at them, while he rode the subway and responded to bumps, starts, and stops.[3]

Building on the examples listed above, this chapter examines the body as a drawing instrument through performance, land art, technology usage, and the use of tracing and traces.

EXERCISE: Found Drawings

Take a walk and keep an eye out for found drawings (lines in various arrangements and combinations). You are not interacting with any lines, just documenting interesting existing arrangements by capturing them with your camera. It might take time to find something that interests you. Any camera is fine. You will then share your images online, creating a sharable gallery of found drawings. This exercise will enhance close observational skills of focus and attention.

Reflection questions:

• If you're doing this exercise with others, did you notice any trends in where people found their drawings?

• What types of lines were you attracted to?

• Was it easy or difficult to spot the drawing? Why?

• Depending on what you used to take photos, what role did the viewfinder (on a camera) or the rectangle of the phone screen play in creating the drawings?

Performance Links

Above, several artists are mentioned who use their feet to draw while walking, which is inherently performative. There are many other artists who have worked in this way, and with a live audience present. Take for example *Vagina Painting* (1965) by **Shigeko Kubota** (1937–2015), who used a paint brush attached to the underwear she was wearing to draw on the ground with red paint as she walked around the floor in a squatting position. This performative walking and drawing work was presented as part of the Perpetual Fluxfest at Cinematheque in New York.[4]

Other artists also use depictions of blood and actual blood in their performative walking and drawing works, such Regina José Galindo's *Who Can Erase the Traces* (2003), mentioned in chapter six, or *I Miss You* (1999–2005) by **Franko B.** (1956–). In this work, which was reperformed several times for large crowds, the artist walked up and down a catwalk in the nude, covered in white body paint, allowing drips of blood from his arms to mark his walking path onto a canvas that has been laid down. The artist later uses the bloodied canvas to create collages and objects coated with pieces of the canvas.[5] Conceptually, the work engages with ideas of fashion and spectacle, as well as the vulnerability of the body. Through repetition of walking back and forth in a single line with controlled lighting and coordinated color choices between the body and the canvas, Franko

B. creates a carefully controlled environment for audience members to experience this walking-based live drawing experience.

Another work resulting in a long parallel-line drawing is *Saddledrag* (2006–) by **Anna Campbell** (1979–), specifically the 2008 iteration (see figure 9.1 for 2006 iteration). For this work, the artist dressed as a cowboy, and pulled a cast-plaster saddle for the duration of a public parade route, which was choreographed by artist Fritz Haeg and entitled, *East Meets West Interchange Overpass Parade*. As the parade proceeded, Campbell left a long double line behind, eventually fully eroding the plaster saddle. The artist stated she hopes "to critique both the construct of the American cowboys, as well as nostalgia for a romantic past that never existed."[6] The ephemeral nature of the line left behind through the labor of walking and plaster dust helps underscore the disappearance of that nonexistent romantic past.

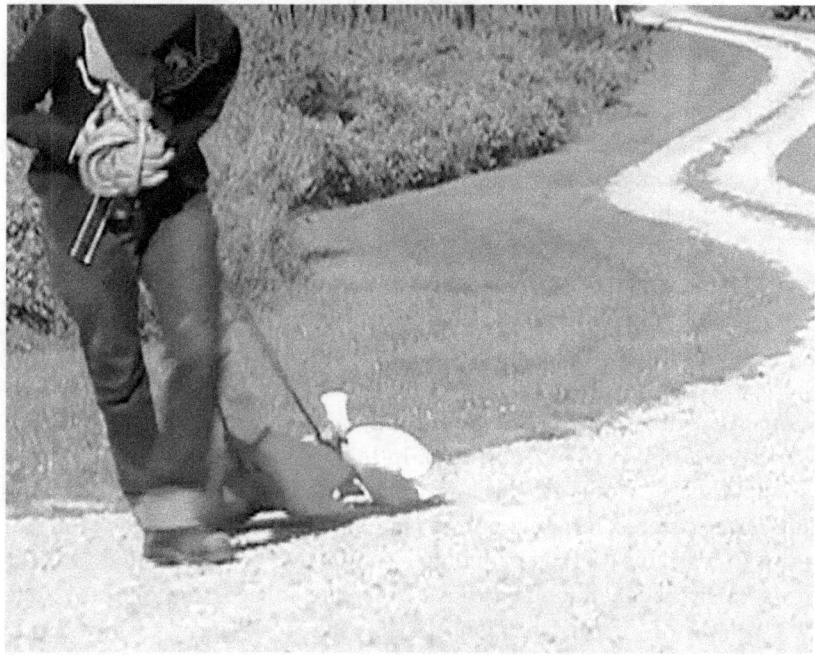

Figure 9.1. Anna Campbell, Still from *Saddledrag: Trail*, 2006, documented by Chele Isaac and Rachel Manderfeld, © Anna Campbell. *Source*: Courtesy of Anna Campbell.

Francis Alÿs has a similar walking and disappearing drawing performance entitled *Paradox of Praxis 1 (Sometimes Making Something Leads to Nothing)* (1997), also mentioned in chapter six. For this work he pushed a block of ice throughout the streets of Mexico City until it fully melted. The walk lasted more than nine hours, leaving a wet evaporating line behind him. Onlookers of this performative walk and fleeting drawing were chance members of the public. The scale of the ice block helped draw attention to the performative walk and create a noticeable line on the street. As the scale shifted with the melting, Alÿs had to also adjust his body position, creating further visual interest.

Unlike those mentioned above, **Lygia Pape** (1927–2004) created a massive performative walking-drawing in 1968 with *Divisor (Divider)*, which used points, rather than lines, to draw. This work consisted of a giant white sheet with periodic holes for people to poke their head through. Once the holes were filled, the walking participants moved down the street as a giant series of walking head-points, as their bodies were all hidden beneath the fabric. The work built on other geometric abstract art from the Brazilian Neo-Concrete movement in the 1950s. Conceptually, the work reflected on the struggle between individualism and collectivism.[7]

Lastly, La Monte Young created *Composition 1960 #10*, a popular walking and drawing score that is often performed. This work simply states, "Draw a straight line and follow it." Similar to other Fluxus scores, it is short and almost infinitely interpretable. Artist Nam June Paik famously performed Young's score at Fluxus Festspiele Neuester Musik in Wiesbaden, Germany, using his head dipped in paint for *Zen for Head* (1962). Others continue to perform this drawing work, frequently incorporating walking and walking-adjacent moves.

Altogether, it's clear that performance has a long and ongoing intersection with the combination of drawing and walking. Audiences can be large or small, indoors or outdoors, organized or chance encounters, and so on. Scores can also be incorporated with this triad of concepts to create fascinating new results.

Dance and Choreography

As mentioned in chapter one, choreography, and modern dance specifically, have had a long-standing interest in walking and other everyday movements. Several projects mentioned in previous chapters include an intersection between walking and choreography, such as *Street with a View* (2008) by Robin Hewlett and Ben Kinsley (chapter four), *Walk the Walk* (2010) by Kate Gilmore (chapter eight), several of the reenactment works from chapter eight, or *Slowalk (In Support of Ai Weiwei)* (2011) by Hamish Fulton (chapter eight). This section examines specifically the intersection of dance and choreography with walking and drawing. Some of the works take a generous view of what a line can be, how one defines drawing, and where these drawings take place.

For instance, in *Violin Phase from Fase: Four Movements to the Music of Steve Reich* (1982) by Anne Teresa De Keersmaeker (first mentioned in chapter two), the walking, shuffling, and spinning performer is drawing with their feet in a carefully laid bed of sand. As the music and the movement progresses, a large-scale drawing of a circle with several pie-shaped sections is slowly revealed. The careful choreographed walking choices clearly use the body as a drawing instrument. Similarly, *It's a Draw/Live Feed* (2003, 2008) by Trisha Brown results in a large-scale drawing from using charcoal and pastel held in her feet as she moves across a sheet of paper laid on the floor. Marks include lines, smudges, smears, spins, and rolling of the drawing media. The resulting drawings exist because of this intersection of walking, improvised choreography, and drawing.

In a slightly different approach to the triad of choreography, walking, and drawing, **Eric Andersen** (1940–) orchestrated *The MassDress* (1985). In this case, the shapes and lines created were formed by a shared piece of stretchy blue custom-date clothing connecting thirty walking participants. This three-dimensional drawing morphed and changed for two hours as the walkers moved through extensive choreography, including climbing a fire engine ladder. An aerial view of the performance would have provided views of all sorts of zigzags, circles, and meandering blue lines in space.[8]

Similar to Andersen's use of choreographed bodies to create lines and shapes in space, **Melanie Manchot** (1966–) created *Walk (Square)* (2011) by inviting one thousand children from Hamburg, Germany, to participate in movements inspired by Bruce Nauman's famous video work, *Walking in an Exaggerated Manner Around the Perimeter of a Square* (1968), which is discussed further in chapter ten. This work brings up issues of collective identity and walking as a form of speech. Visually, it highlights lines, circles, and squares as the participants move through public space, which can be seen in stills from the resulting video.[9]

Another example of drawing with bodies in space is *Guards* (2004–2005) by Francis Alÿs. In this case, Alÿs's participants, sixty-four Coldstream guards, were highly trained in tightly synchronized movements, and aerial views reveal marching lines and rectangles throughout the streets of London. The guards started out this work individually and were given directions to walk until they encountered others, at which time they would fall into formation until a group of at least eight by eight guards was assembled. Once they had achieved the minimum formation, they were to march to the closest bridge and disperse. In this case the work functioned much more like a formal study due to the matching attire and clean formations.

EXERCISE: Reprise of Painting to Be Stepped On

Consider *Painting to Be Stepped On* by Yoko Ono, which states, "Leave a piece of canvas or finished painting on the floor or street."

Find a piece of canvas, paper, or a painting, photograph, etc. that you will collect footprints on.

Locate a high-traffic area to place the item. For example, a doorway.

Allow passersby to step on the item for a predetermined amount of time.

Display the work.

Discuss the role of chance in its creation. How does this exercise relate to performance art?

Land Art Relationships

Many texts on the topic of walking mention desire lines, sometimes also referred to as free-will ways, game trails, social trails, herd paths, use trails, bootleg trails, cow paths, olifantenpad (elephant trails), pirate paths, social trails, kemonomichi (best trails), or chemins de l'âne (donkey paths).[10] These lines are created when people or animals erode a path from continuous use, and they often follow the shortest or most easily navigated path between two points. While these lines are most often made out of an urge for efficiency or to avoid walking in certain areas, others characterize them as a collective record of civil disobedience.[11] However a viewer chooses to characterize the motivation behind their creation, desire lines are all visually characterized as lines on the ground created by repetitive walking. In this way, they operate as large-scale drawings created by human bodies, similar to some land artworks.

Perhaps the most well-known example of this approach is Richard Long's *A Line Made by Walking* (1967), mentioned in chapter one, however there are many other examples of walking paths becoming large-scale drawings. Other artists have also used this method of creating lines along the ground with their feet. For instance, **Michael Heizer** (1944–) used walking to trace out the pattern for his large-scale drawing, *Circular Surface Planar Displacement Drawing* (1970), in a dry lake bed in Nevada. He first walked the perimeter of each circle, the largest of which was four hundred feet in diameter, using a string affixed to its center, becoming a human compass. Then, he retraced his steps with a motorcycle to make the lines more pronounced.[12]

Other land art works, like *Spiral Jetty* (1970), mentioned in chapters four and six, often become large-scale drawings activated by walking along them. Similarly, **Walter De Maria** (1935–2013) created earthworks such as *Mile Long Drawing* (1968) (which featured two parallel lines of chalk, each one mile long, in the Mojave Desert in California) and *Las Vegas Piece* (1969) (which consisted of shallow six-foot-wide cuts in the earth forming a half-mile square with two extended sides in the desert north of Las Vegas, Nevada). These works are drawings in remote, wide-open spaces that could only be experienced by walking along them or flying over them. Additionally, these land art drawings have an ephemeral nature to them, much like an unsealed charcoal drawing. *Spiral Jetty* moves in and out of accessibility as the water of the Great Salt Lake rises and falls; the chalk from *Mile Long Drawing* blew away; and the trenches from *Las Vegas Piece* were filled in via natural erosion and wind, and are no longer visible.[13] In this way, these land art drawings tie back to discussions of liveness, mentioned in chapter four.

Other land artworks like *Stephen Long* (1968) by **Patricia Johanson** (1940–), were so extensive, that walking was required to take in the 1600-foot-long red-, yellow-, and blue-striped drawing laid along an abandoned Boston and Maine railroad bed in Buskirk, New York. This is another work that was not visible from a single point on the ground, requiring aerial views unless one chose to walk the length of the work.[14]

EXERCISE: Grass Drawing

This is a group walking project. As a collective, find a location to draw a line in the grass using the group's walking bodies as the drawing instrument. The repeated vigorous walking (sometimes shuffling to create greater friction), will create the line. Don't worry, the grass will grow back soon. The line can be squiggly or straight, long or short—it's up to the group. Make sure to designate someone to document the process during and afterwards using photo, video, drawing, or other means. This exercise will build collaborative skills, observational skills, and documentation skills as well as result in a drawing in the grass.

Technology and Mapping

Several of the works in previous chapters have included maps and mapping technology, such as GPS (global positioning system) mapping, as in *All GPS Traces in Berlin in 2011–2012* (2012) by plan b (see chapter two), or *3 Months New York/Toronto* (2004) by Gwen MacGregor (see chapter six). These GPS maps can be printed, animated, and/or shared online. Chapter two includes a diagram of basic mapping components. In this section, the focus is on cartography, or mapmaking, as a form of drawing resulting from walking. This approach may be familiar as many exercising walkers, runners, and bicyclists use common GPS applications to create drawings along their routes.

Take for instance Richard Long's works in the vein of *A Walk of Four Hours and Four Circles* (1972), which consists of a map with four concentric circles indicated, along with the title. Writer Rebecca Solnit observes, "On the maps the route of the walk is drawn in to suggest that the walking is drawing on a grand scale, that his walking is to the land itself as his pen is to the map, and he often walks straight lines, circles, squares, spirals."[15] This work is a very direct example of using the body as a drawing instrument for large-scale environmental drawings.

Tim Knowles (1969–) takes a similar approach but ends up with very different erratic-looking drawings in his work *From Windwalk—Seven Walks from Seven Dials* (2009) because his drawings are not planned. This project begins with Knowles wearing a custom bicycle helmet featuring a sail mounted on top to catch the wind. As he cycled through London, he followed as closely as possible the path on which the wind directed him. He used GPS to trace these bike rides, resulting in meandering and jagged-looking drawings.[16] In contrast with Long, who pre-plotted his route on an existing map, Knowles follows a chance route determined by the environment and existing architecture.

Artist **Jeremy Wood** (1976–) creates a variety of GPS drawings from his walking, and other movements, such as flying. His long-term project *My Ghost* (2000–2016) resulted in several different printed series featuring collected pathways from different time frames in his life, such as 2000–2006, 2000–2009, 2000–2012, 2000–2014, and so on.[17] The printed imagery looks like any aerial map, but with some paths thicker or thinner based on how frequently they were traversed.

A similar project to Wood's is *Amsterdam RealTime* (2002) by **Esther Polak** (1962–), **Jeroen Kee**, and **Waag Society** (1994–). This project also traced everyday trips but engaged ten different people each week. Participants across professions and age groups held a GPS device on their commutes to and from the city center of Amsterdam, and their movements were live-tracked on a wall-sized projection. The work was not available online, so viewers had to travel to the museum to see the paths unfold in real time. The trips also accumulated on a map, showing frequently traveled paths more brightly.[18]

Unlike the above examples, artist **Stanley Brouwn** (1935–2017) used mapping to create drawings in a slightly different way with *This Way Brouwn* (1960–1964). For this project, he asked people in the street to draw directions to a particular location for him, resulting in a range of different-looking quick drawings. While these drawings are not as precise as GPS drawings, they rely on a collective knowledge and vision of space that is visually compelling when juxtaposing all the drawings against one another.

EXERCISE: GPS Shape Walk

Using a map, plan a walk that will create a recognizable shape from a bird's eye view. You will use a GPS tracking app on your phone or other mobile device to follow the shape you've planned, and a GPS map will be created as you walk the path.

After the walk, reflect on what the walk was like. Did you notice anything in particular as you created this large-scale drawing? Were you thinking about the idea behind the drawing at all? If you were to do it again, would you do anything differently?

Leaving Traces or Tracing

Some works previously mentioned include the use of tracing, such as Michael x. Ryan's *Roadstains* (2007) mentioned in chapter six or Larsen Husby's *Long Trace of Minneapolis* (2016–2018) mentioned in chapter seven. Here, further tracing and trace-leaving works are explored in depth.

LEAVING TRACES

Walking artists often find ways to leave a trace in the landscape, and some of those could be classified as drawings. For example, *The Green Line* (2004) by Francis Alÿs was a twenty-four-kilometer-long line created by the poking a hole in cans of paint (fifty-eight liters total), which dribbled out as the artist walked along the "Green Line" that marks a border that runs through the municipality of Jerusalem, indicating "the ceasefire demarcation line separating Palestinian and Israeli communities since the end of the 1948 Israel War of Independence . . . but officially lost its boundary position in 1967."[19]

Other artists have created similarly politically charged walking-based drawings, such as *Land Mark (Foot Prints)* (2001–2002) by **Jennifer Allora** (1974–) and **Guillermo Calzadilla** (1971–). This work responded to disputed territory, a beach in Vieques, Puerto Rico, used by the US Military and NATO for military exercises. The artists collaborated with activists to create shoes with custom-engraved soles that would leave messages in the sand on the beach, communicating their concerns to the military personnel working there. These shoe-print drawings in the sand helped amplify the activists' voices.[20]

Dennis Oppenheim (1938–2011) created a similar project using shoes as a form of printmaking and drawing in *Ground Mutations—Shoe Prints* (1969). This project was not as politically charged as Allora and Calzadilla's work, but still explored walking and leaving a trace. Oppenheim's custom shoe soles featured ¼" diagonal grooves. He wore the shoes for three winter months and envisioned his individualized marks as interacting with many others.[21]

Another example of an artist leaving traces and drawings from walking is *Stamp Sticks* (2007) by Barbara Lounder in which she created a series of walking sticks with various carved linoleum stamp shapes attached to their ends (see figure 9.2). These were approximately one to two-inches and could be used to leave a specific marking behind during a walk.[22] While the concept of this work might not be as politically overt as the work of Alÿs or of Allora and Calzadilla, it brings attention to the idea of humans leaving traces behind during their interactions with the environment.

In a slightly different approach, artist **Jennifer West** (1966–) created a work that captured the traces of walkers in *One Mile Parkour Film* (2012). For this project, she laid one mile of analog film on the ground along the High Line Park in New York City, from Gansevoort to West Thirtieth Street. Visitors walked over the film, and later the film was further treated and integrated into a finished film piece.[23] Here the community's walking traces are captured and played back for further consideration.

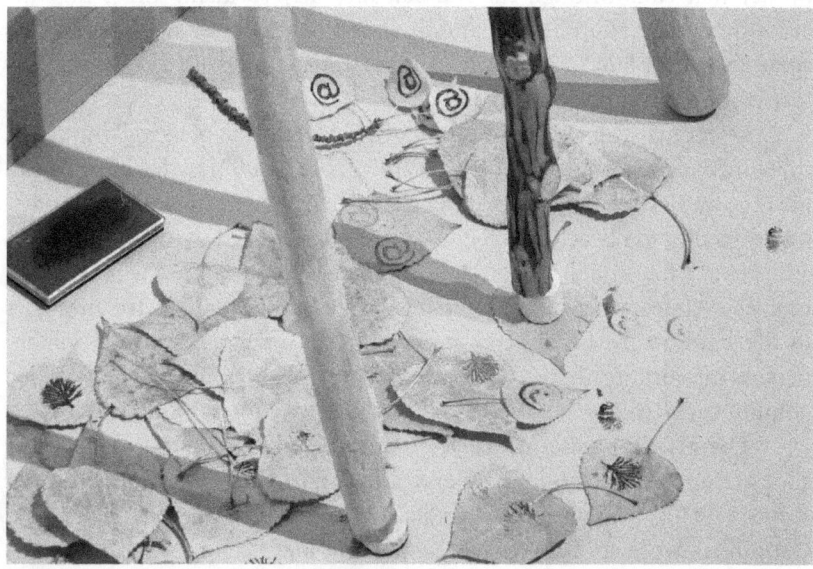

Figure 9.2. Barbara Lounder, *Stamp Sticks*, 2007, walking sticks with carved linoleum, © Barbara Lounder. *Source*: Courtesy of Barbara Lounder.

EXERCISE: Leave a Trace

Take a walk where you leave a trace in the environment, and then take another walk where the environment leaves a trace on you.
 Reflection questions:

- Is it possible to leave a trace that will disappear? What might that look like?

- If you leave a lasting trace in the environment, is that ethically okay?

- In what ways can the environment leave a trace on a walker?

TRACING

Other walking artists use the idea of tracing, rather than leaving a trace to create drawings. For example, **Francisca Benítez** (1974–) created a series of rubbings from private property line plaques embedded in the sidewalks of New York City. The work is entitled *Property Lines, New York* (2008). There are seventy rubbings in the series, and they were installed as a grid on the wall with varying dimensions depending on the location. The simple act of tracing in this set of walking-based drawings asks questions about borders, public versus private space, and how people mark space.
 Artist **Reg Carremans** (1981–) took a slightly different approach to tracing his walk and the resulting drawing in *Pathscape* (2012). In this work, the artist added specially designed canvas to the soles of his shoes, which he then wore on a 375-kilometer walking route. He regularly changed the canvas, and later displayed the shoe-sized rectangles as a grid, calling them "landscape paintings." Each rectangle showed different traces of wear and tear, reflecting changes in the path during the month-long walk.
 Artists have also captured the intersection of walking and tracing in video formats. For instance, in *Touch* (2002) by **Janine Antoni** (1964–), the artist frames a view of the beach, ocean, and sky with a slackline suspended slightly above the horizon. She then proceeds to walk from left to right across the frame, and with each step, the slackline touches and traces the line of the horizon. This work brings up ideas trying to attain balance or perfection in life, or of accepting a constant state of imbalance.[24]
 Michèle Magema (1977–) also uses video to capture a moment of walking and tracing in her piece *Across the Souvenirs* (2010). This is a

video piece in three parts, each one featuring doubled and reflected images of the artist walking in various settings, which in and of itself could be interpreted as a type of tracing. In the third part, the artist holds chalk, tracing a line as she walks along a black wall. Finally, she erases the line as she walks back along the wall, and the image is not doubled and reflected. This work is inspired by Magema's background, having parents from both France and Democratic Republic of Congo.[25] Themes of personal versus cultural history, as well as tracing and erasure, are present in the work.

Other artists complete tracing walks, which result in drawings such as *Walking Amsterdam 9–5* (2002) by **Danica Phelps** (1971–). This work resulted in 116 small drawings of situations or objects the artist spent money on during the thirteen days of walking (for eight hours each day). Each walk started in Amsterdam's Central Station, and Phelps attempted to trace, through walking, as straight a line as possible away from the station. Each day, she shifted her walking line to be twenty degrees off the line taken the previous day. When the work is exhibited, the drawings are clustered by day and marked with a system of colored stripes indicating dollars spent, price of the work, and iteration of the work (as she sold a piece in the series, she replaced it with a copy).[26] Here, the tracing took place through the act of walking, and the resulting drawings focused on other interactions that occurred during the walks.

Susan Stockwell (1962–) similarly used tracing in her piece *Taking a Line for a Walk* (2002–2003). This work involved the artist wearing a line-drawing machine on her back as she traced the outline of Stockwell district in South London, leaving a stripe of temporary white paint behind herself as she walked. The line was 2.7 miles long and took three hours to draw. By tracing the perimeter of this district, the artist hoped to highlight the border of the neighborhood and details of the everyday that are easily overlooked. The entire process was documented on video and is available as a short film.

EXERCISE: Developing Personal Marks

Start by planning to follow one of your short everyday walks. Take a pen and paper with you. You will develop a series of marks that represent different actions in your journey. Develop a mark for:

- Your feelings as you begin the walk

- The act of pausing

- When you encounter an obstacle along the walk

- The act of continuous walking in a familiar location

- Your feelings as you end the walk

Take your collection of five marks, arrange them on a single piece of paper, and share with others.

This walk is inspired by **Wayne Koestenbaum**'s (1958–) "Making Marks" in *Prompts for Participatory Walks* (2019) edited by Todd Shalom.

Summary

In this chapter, walking and drawing are the focus. This is a wide-ranging area of research with a broad interpretation of drawing. Topics link to performance, dance, and choreography, as well as relationships to land art. Technology and mapping are considered alongside considerations of leaving traces, or the act of tracing. Selected exercises open up space for further exploration.

Chapter 10

Embodiment

A vulnerable body seeks other bodies willing to become vulnerable
with it, not as the surrendered raw material of public art, but as
collaborators, partners, performers, volunteers, and audiences in a
humble, strong practice. Socially engaged art practice is not about
the author's body but about all the participants' bodies.

—Ernesto Pujol[1]

Walking as artistic practice often includes the embodiment, or heightened
physical awareness of one's body and sensations, of both the artist and
participants. Embodiment has come up before in regard to the senses and
phenomenology in chapter three, and it necessitates a heightened awareness of ability in order to be inclusive. Issues of pace or speed, balance,
duration, and energy dynamics become particularly important. Humanistic
geographer David Seamon points out this heightened awareness can lead
to "the mobilities of bodies combin(ing) in space and time to produce
an existential insideness—a feeling of belonging within the rhythm of life
in place."[2] These elements of embodiment set walking apart from other
artistic media that focus more prominently on visual experiences.

An example of a walking project focused on embodiment and pacing is *The Slow Walkers of Whycocomaugh* (2012) and *The Fast Walkers
of Whycocomaugh* (2012) developed by **Aislinn Thomas** (1981–) as part
of the Whycocomagh Skillshare. This skillshare provided free workshops,
presentations, and activities in response to a rural community that intentionally centers around a person with intellectual disabilities. Conceptually,

the work posed questions about expertise and value, while contextually, the work wrestled with subjective embodied understandings of speed in different landscapes, from riversides to mountain trails, to inside a mall in Mississauga.[3]

In recent years, embodiment has been a popular lens for artists, creative leaders, and anti-racist advocates to work with. Books like *Making and Being* (2019) by **Susan Jahoda** (1952–) and **Caroline Woolard** (1984–) bring a visual-arts focus to embodiment, while projects like MoMA's "Artful Practices for Well-Being" (2020–) provide embodied activities in response to the COVID-19 pandemic, such as mindfulness walks for connectedness and healing through art. Similarly, *The Nap Ministry* (2016–) headed by **Tricia Hersey** (1974–), examines rest as a form of embodied resistance via performance art, site-specific installations, and community organizing.

Leadership strategist **Ginny Whitelaw** proposes this lean towards embodiment comes from deep cultural divisions and discontent, as well as "dissociations of head from heart, of talk from walk . . ."[4] This analysis points to the deep and lasting impact that philosopher **René Descartes** (1596–1650) has had via the concepts of Cartesian dualism (the separation of mind and body) and mechanistic theory (the body is a machine).[5] These ideas have gone on to deeply affect the development of Western notions of health and medicine, ignoring the fact that humans "are not disembodied brains traveling through space and time . . ."[6] and that, "the inputs and outputs to and from our brains are mediated by our bodies."[7] These Western ideas are quite different from other bodily understandings and holistic practices, such as Traditional Chinese Medicine (TCM), which focuses on vital energy (Qi) and harmony of opposite elements and forces (yin and yang),[8] or Native-American healing traditions that embrace bio-psycho-socio-spiritual approaches and traditions, among others.[9]

Walking artists have touched on all these ideas, including mind-body connections, health, meditative qualities, thinking and perspective taking, and examining when the body fails us, as in falling. Below is a selection of those works.

Connections to Health

Walking has well-recognized health benefits, both physically and mentally. Scholar **Karein K. Goertz** (1966–) states, "Recent empirical findings in (neuro)physiology validate the curative properties of walking with variables relative to duration, intensity and frequency: it clears the body of stress hormones, boosts endorphins, strengthens the immune system, increases energy, elevates mood and promotes restful sleep." She goes on to add, "The flow of oxygen to the brain heightens mental alertness, concentration and memory. Walking enhances connectivity of brain circuits and boosts performance on cognitive tasks."[10] Other scholars concur, including **Shane O'Mara**, who has examined many scientific walking-related studies. He points out that walking can improve how people feel, help protect and repair organs, enhance the gut by helping food pass through, and pause and reverse aging in the brain.[11]

These findings back up what thinkers, creators, and activists of all types throughout history have anecdotally noted—that walking can be a useful mind-body balancing practice. Author Kerri Andrews notes that recognized walkers have used the physical act of walking for a range of mind-body benefits for years, including self-discovery, escaping personal difficulties, communing with the dead, defying convention, and stepping beyond the self.[12] Existentialist philosopher Søren Kierkegaard noted in a letter to his eighteen-year-old niece, "Above all, do not lose your desire to walk: every day I walk myself into a state of well-being and away from every illness."[13] British historian **George Macaulay Trevelyan** (1876–1962) called his legs his "two doctors" and referenced them accordingly, "When body and mind are out of gear . . . I know that I have only to call in my doctors and I shall be well again."[14] While these examples are purely subjective, they demonstrate awareness of the benefits of walking among various thinkers, stretching back hundreds of years.

EXERCISE: Thirty-Day Walk

Select a walking route you can commit to for thirty days. This means it should not be too long or rigorous, and should fit into your daily routines. Walk that route each day for thirty days. After each iteration of the walk, record your brief reflections on how you feel physically and emotionally. At the end of the thirty days, review all your reflections. What do you notice?

Writer Sarah Stoddart Hazlitt, first mentioned in chapter one, wrote about these mind-body benefits, especially in relation to emotional versus physical exhaustion. As previously stated, London-based Hazlitt was pressured to support her husband's divorce, causing significant emotional distress. Her situation began when he cheated on her, and then bullied her into committing perjury to obtain a divorce in Scotland, where he planned for Hazlitt to "catch" him with a prostitute. During the prolonged legal proceedings, walking great distances (twenty–thirty miles per day) brought her comfort and focus, using the physical intensity to distract from the emotional toll. By focusing on the bodily walking practice, and the inherent mental release of washing up, eating, and sleeping afterwards, she was temporarily able to free herself from the limitations of deeply sexist laws and social norms. Her meditative walking became about self-care, self-assertion, and self-knowledge.[15]

While Hazlitt might not have characterized herself as a walking artist in the contemporary understanding of the term, her reflective writing on her personal experience of walking and wellness aligns with current practitioners and authors, such as Cheryl Strayed, who in 1995 took a similar long-distance walk along the Pacific Crest Trail with emphasis on physical strain as a portal towards reconnecting with the self, resulting in the memoir *Wild* (2012), and later a movie adaptation. Another example is *Effugio c, you're always only half a day away* (2011) by artist Guido van der Werve, mentioned in chapter six. In this work, he spent twelve hours running around his house (sixty-five miles in total), an exercise in extreme self-reflection and self-exertion.

A similar running-based work is *Epic Ravine Marathon* (2015), organized by Amish Morrell, **Henri Fabergé**, and **Christine Atkinson** (1986–), which took place in Toronto's ravine system. There were more than thirty participants of widely varying backgrounds. Only two finished the entire fifty-five-kilometer route, which took more than nine hours to complete. However, the work was less about competition and running times, and more about new ways to move through and observe the city. Here, the format of what is normally a health-oriented running race helped facilitate deeper looking and reflection.

Meditative Qualities

Meditation practice seeks to discern the purpose of every step we wish to take, and the effect of every step taken, seeking the meaning of it all. All steps, fast or slow, in any direction, amount to meaning.

—Ernesto Pujol[16]

The meditative qualities of walking are well documented. For example, there is a group of Tendai Buddhist monks in Japan who run or walk a marathon every day for one hundred days. This practice is known as *kaihogyo* and has evolved from 1310 CE to present.[17] Some walking artists have adapted walking exercises, such as the marathon, into their creative practice. For example, in addition to the works mentioned in this chapter, Mihret Kebede's *Slow Marathon* or May Murad and Rachel Ashton's *Walking without Walls*, both mentioned in chapter five, use the format and length of a marathon to frame their meditative walking works.

Other artists and writers use walking to meditate on physical activity to distract from, or alter, one's mood or emotions. Author Anaïs Nin wrote about how "city walking offered creativity, escape, fantasy, pleasure and solace." "When I'm sad," she wrote in 1935, "I sometimes tire my sadness away by walking."[18] This connects to other walkers discussed in this chapter, such as Hazlitt and Kierkegaard. More recently, in *A Walk around the Block* (2010) in Huntly, Scotland, Hamish Fulton instructed walkers to maintain a two-meter distance between themselves as they walked single-file around a city block for two hours. The focus required to maintain this distance and rhythm during this repetitive walk triggered a meditative and relaxed state of mind in some.[19]

A focus on rhythm is a common thread in many meditative walking projects. This is because the rhythm of breath, or the rhythm of the legs continuously changing position as muscles flex and extend over and over, is central to the act of walking. Several artists have made work about the rhythm of walking, including Benjamin Patterson, whose work *Stand Erect* (1961) is a short score that takes the reader through the seemingly simple act of taking steps. By breaking the process down into its component parts, the act of walking becomes more complex and the rhythm is revealed. When the participant is asked to focus on each sub-movement repeatedly, the meditative qualities of the walk are enhanced. In this same way, Marina Abromović draws attention to each walking sub-movement with her work *Shoes for Departure* (1991), which consists of several pairs of shoes carved out of crystals. These very heavy objects would heighten the awareness of the wearer, enhancing a meditative state, or departure state of mind, according to the artist.[20]

Meditation is also emphasized in *Your Temper, My Weather* (2013) by **Diane Borsato** (1973–) (see figure 10.1). This large-scale durational work engaged one hundred beekeepers in five hours of meditation and slow walking. Conceptually, the work highlighted the interconnectedness

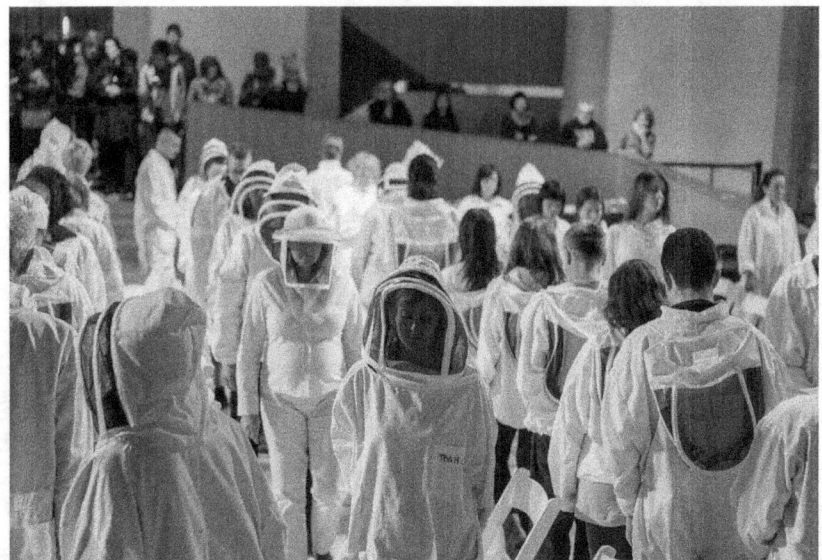

Figure 10.1. Diane Borsato, *Your Temper, My Weather*, 2013, one hundred bee-keepers, five hours, © Diane Borsato. *Source*: Courtesy of Diane Borsato.

of the health and temper of the bees, and those who take care of them, thus also emphasizing environmental concerns that affect both humans and other creatures. Formally, the work had strong cohesion between all the disparate participants due to the use of mostly white uniforms and white chairs. The coordination of their movements and the repetition of the chairs arranged in rows also contributed to a sense of solidarity, supporting the meditative atmosphere.

EXERCISE: Stand Erect

Take a moment to search for Benjamin Patterson's score, *Stand Erect* (1961). By yourself or with a small group, walk through the steps. What do you notice as you move through the directions? Note the last line "Continue sequentially left, right, left, right until the process becomes automatic." How long does it take for the movement to feel automatic?

Not all meditative walking works are linked to a calming state. Some works are meditative because the artist is focused on completing specific challenging walking acts. For instance, *Man Walking Down the Side of a Building* (1970) by Trisha Brown required a great deal of meditative focus due to the physically rigorous walking stance from start to finish. As the title implies, the performer of the work holds their body perpendicular to the side of a building as they are slowly lowered towards the ground by a rope, all the while moving through space as if they were walking on the ground. Similarly, *Walking in an Exaggerated Manner Around the Perimeter of a Square* (1968) by Bruce Nauman, which consisted of a film of exactly what the title describes, required meditative focus to execute the various specific movements over and over, backward and forward.

In some cases, artists create installations or situations that encourage participants to take on a meditative state. For instance, in *120 Doors Pavilion* (2003) by art and architecture studio **Pezo von Ellrichshausen** (2002–), a maze-like interactive installation invites viewers to consider ideas of space, friction, and points of transition. The participant must remain focused in order to successfully move through the work, which is similar to many of the labyrinth works examined in chapter six. Other works, like *The Gates* (mentioned in chapter two), encourage meditative walking without the fully enclosed environment, as in *120 Doors Pavilion*. In the case of *The Gates*, participation and energy dynamics were heightened by the fact that the work would only be installed for sixteen days, encouraging walkers to meditate on both the experience of the work, and its ephemerality.

EXERCISE: Walking without Thoughts

Start with a short walk—five minutes or less. Attempt to take a walk without any thoughts. It can help to focus on your breath instead. As a thought arises, let it pass by and out of your mind, and redirect your attention to your breath. Do not be discouraged if thoughts continue to arise. Observe them and let them go as you continue walking.

Afterwards, reflect on what you notice about the walk and the thoughts that arise. How frequently do thoughts interrupt your walk? Are you successful at letting them pass on? Does the focus on your breath help?

Try repeating this short five-minute exercise several days in a row. Do you notice any shifts in your ability to focus on the breath, or on the frequency of thoughts arising?

Other artists might take advantage of existing nature preserves or hiking trails to induce a meditative or thoughtful quality, similar to the reflections achieved by Matsuo Bashō, discussed in chapters one and three. For example, in *Footnotes: Cape Jourimain* (2008) by **Kay Burns**, the artist used audio to lead participants along the Lighthouse Trail, a two-kilometer loop at Cape Jourimain Nature Centre in New Brunswick, Canada. The audio shared fragments of narratives related to four generations of the same family who lived at the lighthouse. Concepts for meditation included a recurring sense of isolation, as well as the pleasures and hardships of living at the lighthouse.[21]

Another example is *The New Field* (2017) by the group **Public Studio** ([2009–], founded by **Elle Flanders** [1966–] and **Tamira Sawatzky** [1971–]), in which they walked the entire Bruce Trail, located in Ontario, Canada, connecting Niagara to Tobermory (900 km). As they walked, Public Studio invited artists, activists, scientists, writers, curators, philosophers, and youth groups to walk with them and complete a variety of activities while discussing wide-ranging topics, from land acknowledgments, geology, botany, Indigenous knowledge, poetry, and more.[22] The meditative quality of hiking helped enhance the thoughtful approach to all these topics, each of which were directly linked to different facets of the trail.

Thinking and Perspective Taking

Similar to Public Studio's work above, people have long used walking to sharpen thinking, wrestle with new ideas, and shift perspectives (consider the history of thinkers in chapter one, or the pilgrimage examples in chapter six). Both rhythm and pacing (speed, or in this case, slowness) contribute to walking's ability to enhance thinking, memory,[23] and creativity.[24] Artists and writers throughout history have observed this effect firsthand. Take for instance author Virginia Woolf, who wrote about walking's ability to facilitate ". . . access to profound and unsettling questions about identity, about the nature of self, and the essence of our purpose as human beings on this earth."[25] Similarly, Garnette Cadogan reminds, "Walking is, after all, interrupted falling. We see, we listen, we speak, and we trust that each step we take won't be our last, but will lead us into a richer understanding of the self and the world."[26] Rebecca Solnit adds, "Walking can also be imagined as a visual activity, every walk a tour leisurely enough both to see and to think over the sights, to assimilate the new into the known."[27]

Several walking artists and collectives have built on this thoughtful function of walking. For instance, *Free Range Trials* (2018) by **Cecilia Ramón** (1965–) is a mown-grass earthwork inviting walking participants to reflect on ocean currents, water movements, and aquatic organisms by walking the planetary path of the Thermohaline Ocean Global Current. Ramón recognizes the value of walking to both enable and encourage thinking and perspective taking in relationship to global connectivity.

Scholar Rebecca Solnit points out that the benefits of walking for thinking haven't historically been distributed equally.

> A mode of contemplation and composition, from Aristotle's peripatetics to the roaming poets of New York and Paris. It has supplied writers, artists, political theorists, and others with the encounters and experience that inspired their work as well as the space in which to imagine it, and it is impossible to know what would have become of many of the great male minds had they been unable to move at will through the world. Picture Aristotle confined to the house, Muir in full skirts . . . If walking is a primary cultural act and a crucial way of being in the world, those who have been unable to walk out as far as their feet would take them have been denied not merely exercise or recreation but a vast portion of their humanity.[28]

While Solnit is making an important point about imbalanced, gender-based participation in the world, it's important to explicitly state that some of the emphasis on romantic notions of walking-based creativity also perpetuate harmful ableist narratives. Those with disabilities that prevent them from walking are just as capable of creativity and thoughtful work. Author Kerri Andrews builds on Solnit's point adding, "If walking is central to an individual's 'humanity,' understanding how walking is experienced by different people will enable a better comprehension of our shared humanity,"[29] which speaks to the importance of perspective taking through walking practice.

Viv Corringham (1951–) has used walking to very directly consider another person's perspective in her *Shadow-Walks* (2003–), which involve the artist arriving in a new place and asking a local person to take her on a special walk that the person has repeated many times. The pair walk and talk together along the route, recording the audio of their conversation. Then Corringham returns to the route alone to sing wordless improvisations and record environmental sounds. All the audio is edited together to create a final audio track that can take forms such as audio-walks, concerts, radio works, an iPhone app, and/or sound installations. Corringham describes these recordings, stating, "If a person walks through certain places repeatedly, along the same route, does that act of walking leave a trace? In a sense *Shadow-Walks* is an attempt to make a person's traces, their shadow, audible through my singing, improvising voice."[30]

Taking a slightly different approach, **Deirdre Heddon** (1969–) and **Misha Myers** (1967–) engage with thinking and perspective-taking in the ongoing project, *The Walking Library* (2012–), in which they prompt specific groups to create collections of books to take on specific walks, or on walks for specific groups of people. The books are put in special sacks and carried along on the walk to see how reading at a particular site affects the experience of a walk. Walkers are also encouraged to write and reflect on their experiences. In this way, *The Walking Library* brings focus to perspective-taking by explicitly prompting participants to do so.

EXERCISE: Walking with a Book

Both historical walkers, such as the Romantics and Naturalists, and contemporary walkers, like **Alec Finlay** (1966–), have suggested taking a book for a walk. Select a book for a specific walking route. Trade recommendations with a partner. After you each go for your walk and read on site, meet up to talk about your reflections. Did the book seem well suited for the walk? Can you think of another book to pair with that walk?

Another collective who uses walking to wrestle with new ideas is the Walking Reading Group (previously mentioned in chapter four). This collective runs structured walks that reflect on preselected topical texts, and aims to override dominant discussion voices by having participants walk in conversation pairs that change throughout a walk. The act of walking contrasts with a classroom setting or a conference table that a group of readers might normally gather in or around to discuss readings.[31] Their carefully predetermined format helps the group to clearly set expectations for participants, and cycle through a variety of topics.

EXERCISE: Walking Text Reflection

Similar to the Walking Reading Group, think of a topic you'd like to learn about and discuss. Select three short texts from diverse points of view and make PDFs available to a group of invited walkers. Have the walkers read the texts before gathering for a walk. On the walk, split people into pairs to talk through the texts, changing partners every ten to fifteen minutes. End after three rotations. Regroup as a whole for people to reflect on their experience.

In terms of using walking to wrestle with new ideas, Barcelona-based *Deriva Mussol* (its literal translation would be "owl drift") led by artists **Jordi Lafon** (1967–) and **Eva Marichalar-Freixa** (1973–) in collaboration with **Aula de Teatre**, a theatre group from the University of Vic, directed a series of twelve night-walks in 2013. The purpose of the walks was to use collective processes and reflection to research and create a new performative work examining place and public space. Using the diversity of feedback after each walk, the group reflected on each experience sharing photos, videos, drawings, maps, thoughts, and so on, eventually presenting a street art performance.[32] Without the medium of walking to grapple with their wide-ranging ideas, the eventual performance would not have been possible.

EXERCISE: Vigorous Walking Collaboration

Taking inspiration from filmic collaborators **Eric Butler** (1993–) and **Alexander MacAlpine** (1994–), take a vigorous walk with a creative collaborator to help focus your thinking around a possible future joint creative endeavor.

Select a level of physical rigor appropriate to both of you (safe yet challenging). Allow the physical challenge of the walk to focus your conversation about the creative project. Between the walking and the conversation, all other mental distractions can float away. At the end of the walk, record the highlights of your conversation for future reference.

Falling

An important part of embodied awareness during walking is falling, a moment where the vulnerability of the human body is highlighted. Scientists have pointed out that every step in the walking process is a tiny fall.[33] Artist **Amy Sharrocks** has written and presented on this topic, and identified five phases to any fall: approach, letting go, falling (out of control), crash, and recovery.[34] While not all of the works discussed here will adhere to these five phases, they can be helpful to keep in mind while considering the pieces below.

Scholars Alyson Hallett and Phil Smith note that falling, as well as stumbling and limping, have some ties to disability,[35] discussed in chapter five. Artist **Jesse Darling** (1981–) explores this concept with their sculptural works *Crawling Cane* (2017) and *Collapsed Cane* (2017), both of which strongly reference the material language of walking aids with the use of steel, aluminum, rubber, and lacquer.[36] These bent and drooping objects enhance ideas of falling, limping, crawling, or sitting.

In some of the works mentioned in previous chapters, the potential for a fall or stumble is key to the content and form of a work. Take for example, Amanda Heng's *Let's Walk* (1999), mentioned in chapter five, in which participants were asked to walk backward with a shoe in their mouth, using a hand mirror or phone camera to guide themselves. The potential for a fall or stumble was quite high, and the risk enhanced the artist's message about the difficulty of navigating the world as a woman. Similarly, Trisha Brown's *Walking on the Wall* (1971), mentioned in chapter one, had a greater visual impact due to the walkers' potential for falling as they walked suspended, perpendicular to the gallery walls.

Additional works that use the potential for a fall to enhance impact include *High Wire* (2008) by **Catherine Yass** (1959–), in which she video recorded a high-wire artist, a person with highly attuned embodiment skills, attempting to walk a line suspended at ninety meters between two social-housing blocks in Glasgow, Scotland. These buildings were the tallest in all of Europe at one point. Conceptually, Yass was drawing connections between modernist architecture and failed utopian visions when she stated, "The dream of reaching the sky is also a modernist dream of cities in the air, inspired by a utopian belief in progress."[37] Formally, the completed video installation occupies a room and includes four projections of the event from different angles and two lightboxes. The duration is just short of seven minutes and begins with the wire-walker starting his walk, then getting about one-third of the way out, before he is forced to return due to the risk of falling, as the rope was shaking too dangerously.[38]

Hiwa K (1975–) similarly uses the precariousness of a balancing act to enhance the conceptual content of his walking work in *Pre-Image (Blind as the Mother Tongue)* (2017) (see figure 10.2). This video piece documents the artist as he retraced the route he took when he fled Iraqi Kurdistan in the mid-1990s, all while balancing an elaborate mirrored device on his head. The mirrors were pointed in various directions mimicking a sense of disorientation. The focus required to walk and balance this device alluded to the effort required to continuously "recalibrate oneself to new contexts."[39] The ongoing risk of the device falling helped enhance the emotional engagement of the work, encouraging viewers to consider refugees' experiences.

Other artists use falling to enhance humor, as in *Stoat* (1999) by Marcus Coates, mentioned in chapter eight. In this work, the humor of a man stumbling while he attempts to walk like a stoat opens the door for deeper conversations of environmental awareness. Similarly, artist **Martin Kersels** (1960–) uses tripping and humor to highlight issues of body stereotyping in *Tripping* (1995) (see figure 10.3). This series of photos feature Kersels, who might otherwise be assumed to be threatening at

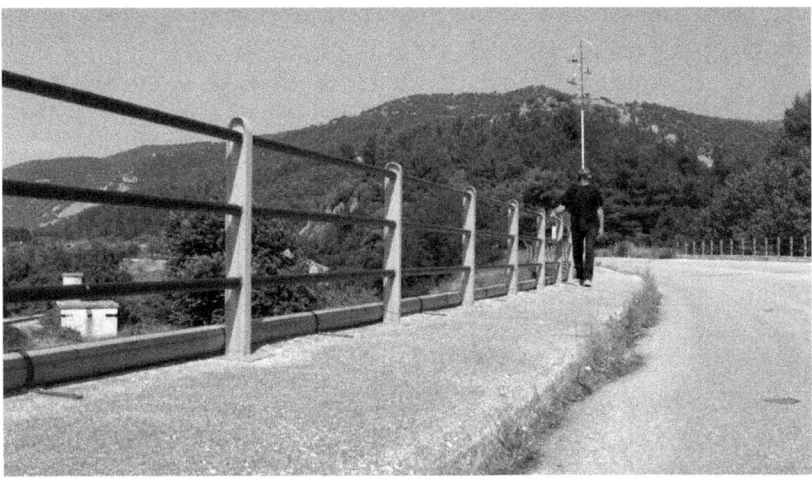

Figure 10.2. Hiwa K, *Pre-Image (Blind as the Mother Tongue)*, 2017, Single channel HD video, 16:9, color, sound (with English language), 18 min; KOW Berlin and Prometeo Gallery Ida Pisani, Milano. *Source:* Courtesy of Hiwa K.

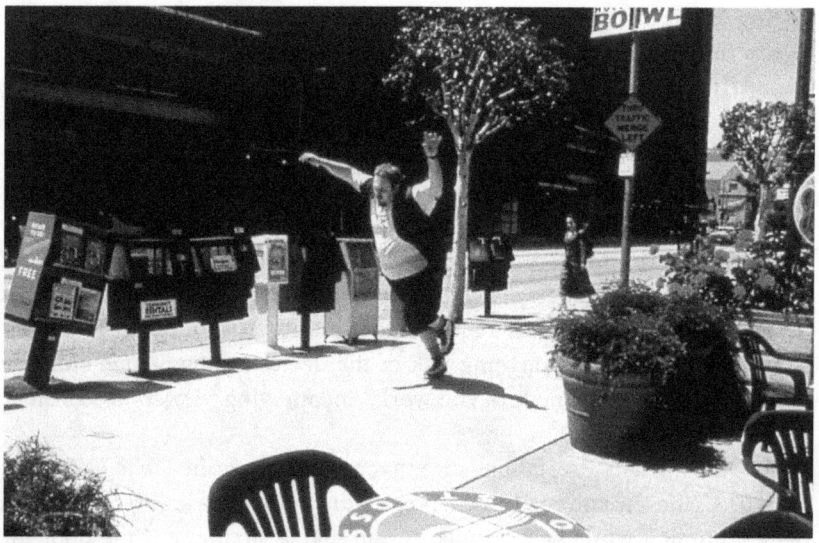

Figure 10.3. Martin Kersels, *Tripping photos #1 (A) Beverly Center*, 1995, C-print, 20" × 30", 50.8 cm × 76.2 cm, © Martin Kersels. *Source*: Courtesy of Martin Kersels and Mitchell-Innes & Nash, New York.

6'7" tall and 300 pounds, in mid-trip. He uses this moment of shared embarrassment and vulnerability to engage in a type of slapstick, knowing that humor can draw viewers into a work, and further consider serious assumptions about body size.[40]

Whether using falling for its humor or suspense, all of these artists rely on a sense of embodied awareness combined with disrupted walking to bolster the impact of their works.

EXERCISE: Slipping

Taking inspiration from *Falling Down on the Icy Sidewalk* (date unknown) by **Brian Buczak** (1954–1987), which consisted of "slipping and falling down on the sidewalk when least expected to do so,"[41] reflect on some of the slipperiest spots you can remember (they don't necessarily have to be icy). Make a map of at least three of these locations; feel free to add more. How far apart are these locations? Do you typically avoid them, or are some of them unavoidable? How might you visually represent slipperiness if you were to share this map with someone else?

Summary

In this chapter, walking and embodiment are the focus. Topics include connections to health, meditative qualities, thinking and perspective taking, and falling. Selected exercises open up space for further exploration.

Appendix

Tips and Resources for Documentation

The following tips could be helpful depending on the type of documentation you are aiming for.

PHOTOGRAPHY

Visit the site ahead of time. Look around to see what you might need to be prepared for. Do you need electricity? Is the ground stable? Where might you situate yourself to best document the work? What types of shots are you hoping for? Make a shot list or storyboard so you have a plan you can remember and/or communicate to an assistant.

Use a tripod. Phones often have great cameras, but sometimes don't have great stabilization. When shooting documentary photos, use a tripod to ensure a sharp image.

Check your settings. Whether you're shooting with a phone or a manual camera, try to ensure the camera is set to take the largest possible resolution images. This allows for more flexibility when editing the images later. Similarly, if your camera has adjustable white balance, make sure you've selected the correct setting for your current light.

Check your lighting. Try to avoid using a flash due to the harsh direct light it creates. The best light is indirect natural light. If that's not available, you can use reflectors or sheets of diffusion to help control light. A reflector is used to bounce and direct light on your subject and can be as simple as a large piece of white cardboard or a professional-grade version (available online). Similarly, a sheet of diffusion helps reduce glare from an intense light source. Inexpensively, one could use a matte finish plastic shower curtain or a piece of ceiling light panel (used for covering fluorescent bulbs and available at most home remodeling stores), or again search for professional grade online.

Remember framing. Use the rule of thirds to ensure you are making the best use of the frame.

Check your focus. Make sure your subject is in focus, rather than your background or another object.

Take a lot of photos. It is always a good idea to take more photos than you think you will need. Errors can happen (something is blurry, the lighting was bad, etc.), and it's better to have options.

Engage an assistant. Even if you aren't directly participating in the walking work you are documenting, you might be called on to troubleshoot, and you don't want to leave your documentation responsibilities in that case.

VIDEO

Follow the recommendations for taking strong documentary photos—they all apply to video work too.

Have **extra memory cards and charged batteries** with you if you are working with any camera that is not a phone.

Consider multiple cameras from multiple angles to provide options when editing the documentation.

Try to film **five seconds before and after** each clip to make editing easier.

AUDIO

Many phones have adequate audio recording ability, but it's best to **test it first**.

If you have the option, select a **directional microphone** instead of an omnidirectional microphone. This will help avoid capturing too much background noise.

Try to **maintain similar conditions** for each recording. This will help when editing.

If it is windy, it can be helpful to **use a windscreen or muff** to ensure you get the best possible recording.

If you are doing interviews, **a lapel mic can be helpful**.

Sample Syllabi

15-WEEK OUTLINE

Week 1	Create a Group Agreement together (practicing community engagement skills)
	In class: Do one or two exercises together
	Assign: Read chapter one
	Assign: Execute one exercise from chapter one and write about in a reflection journal
Week 2	In class: Talk about how the reading and exercises went
	In class: Analyze a few walking works from chapter one or two together; practice using the vocabulary together
	Assign: Read chapter two
	Assign: Execute one exercise from chapter two and write about in a reflection journal
Week 3	In class: Talk about how the reading and exercises went
	In class: Do one or two exercises together
	Assign: Read chapter three
	Assign: Execute one exercise from chapter three and write about in a reflection journal
Week 4	In class: Talk about how the reading and exercises went
	In class: Do one or two exercises together
	Assign: Read chapter four
	Assign: Execute one exercise from chapter four and write about in a reflection journal
Week 5	In class: Talk about how the reading and exercises went
	In class: Do one or two exercises together
	Assign: Read chapter five
	Assign: Execute one exercise from chapter five and write about in a reflection journal

continued on next page

Week 6	In class: Talk about how the reading and exercises went In class: Do one or two exercises together Assign: Read chapter six Assign: Execute one exercise from chapter six and write about in a reflection journal
Week 7	In class: Talk about how the reading and exercises went In class: Do one or two exercises together Assign: Read chapter seven Assign: Execute one exercise from chapter seven and write about in a reflection journal
Week 8	In class: Talk about how the reading and exercises went In class: Do one or two exercises together Assign: Read chapter eight Assign: Execute one exercise from chapter eight and write about in a reflection journal
Week 9	In class: Talk about how the reading and exercises went In class: Do one or two exercises together Assign: Read chapter nine Assign: Execute one exercise from chapter nine and write about in a reflection journal
Week 10	In class: Talk about how the reading and exercises went In class: Do one or two exercises together Assign: Read chapter ten Assign: Execute one exercise from chapter ten and write about in a reflection journal
Week 11	In class: Talk about how the reading and exercises went In class: Do one or two exercises together (select from those not completed yet) Start planning for final project (everyone designs a walking project for the class, and have people present/participate for remaining meetings of the class)
Week 12	Final Projects
Week 13	Final Projects
Week 14	Final Projects
Week 15	Final Projects

10-WEEK OUTLINE (COVER FULL BOOK)

Week 1	Create a Group Agreement together (practicing community engagement skills) In class: Do one or two exercises together Assign: Read chapter one Assign: Execute one exercise from chapter one and write about in a reflection journal
Week 2	In class: Talk about how the reading and exercises went In class: Analyze a few walking works from chapter one or two together; practice using the vocabulary together Assign: Read chapter two Assign: Execute one exercise from chapter two and write about in a reflection journal
Week 3	In class: Talk about how the reading and exercises went In class: Do one or two exercises together Assign: Read chapter three Assign: Execute one exercise from chapter three and write about in a reflection journal
Week 4	In class: Talk about how the reading and exercises went In class: Do one or two exercises together Assign: Read chapter four Assign: Execute one exercise from chapter four and write about in a reflection journal
Week 5	In class: Talk about how the reading and exercises went In class: Do one or two exercises together Assign: Read chapter five Assign: Execute one exercise from chapter five and write about in a reflection journal
Week 6	In class: Talk about how the reading and exercises went In class: Do one or two exercises together Assign: Read chapter six Assign: Execute one exercise from chapter six and write about in a reflection journal

continued on next page

Week 7	In class: Talk about how the reading and exercises went
	In class: Do one or two exercises together
	Assign: Read chapter seven
	Assign: Execute one exercise from chapter seven and write about in a reflection journal
Week 8	In class: Talk about how the reading and exercises went
	In class: Do one or two exercises together
	Assign: Read chapter eight
	Assign: Execute one exercise from chapter eight and write about in a reflection journal
Week 9	In class: Talk about how the reading and exercises went
	In class: Do one or two exercises together
	Assign: Read chapter nine
	Assign: Execute one exercise from chapter nine and write about in a reflection journal
Week 10	In class: Talk about how the reading and exercises went
	In class: Do one or two exercises together
	Assign: Read chapter ten
	Assign: Execute one exercise from chapter ten and write about in a reflection journal (final assignment)

10-Week Outline (cover selected chapters)

Week 1	Create a Group Agreement together (practicing community engagement skills)
	In class: Do one or two exercises together
	Assign: Read chapter one
	Assign: Execute one exercise from chapter one and write about in a reflection journal
Week 2	In class: Talk about how the reading and exercises went
	In class: Analyze a few walking works from chapter one or two together; practice using the vocabulary together

	Assign: Read chapter two Assign: Execute one exercise from chapter two and write about in a reflection journal
Week 3	In class: Talk about how the reading and exercises went In class: Do one or two exercises together In class: As a group, decide on three more chapters the class would like to cover Assign: Read chapter XXX Assign: Execute one exercise from chapter XXX and write about in a reflection journal
Week 4	In class: Talk about how the reading and exercises went In class: Do one or two exercises together Assign: Read chapter YYY Assign: Execute one exercise from chapter YYY and write about in a reflection journal
Week 5	In class: Talk about how the reading and exercises went In class: Do one or two exercises together Assign: Read chapter ZZZ Assign: Execute one exercise from chapter ZZZ and write about in a reflection journal
Week 6	In class: Talk about how the reading and exercises went In class: Do one or two exercises together (select from those not completed yet) Start planning for final project (everyone designs a walking project for the class, and have people present/participate for remaining meetings of the class)
Week 7	Final Projects
Week 8	Final Projects
Week 9	Final Projects
Week 10	Final Projects

Suggested Readings and Resources

A variety of intriguing texts are cited in each chapter of this book, and readers are encouraged to peruse those titles. Here are a few more focused reading and resource lists:

SELECTED EXHIBITION CATALOGS

Adams, Rachel. *Wanderlust: Actions, Traces, Journeys 1967–2017*, 2017.
Denison, Jane, and Sharne Wolff. *From Here to There: Australian Art and Walking*, 2018.
Hesse, Fiona, Marie Oucherif, and Matthias Ulrich. *Walk!*, 2022.
Horodner, Stuart. *Walk Ways*, 2002.
Miller, Earl. *Artists' Walks: The Persistence of Peripateticism*, 2013.
Morrison-Bell, Cynthia, and Alistair Robinson. *Walk On: From Richard Long to Janet Cardiff—40 Years of Art Walking*, 2013.
Sullivan, Lexi Lee. *Walking Sculpture 1967–2015*, 2015.

SELECTED COLLECTIONS OF SCORES, DIRECTIONS, EXERCISES, ACTIVITIES

Antony, Rachael, and Joël Henry. *The Lonely Planet Guide to Experimental Travel*, Footscray: Lonely Planet Publications, 2005.
Brotchie, Alastair, and Mel Gooding. *A Book of Surrealist Games*. Boulder: Shambhala, 1995.
Eno, Brian. *Oblique Strategies*. Brian Eno, 1975.
Hanh, Thich Nhat. *How to Walk*. Berkeley: Parallax Press, 2015.
Hind, Claire, and Clare Qualmann. *Ways to Wander*. Axminster: Triarchy Press, 2015.
July, Miranda, and Harrell Fletcher. *Learning to Love You More*. Munich: Prestel, 2007.
Monsoon, Jennifer. *A Field Guide to iLANDing*, Brooklyn: 53rd State Press, 2017.
Ono, Yoko. *Grapefruit*. New York: Simon & Schuster, 2000.
Shalom, Todd. *Prompts for Participatory Walks*. Elastic City, 2019.
Shared Walks. 2018. http://sharedwalks.com
Smith, Phil. *Counter-Tourism: The Handbook*. Axminster: Triarchy Press, 2012.
Wrights & Sights. *A Mis-Guide to Anywhere*. Wrights & Sights, 2006.

Selected Websites

Walking Artists Network, https://www.walkingartistsnetwork.org/.
Museum of Walking, https://www.museumofwalking.org/.
walk · listen · create, https://walklistencreate.org/.
Interartive, Walking Art, https://walkingart.interartive.org/.

Idea Generation Tips

Set a goal for your idea generation. A good goal is specific, measurable, attainable, relevant, and time-bound (SMART). This can take some time and effort to formulate, but it's important as a first step.

Set a time limit. There's no perfect amount of time, and it will shift for each project or person participating. Try a shorter period of time to begin with; if necessary you can add more time.

Consider the format for collecting your ideas. Some people like to write a long list, adding item after item, using up many pages in a notebook. Others like to put each idea on a sticky note, which can be repositioned on a wall or table, possibly in combination with others' ideas. Others might like note cards pinned to a board, while some might like to use an online resource that mimics sticky notes (there are several free options available with a quick internet search). Others yet prefer mind-mapping, either analog on paper or on a white board, or using an electronic application (again, there are several free options available online).

Remind yourself there is no judgment during the idea generation time period. Quantity is the goal. Don't worry about quality at this point. There are no good ideas or bad ideas. You are specifically looking for a large number of ideas, so just keep going until you hit your time limit. Get every single idea out, no matter how silly or absurd you might normally think it is. If you're working as a collaborative group, and someone is shooting down other people's ideas, remind them of the "no judgment" rule.

If you need a prompt to get things started, consider adapting one of the following questions:

- What if . . . ?
- If we had limited resources, such as . . . what could we . . . ?
- What would . . . do in this scenario?
- If we could break the rules, what would we . . . ?

After all the ideas have been collected and the idea generation period is over, you can begin to narrow down. You might group ideas by similarities, or you might match ideas that could reinforce or strengthen one another. You can let go of the completely impossible ideas and start to focus on what your solution might be.

Community Engagement

Artist and scholar Kate McLean mentions the importance of engaging local communities in her work on "smellwalking." She suggests walking in pairs with local residents ". . . to afford greater insight into the smells-cape. Not only did my smell buddy indicate indigenous plants, religious customs, and food dishes, but she also indicated where smell encounters might take place."[1]

Here is a collection of tips for effective community engagement as it relates to walking projects. Not all the tips are applicable in all situations, so it is important to be thoughtful and considered in applying them.

- Secure an invitation to be there if possible, and work with community-based entities (people or organizations) that can provide a through line for the work.

- Be aware of your own bias and privilege.

- Recognize and value local expertise, knowledge, and cultural practices (as McLean mentions above).

- Practice creative, mindful, sustainable adaptive reuse of everything at hand as a means of being local.

- As appropriate, consider leaving some open or unstructured time for new ideas and reflections from participants.

- Practice reciprocity via genuine exchange and sharing of power between the artist and community at all stages of the process, from idea generation to aesthetic choices to implementation.

- Practice generosity by recognizing that people's time and energy are precious and making sure to provide something of real value in exchange.

- Equitably compensate and recognize community members as cocreators.

- Adjust the scale of your walking projects to be appropriate to the available resources (people, funding, space, time, etc.).

"Of course, ignorant and innocent mistakes are acceptable as long as they are accompanied by a profusion of humble private and public apologies. However, the failure of an entire project to which life stories have been entrusted and on which the sustainable development of a community may depend, is not acceptable. The project may not succeed fully, but it cannot afford to fail completely."[2]

Many of these ideas are borrowed from ArtMakingChange.org, MildredsLane.com, and *Open Field: Conversation on the Commons* (2012).

If you are interested in building your community engagement skills, there are a number of skill sets you can develop:

- Communication (written, oral, visual)

- Facilitating discussion/meetings

- Community building/organization/leadership

- Active listening

- Practicing humility and empathy

- Conflict resolution

- Reflection/analysis/assessment

- Language learning

- Collaboration

- Cultural competency

- Understanding privilege and difference

- Negotiating

- Methods of radical pedagogy

- Methods of restorative justice

Tips for Walking During Travel-Based Study
or General Tourism

First and foremost, be prepared with comfortable walking shoes and cloth-ing that can last for long distances and varied weather. You don't want to be worrying about foot pain while you're walking, or a jacket that lets the rain soak through. You will also want to get a good bag to carry your essentials, whether that's a hip-pack, backpack, or cross-body bag. Second, you might want to do some preparatory walking before your trip to ease into walking longer distances. You can ease into this exercise over several weeks, and it can be fun to partner with a friend for accountability. Third, do some research ahead of time. Many locations have free walking tours online, and if you're prepared, you can plan for them.

If you are staying in a location for multiple days, and you have time to explore, it can be fun to walk around to get a first impression of the location. Then, select an observational walking exercise to look, listen, taste, smell, and feel more deeply in the same place. Journal about what you noticed with each visit.

Other tips include learning a bit of the local language if you're trav-eling to another country with a different language. Remember to enjoy the popular tourist attractions if that's what you're after, but to also plan time to get to know local interests. This is where walking can come in handy as you move away from well-trod tourist stops. Also, be safe and prepared—have a phone for maps, translation, photos, and so you can call for assistance. Be respectful of local laws and culture—a quick internet search will reveal any top issues you should be aware of. Lastly, keep a journal of your experiences—you will enjoy reading it later.

Types of Walking—A List to Inspire

Ambling
Arriving
Breaching
Bushwhacking
Crossing
Dérive / Drifting
Descending
Flânerie

Following
Geocaching
GPS drawing walks
Group walks
Guided walks
Haunting (as in Virginia Woolf's "street haunting")
Hiking
Hopping on one foot
Investigating
Jaunting
Journeying
Leading
Leaving
Meandering
Migrating
Moon walking
Mythogeography (as in Phil Smith's book, *Mythogeography: A guide to walking sideways*)
Navigating
Nomadism
Orienteering
Parkour
Pilgrimage
Perambulating
Procession
Promenading
Protests
Psychogeography
Pub crawling
Questing
Rambling
Retracing your steps
Roaming
Rolling
Sauntering
Scored walks (following directions)
Sensory walks
Shuffling
Skipping

Sleepwalking
Smellwalking
Solo walking
Spacewalking
Speed walking
Stamping
Stilt walking
Stomping
Strolling
Tailing
Three-legged walking
Tightrope walking
Tiptoeing
Tracing
Tracking
Trailing
Tramping
Traversing
Treading
Trekking
Troubadouring
Visiting
Walking for mental health
Walking for physical health
Wandering
Wayfaring

Notes

Introduction

1. Francesco Careri, *Walkscapes: Walking as an Aesthetic Practice* (Ames, IA: Culicidae Architectural Press, 2017), 26.

Chapter 1

1. Lani Seelinger, "10 Nomadic Communities and Their Fascinating Lives," *Culture Trip*, July 2017, accessed October 15, 2021, https://theculturetrip.com/africa/articles/10-nomadic-communities-and-their-fascinating-lives/.

2. Francesco Careri, *Walkscapes: Walking as an Aesthetic Practice* (Ames, IA: Culicidae Architectural Press, 2017), 56.

3. Careri, 29.

4. Howard Norman, "On the Trail of a Ghost," *National Geographic* 213, no. 2 (February 2008): 136–49.

5. "Samuel Taylor Coleridge, A Walking Tour of Cumbria." British Library, accessed October 9, 2021, https://www.bl.uk/collection-items/samuel-taylor-coleridge-a-walking-tour-of-cumbria.

6. Joanna Taylor, "Dorothy Wordsworth, Mountaineering Pioneer," *BARS Blog*, September 2018, accessed October 3, 2021, https://www.bars.ac.uk/blog/?p=2200.

7. Chelsea Kidd, *The Sarah Stoddart Hazlitt Project,* accessed February 11, 2022, https://sarahstoddarthazlitt.wixsite.com/theproject/about-ssh.

8. Helena Whitbread, "Anne's Travels," accessed February 11, 2022, https://www.annelister.co.uk/annes-travels/.

9. Henry David Thoreau, "Walking," *The Atlantic*, June 1862, accessed October 3, 2021, https://www.theatlantic.com/magazine/archive/1862/06/walking/304674/.

10. Russell Goodman, "Transcendentalism," *Stanford Encyclopedia of Philosophy*, accessed October 3, 2021, https://plato.stanford.edu/entries/transcendentalism/.

11. "Art Term: Flâneur," *Tate Modern*, accessed October 9, 2021, https://www.tate.org.uk/art/art-terms/f/flaneur.

12. Aggie Toppins, *Critical Theory Cocktails*, vol. 4, Aggie Toppins, 2018.

13. Bobby Seal, "Baudelaire, Benjamin and the Birth of the Flâneur," *Psychogeographic Review*, November 2013, accessed October 9, 2021, https://psychogeographicreview.com/baudelaire-benjamin-and-the-birth-of-the-flaneur/.

14. Clare Qualmann and Amy Sharrocks, "WALKING WOMEN: A Study Room Guide on Women Using Walking in Their Practice," (London: Live Art Development Agency, 2017), p. 53, accessed February 26, 2022, https://www.thisisliveart.co.uk/resources/catalogue/walking-women-a-study-room-guide-on-women-using-walking-in-their-practice/.

15. Emily Thomas, "Five Philosophers on the Joys of Walking," *OUPblog*, February 2020, accessed October 9, 2021, https://blog.oup.com/2020/02/five-philosophers-on-the-joys-of-walking/.

16. Michel de Certeau, *The Practice of Everyday Life*, trans. Steven F. Rendall (Berkeley: University of California Press, 2011), 98.

17. Joshua J. Mark, "The First Labor Strike in History," *World History Encyclopedia*, July 2017, accessed March 5, 2022, https://www.worldhistory.org/article/1089/the-first-labor-strike-in-history/.

18. Karen, Harris, "When the Peasants Went on Strike: Ancient Rome's Secessions of the Plebs," *History Daily*, September 2019, accessed Dec 31, 2021, https://historydaily.org/when-the-peasants-went-on-strike-ancient-romes-secessions-of-the-plebs.

19. Chad Bryant, Arthur Burns, and Paul Readman, "Introduction: Modern Walks," *Walking Histories, 1800–1914* (London: Palgrave Macmillan, 2016), 11.

20. Careri, 78.

21. Michèle Bernstein, *The Night*, ed. Everyone Agrees, trans. Clodagh Kinsella (Book Works, 2013, original publication, 1961), 13.

22. Guy-Ernest Debord, "Theory of the Dérive," *Les Lèvres Nues* #9, November 1956, accessed February 11, 2022, https://www.cddc.vt.edu/sionline/si/theory.html.

23. Paul Walsh, "The Naked City," *Photowalk*, July 2013, accessed October 17, 2021, https://paulwalshphotographyblog.wordpress.com/2013/07/08/the-naked-city/.

24. Guy-Ernest Debord, "Introduction to a Critique of Urban Geography," *Les Lèvres Nues* #6, 1955, accessed February 11, 2022, http://library.nothingness.org/articles/SI/en/display/2.

25. Ibid.

26. Merlin Coverley, *Psychogeography* (Harpenden: Pocket Essentials, 2018), 9.

27. Morag Rose, "Celebrating 10 Years of Creative Mischief at the Peoples History Museum," *The LRM*, 2016, accessed April 2, 2022, http://thelrm.org/loitering-with-intent.

28. "Walking with Contrapposto," *Smithsonian American Art Museum*, accessed July 17, 2022, https://americanart.si.edu/artwork/walk-contrapposto-77197.

29. Lori Waxman, *Keep Walking Intently: The Ambulatory Art of the Surrealists, the Situationists, and Fluxus* (Berlin: Sternberg Press, 2017), 245.

30. Waxman, 200.

31. Waxman, 213.

32. "Beverly Buchanan," *Art Papers*, Fall/Winter 2020, accessed July 17, 2022, https://www.artpapers.org/beverly-buchanan-2/.

Chapter 2

1. Francesco Careri, *Walkscapes: Walking as an Aesthetic Practice* (Ames, IA: Culicidae Architectural Press, 2017), 145.

2. JeeYeun Lee, *Walking Detroit* (2020), 11.

3. Lucy R. Lippard, *The Lure of the Local* (New York: The New Press, 1997), 78.

4. JeeYeun Lee, " 'Don't Look to My Work for Reconciliation': A Conversation with Andrea Carlson," *Monument Lab*, July 2021, accessed February 13, 2022, https://monumentlab.com/bulletin/dont-look-to-my-work-for-reconciliation-a-conversation-with-andrea-carlson.

5. *Weird Walk*, accessed February 13, 2022, https://www.weirdwalk.co.uk/.

6. "Parallel Walking," *Walkspace*, accessed February 13, 2022, http://walkspace.uk/parallel-walking/,

7. Lori Waxman, *Keep Walking Intently: The Ambulatory Art of the Surrealists, the Situationists, and Fluxus* (Berlin: Sternberg Press, 2017), 233.

8. "The Difference between 'Race' and 'Ethnicity,' " *Merriam-Webster*, accessed May 16, 2022, https://www.merriam-webster.com/words-at-play/difference-between-race-and-ethnicity.

9. "The Difference between 'Race' and 'Ethnicity,' " *Merriam-Webster*, accessed May 16, 2022, https://www.merriam-webster.com/words-at-play/difference-between-race-and-ethnicity.

10. Laurel Wamsley, "A Guide to Gender Identity Terms," *NPR*, June 2, 2021, accessed February 6, 2022, https://www.npr.org/2021/06/02/996319297/gender-identity-pronouns-expression-guide-lgbtq.

11. "Disability," *Merriam-Webster.com Dictionary*, Merriam-Webster, accessed March 5, 2022, https://www.merriam-webster.com/dictionary/disability.

12. "Citizen," *Merriam-Webster.com Dictionary*, Merriam-Webster, accessed May 16, 2022, https://www.merriam-webster.com/dictionary/citizen.

Chapter 3

1. Howard Norman, "On the Trail of a Ghost," *National Geographic* 213, no. 2 (February 2008): 136–49. https://search.ebscohost.com/login.aspx?direct=true&db=aph&AN=28572143&site=ehost-live.

2. Guy Debord, "Theory of the Dérive," *Situationist International Anthology*, trans. Ken Knabb (Berkeley: Bureau of Public Secrets, revised and expanded edition, 2006), http://bopsecrets.org/SI/2.derive.htm.

3. Todd Shalom, *Prompts for Participatory Walks* (Elastic City, 2019).

4. Shane O'Mara, *In Praise of Walking* (New York: W. W. Norton & Company, 2019), 80.

5. O'Mara, 74.

6. Christian Jarrett, "Psychology: How Many Senses Do We Have?" *BBC.com*, November 19, 2014, accessed April 17, 2022, https://www.bbc.com/future/article/20141118-how-many-senses-do-you-have.

7. Oliver Wainwright, "Victoria Henshaw Obituary," *The Guardian*, October 19, 2014, accessed April 10, 2022, https://www.theguardian.com/cities/2014/oct/19/victoria-henshaw.

8. Ellen Mueller, *Elements and Principles of 4D Art and Design* (Oxford: Oxford University Press, 2017), 180.

9. "The Center for Deep Listening," accessed January 16, 2022, https://www.deeplistening.rpi.edu/deep-listening/.

10. CSU Global, "What Is Active Listening? 4 Tips for Improving Communication Skills," May 10, 2021, accessed January 16, 2022, https://csuglobal.edu/blog/what-is-active-listening-4-tips-for-improving-communication-skills.

11. Pauline Oliveros, *Sonic Meditations* (Smith Publications, American Music: March–November 1971).

12. Leah Sandals, "Step by Step: Artists Walk to Resist Colonization, Ableism and More," *canadianart*, June 22, 2017, accessed January 16, 2022, https://canadianart.ca/features/step-step-artists-walk-resist-colonization-ableism/.

13. "walk · listen · create," accessed January 16, 2022, https://walklistencreate.org/about/what-is-a-sound-walk/.

14. "Award 2017—Longlisted: Blind Field Shuttle—Carmen Papalia," *Visible Project*, accessed May 1, 2022, https://www.visibleproject.org/blog/project/blind-field-shuttle/.

15. Tanya Lewis, "The Nose Knows: Humans Can Smell More Than 1 Trillion Scents," *LiveScience*, accessed January 16, 2022, https://www.livescience.com/44240-human-nose-distinguishes-1-trillion-scents.html.

16. Katherine Jane McLean, *Nose-First: Practices of Smellwalking and Smellscape Mapping* (Royal College of Art: January 2019), 149.

17. McLean, 3.

18. Constance Classen, *Aroma: The Cultural History of Smell* (Routledge, 1994), 3.

19. Jim Drobnick, "Reveries, Assaults and Evaporating Presences: Olfactory Dimensions in Contemporary Art," *PARACHUTE* #89 (Winter 1998): 10–19, accessed May 1, 2022, http://www.david-howes.com/senses/Drobnick.htm.

20. McLean, 37.

21. Colleen Walsh, "What the Nose Knows," *The Harvard Gazette*, accessed January 16, 2022, https://news.harvard.edu/gazette/story/2020/02/how-scent-emotion-and-memory-are-intertwined-and-exploited/.

22. Ewa Malgorzata Tatar, "Procession—performance by Teresa Murak," *Parallel Chronologies: An Archive of East European Exhibitions*, accessed January 17, 2022, https://tranzit.org/exhibitionarchive/procession-performance-by-teresa-murak/.

23. Luca Maria Aiello, Rossano Schifanella, and Daniele Quercia, "Smelly Maps," *Good City Life*, accessed April 10, 2022, http://goodcitylife.org/smellymaps/.

24. Alina Bradford and Ailsa Harvey, "The Five (and More) Human Senses," *LiveSience*, accessed January 16, 2022, https://www.livescience.com/60752-human-senses.html.

25. Manu J. Brueggemann, Vanessa Thomas, Ding Wang, "Lickable Cities: Lick Everything in Sight and on Site," CHI EA '18: Extended Abstracts of the 2018 CHI Conference on Human Factors in Computing Systems, April 2018, paper no. alt06, p. 2, https://doi.org/10.1145/3170427.3188399.

26. SPURSE, *Eat Your Sidewalk*, accessed January 16, 2022, https://eatyoursidewalk.org/products/eat-your-sidewalk-cookbook.

27. Brueggemann et al., 1.

28. Brueggemann et al., 4.

29. Brueggemann et al., 7.

30. Aggie Toppins, *Critical Theory Cocktails*, vol. 4, Aggie Toppins, 2018.

31. Luis Carlos Sotelo-Castro, "Participation Cartography: Blurring the Boundaries of Space, Autobiography, and Memory by Means of Performance," *RiDE: The Journal of Applied Theatre and Performance* 15, no. 4 (November 2010): 593–609.

32. Pau Catà, "Beyond Qafila Thania: Walking as Immediate and Preterit Empathy," *Walking Art / Walking Aesthetics*, accessed May 15, 2022, https://walkingart.interartive.org/2018/12/Beyond-Qafila-Thania.

33. Allan Kaprow, "The Legacy of Jackson Pollock," *ARTnews*, Oct 1958.

34. Meghan Moe Beitiks, "End Notes," *The Center for Sustainable Practice in the Arts*, Issue 26 (Fall 2019).

35. Ellen Mueller, *Elements and Principles of 4D Art and Design* (Oxford: Oxford University Press, 2017), 62.

36. Melanie Menard, "'Flâneur' vs. 'Dérive,'" *Inner Worlds / Outer Space*, accessed January 22, 2022, https://melaniemenardarts.wordpress.com/tag/charles-baudelaire/.

37. Stuart Horodner, *Walk Ways* (New York: Independent Curators International, 2002).

38. Tim Cresswell, *Place: An Introduction* (New York: Wiley Blackwell, 2015), 63.

39. "walkwalkwalk," accessed February 13, 2022, http://www.walkwalkwalk.org.uk/thirdlevelpages/E8invite.html.

40. Calvin Tomkins, "Man of Steel," *The New Yorker*, July 28, 2022, accessed July 19, 2022, https://www.newyorker.com/magazine/2002/08/05/man-of-steel.

41. Guy Debord, "Theory of the Dérive," *Internationale Situationniste #2* (Paris, December 1958).

Chapter 4

1. "Why Being Social Is Good for You," *Counseling and Psychology, South University*, May 1, 2018, accessed January 23, 2022, https://www.southuniversity.edu/news-and-blogs/2018/05/why-being-social-is-good-for-you.

2. Anne Bénichou, "Vera Greenwood. L'hôtel Soficalle," *Vox,* no. 05 (November 2003), accessed January 30, 2022, http://centrevox.ca/en/exposition/vera-greenwood-lhotel-soficalle/.

3. Nicole Miller, "Following Sophie Calle," *Hyperallergic*, June 18, 2016, accessed January 29, 2022, https://hyperallergic.com/305869/following-sophie-calle/.

4. iLAND, *A Field Guide to iLANDing*, 53rd State Press, 2017.

5. Karen O'Rourke, *Walking and Mapping: Artists as Cartographers* (Cambridge: The MIT Press, 2013), 47.

6. Katherine Jane McLean, *Nose-First: Practices of Smellwalking and Smellscape Mapping* (Royal College of Art, January 2019), 85.

7. McLean, 90, 93.

8. Morag Rose, "Dis/ability and Walking Art," *The LRM*, accessed April 2, 2022, http://thelrm.org/links.

9. Emily Ladau, *Demystifying Disability* (Berkeley: Ten Speed Press, 2021), 78.

10. Ladau, 82.

11. McLean, 90.

12. Todd Shalom, *Prompts for Participatory Walks* (Elastic City, 2019), 24.

13. Rick Lowe, "Growing Dialogue: What Is the Effectiveness of Socially Engaged Art?" in *Public Servants*, ed. Johana Burton, Shannon Jackson, and Domini Willsdon (Cambridge: The MIT Press, 2016), 446.

14. Lucy R. Lippard, *On the Beaten Track: Tourism, Art, and Place* (New York: The New Press, 1999), 2.

15. Lippard, 4.

16. Camille Turner, "Heritage Walking Tour," accessed February 5, 2022, http://camilleturner.com/project/miss-canadianas-heritage-and-culture-walking-tour/.

17. Rachel Kauder Nalebuff, "Death and Doggie Hamlet," *Culturebot*, October 10, 2016, accessed June 17, 2022, https://www.culturebot.org/2016/10/26293/death-and-doggie-hamlet/.

18. Blake Morris, *Walking Networks* (Lanham: Rowman & Littlefield, 2020), 139.

19. Joy Sleeman, "Nancy Holt 'Trail Markers' (1969) or, the Walk from Wistman's Wood," *Holt/Smithson Foundation*, December 2019, accessed March 26, 2022, https://holtsmithsonfoundation.org/nancy-holt-trail-markers-1969-or-walk-wistmans-wood.

20. Charles Merewether, *The Archive* (Cambridge: The MIT Press, 2006), 10.

21. Jacques Derrida and Eric Prenowitz, "Archive Fever: A Freudian Impression," in *Diacritics* 25, no. 2 (1995): 4.

22. Hal Foster, "An Archival Impulse," *OCTOBER 110* (Fall 2004): 3–22.

23. Merewether, 17.

24. Ellen Mueller, *Remixing and Drawing* (Milton Park: Routledge Focus, 2018), 7.

Chapter 5

1. Morag Rose, *The Loiterers Resistance Movement*, accessed February 26, 2022, http://thelrm.org/.

2. Blake Morris and Morag Rose, "Pedestrian Provocations: Manifesting an Accessible Future," *GPS*, Issue 2.2, 2019, accessed February 26, 2022, https://gps.psi-web.org/issue-2-2/gps-2-2-3/.

3. "Colonialism," *Merriam-Webster.com Dictionary*, Merriam-Webster, accessed May 16, 2022, https://www.merriam-webster.com/dictionary/colonialism.

4. JeeYeun Lee, *Walking Detroit,* 2020, 6.

5. "Capitalism," *Merriam-Webster.com Dictionary*, Merriam-Webster, accessed May 16, 2022, https://www.merriam-webster.com/dictionary/capitalism.

6. "Citizen," *Merriam-Webster.com Dictionary*, Merriam-Webster, accessed May 16, 2022, https://www.merriam-webster.com/dictionary/citizen.

7. Morag Rose, "Celebrating 10 Years of Creative Mischief at the Peoples History Museum," *The LRM*, accessed April 2, 2022, http://thelrm.org/loitering-with-intent.

8. Lucy R. Lippard, *The Lure of the Local* (New York: The New Press, 1997), 243.

9. The United States Department of Justice, "Justice Department Announces New Initiative to Combat Redlining," accessed August 7, 2022, https://www.justice.gov/opa/pr/justice-department-announces-new-initiative-combat-redlining.

10. "Kinder Mass Trespass History," *Hayfield Kinder Trespass Group*, accessed March 4, 2022, https://kindertrespass.org.uk/kinder-mass-trespass-history/.

11. "About the Right To Access Swedish Nature," *Visit Sweden*, August 31, 2021, accessed April 9, 2022, https://visitsweden.com/what-to-do/nature-outdoors/nature/sustainable-and-rural-tourism/about-the-right-of-public-access/.

12. "Stuart McAdam / Lines Lost 2013," *Deveron Projects*, accessed March 2, 2022, https://www.deveron-projects.com/stuart-mcadam/.

13. Lippard, 253.

14. John Jordan, "Case Study: Reclaim the Streets," *Beautiful Trouble* (OR Books, 2017), 350.

15. Lippard, 251.

16. Abdallah Fayyad, "The Criminalization of Gentrifying Neighborhoods," *The Atlantic*, December 20, 2017, accessed March 19, 2022, https://www.theatlantic.com/politics/archive/2017/12/the-criminalization-of-gentrifying-neighborhoods/548837/.

17. Tim Cresswell, *Place: An Introduction* (Hoboken: Wiley Blackwell, 2015), 41.

18. Cresswell, 42.

19. Ana Balona de Oliveiera, *Third Text*, 2016, vol. 30, nos. 1–2, 43–59.

20. "Indigenous," *Oxford Learner's Dictionaries*, accessed July 22, 2022, https://www.oxfordlearnersdictionaries.com/us/definition/english/indigenous?q=indigenous.

21. "Imperialism," *Merriam-Webster.com Dictionary*, Merriam-Webster, accessed May 16, 2022, https://www.merriam-webster.com/dictionary/imperialism.

22. "Colonialism," *Merriam-Webster.com Dictionary*, Merriam-Webster, accessed July 22, 2022, https://www.merriam-webster.com/dictionary/colonialism.

23. "Colonizer," *Merriam-Webster.com Dictionary*, Merriam-Webster, accessed July 22, 2022, https://www.merriam-webster.com/dictionary/colonizer.

24. Elizabeth Prine Pauls, "Trail of Tears," *Encyclopedia Britannica*, accessed March 18, 2022, https://www.britannica.com/event/Trail-of-Tears.

25. Jean M. O'Brien, *Firsting and Lasting: Writing Indians out of Existence in New England* (Minneapolis: University of Minnesota Press, 2010).

26. "Presidential Debate in Baltimore (Reagan-Anderson)," *The American Presidency Project*, September 21, 1980, accessed March 19, 2022, https://www.presidency.ucsb.edu/documents/presidential-debate-baltimore-reagan-anderson.

27. "Dakota Commemorative Walk Remembers 1862 Forced March to Fort Snelling," *Pioneer Press via TwinCities.com*, November 11, 2012, accessed March 18, 2022, https://www.twincities.com/2012/11/11/dakota-commemorative-walk-remembers-1862-forced-march-to-fort-snelling/.

28. JeeYeun Lee, "'Don't Look to My Work for Reconciliation': A Conversation with Andrea Carlson," *Monument Lab*, accessed February 13, 2022, https://monumentlab.com/bulletin/dont-look-to-my-work-for-reconciliation-a-conversation-with-andrea-carlson.

29. Margaret Carrigan, "One Mound at a time: Native American Artist Santiago X on Rebuilding Indigenous Cities," *The Art Newspaper*, September 20, 2019, accessed May 1, 2022, https://www.theartnewspaper.com/2019/09/20/one-mound-at-a-time-native-american-artist-santiago-x-on-rebuilding-indigenous-cities.

30. Darcel Rockett, "Happy Indigenous People's Day: Artist Santiago X Gives Us a Serpent and Mounds That Connect to Illinois' Indigenous Past," *Chicago Tribune,* October 14, 2019, accessed May 1, 2022, https://www.chicagotribune.com/lifestyles/ct-life-santiago-x-mounds-indigenous-peoples-day-2019 1014-20191014-4brj2mikendx7ewjwglcg6ot3i-story.html.

31. Including the murders of Trayvon Martin (1995–2012), an African-American boy walking home, Ahmaud Arbery (1994–2020), an African-American man recreationally jogging, or Vicha Ratanapakdee (1936–2021), an elderly Thai-American man walking in daylight in San Francisco. These are just a small sampling.

32. Morag Rose, "Confessions of an Anarcho-Flâneuse or Psychogeography the Mancunian Way," *Walking Inside Out.* ed. Tina Richarson Rowman and Littlefield International, 34.

33. Lori Waxman, Keep Walking Intently: The Ambulatory Art of the Surrealists, the Situationist International, and Fluxus (Berlin: Sternberg Press, 2017), 232.

34. JeeYeun Lee, *Walking Detroit*, 2020, 5.

35. Amanda Gutiérrez, "Brooklyn League of Women Walkers," *Walk Listen Create*, accessed May 16, 2022, https://walklistencreate.org/walkingpiece/brooklyn-league-of-women-walkers/.

36. *Brooklyn League of Women Walkers*, accessed May 16, 2022, https://tmblr.co/ZTJP9X2gkoXPj.

37. The quote continues, "Among the terms for prostitutes are streetwalkers, women of the streets, women on the town, and public women (and of course phrases such as a public man, man about town, or man of the streets mean very different things than do their equivalents attached to women)."

38. Rebecca Solnit, *Wanderlust: A History of Walking* (London: Penguin Books, 2000), 234.

39. Kerri Andrews, *Wanderers: A History of Women Walking* (London: Reaktion Books, 2000), 263.

40. Laurel Wamsley, "A Guide to Gender Identity Terms," *NPR,* June 2, 2021, accessed February 6, 2022, https://www.npr.org/2021/06/02/996319297/gender-identity-pronouns-expression-guide-lgbtq.

41. Heather Cassell, "Two Trans Women Murdered in First Week of 2022," *GayCityNews.com*, accessed February 6, 2022, https://gaycitynews.com/year-begins-with-pair-of-transgender-murders/.

42. Philomena Epps, "The Unbearable Artist: In Conversation with Kubra Khademi," *Various Artist*, October 9, 2021, accessed February 6, 2022.

43. "Amanda Heng: Let's Walk / I Walk from the South to the North," *Let's Talk About Text, Baby*, January 23, 2018, accessed February 6, 2022, https://letstalkabouttextbby.wordpress.com/2018/01/23/amanda-heng-lets-walk-i-walk-from-the-south-to-the-north/.

44. Emily Ladau, *Demystifying Disability* (Berkeley: Ten Speed Press, 2021), 1.

45. "Disability," *Merriam-Webster.com Dictionary*, Merriam-Webster, accessed March 5 2022, https://www.merriam-webster.com/dictionary/disability.

46. Ladau, 9.

47. Shane O'Mara, *In Praise of Walking* (New York: W. W. Norton & Company, 2019), 105.

48. Ladau, 38.

49. Sunaura Taylor (quoting Taylor in discussion with Judith Butler), *Examined Life*, directed by Astra Taylor, Zeitgeist Films, 2019.

50. Raquel Meseguer Zafe, "A Crash Course in Cloudspotting," *Unchartered ollective*, accessed April 2, 2022, https://www.mayk.org.uk/current/a-crash-course-in-cloudspotting.

51. Blake Morris, *Walking Networks: The Development of an Artistic Medium* (Lanham: Rowman & Littlefield Publishers, 2019), 57.

52. "Carmen Papalia: Mobility Device," *High Line*, accessed May 20, 2022, https://www.thehighline.org/art/projects/carmen-papalia/.

53. Kate Morris, *Shifting Grounds: Landscape in Contemporary Native American Art* (Seattle: University of Washington Press, 2019), 101.

54. "Migrants, Asylum Seekers, Refugees and Immigrants: What's the Difference?" *International Rescue Committee*, accessed February 27, 2022, https://www.rescue.org/article/migrants-asylum-seekers-refugees-and-immigrants-whats-difference.

55. "Mihret Kebede / Slow Marathon," *Deveron Projects*, accessed February 27, 2022, https://www.deveron-projects.com/mihret-kebede/.

56. "Slow Marathon 2020: Under One Sky," *Deveron Projects*, accessed February 13, 2022, https://www.deveron-projects.com/events/slow-marathon-2020/.

57. "The Midnight Run," accessed February 11, 2022, http://www.themnr.com/media.

58. David Taylor, "Working the Line," accessed May 6, 2022, http://www.dtaylorphoto.com/portfolio.cfm?nK=4418#0.

Chapter 6

1. Susie Wise, *Design for Belonging* (Berkeley: Ten Speed Press, 2022), 101.

2. Shane O'Mara, *In Praise of Walking* (New York: W.W. Norton & Company, 2019), 177.

3. Søren Kierkegaard, "I Walk for Health and Salvation," *Beneath My Feet: Writers on Walking*, edited by Duncan Minshull (Notting Hill: Notting Hill Editions, 2022).

4. O'Mara, 10.

5. O'Mara, 136

6. O'Mara, 125.

7. "Amanda Heng: Let's Walk / I Walk from the South to the North," *Let's Talk About Text, Baby*, January 23, 2018, accessed June 17, 2022, https://letstalkabouttextbby.wordpress.com/2018/01/23/amanda-heng-lets-walk-i-walk-from-the-south-to-the-north/.

8. *Jalan Gembira*, accessed June 17, 2022, https://jalangembira.com/.

9. Ernesto Pujol, *Walking Art Practice: Reflections on Socially Engaged Paths* (Axminster: Triarchy Press, 2018), 130.

10. Lee Deigaard, "Feature: Lee Deigaard—Near and Far," *Invert/Extant Press*, November 24, 2020, accessed June 17, 2022, https://www.invertextant.com/post/feature-lee-deigaard-near-and-far.

11. Lee Deigaard, "Quarantine Drawings (March 17–19, 2020)," via PDF provided from the artist, June 24, 2022.

12. New Bedford Art Museum.,"Dérive and Psychogeography Walk: Dog Days," Facebook event, February 24, 2018, accessed June 17, 2022, https://www.facebook.com/events/147511305909388/?_rdr.

13. Douglas McCulloch, "Dog-Guided Walk Considers Place, Man's Best Friend," *Dartmouth Week*, February 24, 2018, accessed June 17, 2022, https://dartmouth.theweektoday.com/article/dog-guided-walk-considers-place-mans-best-friend/32663.

14. O'Mara, 127.

15. Lucy R. Lippard, *The Lure of the Local* (New York: The New Press, 1997), 253.

16. The Editors of Encyclopaedia Britannica, "Japanese garden," *Encyclopaedia Britannica*, accessed April 2, 2022, https://www.britannica.com/art/Japanese-garden.

17. Sotheby's, "The Emperor's Long Mid-Autumn Holiday," September 17, 2019, accessed April 2, 2022, https://www.sothebys.com/en/articles/the-emperors-long-mid-autumn-holiday.

18. Hermann Kern, *Through the Labyrinth* (Munich: Prestel, 2000), 23.

19. Kern, 25.

20. Kern, 143.

21. *Dictionary.com*, accessed April 2, 2022, https://www.dictionary.com/browse/the-troy-game.

22. Erwin Reißmann, "The Troy Towns," *The Mystery Labyrinth*, accessed April 2, 2022, http://mymaze.de/trojaburg_en.htm.

23. Kern, 301.

24. Kern, 81.

25. Ronald J. Onorato, "Richard Fleischner, University of Massachusetts," *Art Forum*, March 1979, accessed April 3, 2022, https://www.artforum.com/print/reviews/197903/richard-fleischner-68115.

26. Kerri Andrews, *Wanderers: A History of Women Walking* (London: Reaktion Books, 2000), 227.

27. Andrews, 249.

28. Kern, 30.

29. Dillon de Give, "The Coyote Walks," *Dillon de Give* website, accessed February 19, 2022, https://www.dillondegive.com/coyote-walks.

30. Andrews, 29.

31. Helena Guzik, "What Is a Pilgrimage?" *National Trust*, accessed March 2, 2022, https://www.nationaltrust.org.uk/features/what-is-a-pilgrimage.

32. C. Devereux and E. Carnegie, "Pilgrimage: Journeying Beyond Self," *Tourism Recreation Research*, 31(1) (2006): 47–56.

33. Lucy R. Lippard, *On the Beaten Track: Tourism, Art, and Place* (New York: The New Press, 1999), 37.

34. Lippard, 119.

35. Warwick Frost and Jennifer Laing, "Long-Distance Walking in Films: Promises of Healing and Redemption on the Trail," *The Routledge International Handbook of Walking*, edited by C. Michael Hall (Milton Park: Routledge, 2017).

36. Guido van der Werve, "Effugio c, you're always only half a day away," accessed April 30, 2022, https://roofvogel.org/effugio-c/.

37. Lexi Lee Sullivan, "Stepping Out," *Walking Sculpture: 1967–2015*, deCordova Sculpture Park and Museum, 2015, 14.

38. Carlos Pérez Marín, "Nomads," *Project Qafila*, accessed May 15, 2022, http://projectqafila.weebly.com/nomads.html.

39. Lisa Jaye Young, "Entering Zig's Reservation: In Conversation with Zig Jackson," *Burnaway*, November 25, 2021, accessed May 8, 2022, https://burnaway.org/magazine/with-zig-jackson/.

40. Kate Morris, *Shifting Grounds: Landscape in Contemporary Native American Art* (Seattle: University of Washington Press, 2019), 96.

41. Phil Smith, "Theatrical-Political Possibilities in Contemporary Procession," *Studies in Theatre and Performance 29*, no. 1 (January 1, 2009): 19.

42. "Top Religious Festivals Around the World," *Leisure Group Travel*, accessed June 17, 2022, https://leisuregrouptravel.com/8-top-religious-festivals-around-the-world/.

43. Joseph Scanlan, "Culture in Action," *Frieze*, accessed July 1, 2022, https://www.frieze.com/article/culture-action.

44. Monika Molnár and Tanja Trampe, "Public Art: Consequences of a Gesture?* An Interview with Mary Jane Jacob," *OnCurating*, issue 19, June 2013, accessed July 1, 2022, https://www.on-curating.org/issue-19-reader/public-art-consequences-of-a-gesture-an-interview-with-mary-jane-jacob.html.

45. Jim Adams, "Activist Roots still Thrive in Canada Border Crossing," *Indian Country Today*, July 28, 2004, accessed May 8, 2022, https://indiancountrytoday.com/archive/activist-roots-still-thrive-in-canada-border-crossing.

Chapter 7

1. Tim Cresswell, *Place: An Introduction* (New York: Wiley Blackwell, 2015), 12.

2. Yi-Fu Tuan, *Space and Place* (Minneapolis: University of Minnesota Press, 1977), 6.

3. Cresswell, 47.

4. Jeff Malpas, "Thinking Topographically: Place, Space, and Geography," *Il Cannocchiale: Rivista di studi filosofici* 42, no. 1–2 (2017): 25–53, accessed March 19, 2022, https://jeffmalpas.com/wp-content/uploads/Thinking-Topographically-Place-Space-and-Geogr.pdf.

5. Cresswell, 69.

6. Cresswell, 17.

7. Sebastián Días Morales, *Pasajes IV*, 2013, Vimeo video, accessed July 10, 2022, https://vimeo.com/174799055.

8. Yi-Fu Tuan, *Topophilia: A Study of Environmental Perception, Attitudes, and Values* (Minneapolis: University of Minnesota Press, 1974), 4.

9. *Folding Landscapes*, accessed March 13, 2022, https://foldinglandscapes.com/.

10. Cresswell, 35.

11. Cresswell, 18.

12. Ernesto Pujol, *Walking Art Practice: Reflections on Socially Engaged Paths* (Bridport, UK: Triarchy Press, 2018), 11.

13. Miriam Kahn, "Your Place and Mine," *Senses of Place*, edited by Steven Feld and Keith H. Basso, School of American Research Advanced Seminar Series, 1996, 178.

14. Robin Wall Kimmerer, *Braiding Sweetgrass* (Minneapolis: Milkweed Editions, 2013).

15. "History and Culture: Boarding Schools," *Northern Plains Reservation Aid*, accessed March 25, 2022, http://www.nativepartnership.org/site/PageServer?pagename=airc_hist_boardingschools.

16. Wakáŋyaŋkéwiŋ/Liz Cates, Written correspondence and spoken reflections, August 2022.

17. Leah Sandals, "Step by Step: Artists Walk to Resist Colonization, Ableism and More," *canadianart*, June 22, 2017, accessed March 26, 2022, https://canadianart.ca/features/step-step-artists-walk-resist-colonization-ableism/.

18. Their names are David Kawapit Jr., Stanley George, Jr., Travis George, Johnny Abraham, Raymond Kawapit, Geordie Rupert, and their guide, Isaac

Kawapit. Source: Michelle Filice, "The Journey of Nishiyuu (The Journey of the People)," *The Canadian Encyclopedia*, December 2, 2015, accessed June 26, 2022, https://www.thecanadianencyclopedia.ca/en/article/the-journey-of-the-people.

19. "Cree Walkers Meet Minister at End of Idle No More Trek," *CBC News*, March 25, 2013, accessed March 26, 2022, https://www.cbc.ca/news/canada/ottawa/cree-walkers-meet-minister-at-end-of-idle-no-more-trek-1.1392239.

20. "About the Movement," *Idle No More*, accessed March 26, 2022, https://idlenomore.ca/about-the-movement/.

21. Rebecca Solnit, *Wanderlust: A History of Walking* (New York: Penguin Books, 2000), 276.

22. Yi-Fu Tuan, *Topophilia: A Study of Environmental Perception, Attitudes, and Values* (Minneapolis: University of Minnesota, 1974), 2.

23. Jeffrey Kastner, *Nature* (Cambridge: MIT Press, 2012), 14.

24. "Podcast Episode 4: Critical and Creative Approaches to Walking in Schools," *WalkingLab*, accessed May 24, 2022, https://walkinglab.org/podcast/critical-and-creative-approaches-to-walking-in-schools/.

25. bell hooks, *Belonging: A Culture of Place* (Milton Park: Routledge, 2009), 7.

26. Sharne Wolf and Jane Denison, "Nici Cumpston," *From Here to There: Australian Art and Walking* (Lismore: Lismore Regional Gallery, 2018), 21.

27. Sarah Rodigari, "Rural Utopias Residency: Sarah Rodigari in Ravensthorpe #2," *Space,* accessed June 19, 2022, https://www.spaced.org.au/spaced-latest/sarah-rodigari-2.

28. Sarah Rodigari, "This Must Be the Place," *SarahRodigari.org*, accessed June 19, 2022, https://sarahrodigari.org/This-Must-be-the-Place.

29. Kate Green, "The Pipe Chronicle," *Kate-Green.co.uk*, accessed June 19, 2022, https://web.archive.org/web/20220120053730/https://www.kate-green.co.uk/walks.

30. Lauren Elkin, *Flâneuse* (New York: Farrar, Straus and Giroux, 2016), 22.

31. "The Concrete Path: A History of Sidewalks," *LB & Sons*, March 1, 2021, accessed July 16, 2022, https://lbsons.com/2021/03/history-of-sidewalks/.

32. Alastair Brotchie and Mel Gooding, *A Book of Surrealist Games* (Boulder: Shambhala, 1995), 120.

33. Hui-min Tsen, "The Pedway," *Hui-min Tsen,* accessed June 19, 2022, https://www.huimintsen.com/pedway-intro.

34. JJ Tiziou, "Walk around Philadelphia," *JJ Tiziou,* accessed July 16, 2022, https://www.jjtiziou.net/project/walk-around-philadelphia/.

35. Rozalinda Borcilă, "Invitation: Walk to the Beach," *Common Places*, accessed June 19, 2022, https://web.archive.org/web/20161110151114/http://commonplacesproject.org/blog/?m=200604.

36. Lucia Monge, *Plantón Móvil,* accessed June 19, 2022, https://www.plantonmovil.org/

37. Lucy R. Lippard, *The Lure of the Local* (New York: The New Press, 1997), 23.

38. Cresswell, 39.

39. Cresswell, 40.

40. hooks, 20.

41. Yi-Fu Tuan, "A View of Geography," *Geographical Review*, 81 (1991): 102.

42. N'Goné Fall, "Today, and Always, I Embrace Your Pain," *Ingrid Mwangi & Robert Hutter: Intruders* (Wien: Moderne Kunst Verlag Fur, 2013).

43. Tavia Nyong'O, "Out of the Archive: Performing Minority Embodiment," *Action and Agency: Advancing the Dialogue on Native Performance Art* (Denver: Denver Art Museum, 2010), 156.

44. Lippard, 7.

45. Lippard, 7.

46. Larsen Husby, "My Mind within My Body, Moving through Space," *Long Trace of Minneapolis*, accessed March 20, 2022, https://longtraceofminneapolis.com/My-Mind-Within-My-Body-Moving-Through-Space.

47. Cresswell, 128.

48. Lippard, 85.

49. Nicholas Slayton, "Time to Retire the Word 'Homeless' and Opt for 'Houseless' or 'Unhouse' Instead?" *Architectural Digest*, May 21, 2021, accessed March 20, 2022, https://www.architecturaldigest.com/story/homeless-unhoused.

50. Cresswell, 174.

51. Zygmunt Bauman, *Life in Fragments: Essays in Postmodern Morality* (Oxford: Blackwell, 1995), 94.

52. Agnieszka Sural, "Homeless Vehicle—Krzysztof Wodiczko," *Culture.PL*, November 30, 2016, accessed March 20, 2022, https://culture.pl/en/work/homeless-vehicle-krzysztof-wodiczko.

53. Maria Popova, "A Field Guide to Getting Lost: Rebecca Solnit on How We Find Ourselves," *The Marginalian*, August 4, 2014, accessed June 20, 2022, https://www.themarginalian.org/2014/08/04/field-guide-to-getting-lost-rebecca-solnit/.

54. Walter Benjamin, "A Berlin Chronicle," *One-Way Street and Other Writings* (London: Penguin Classic, 2009).

Chapter 8

1. Rebecca Solnit, *Wanderlust: A History of Walking* (New York: Penguin Books, 2000), 267.

2. "Marching for Justice in the Fields," *National Park Service*, accessed December 31, 2021, https://www.nps.gov/articles/000/marching-for-justice-in-the-fields.htm.

3. Lynn Conway, "The Most Influential Protest You've Never Heard of: May Day, 1971," *Georgetown University Library*, accessed December 31, 2021, https://www.library.georgetown.edu/exhibition/most-influential-protest-you%E2%80%99ve-never-heard-may-day-1971.

4. David Kaufman, "How the Pride March Made History," *New York Times (online)*, June 16, 2020, accessed December 31, 2021, https://www.nytimes.com/2020/06/16/us/gay-lgbt-pride-march-history.html.

5. "ACT UP Demonstrations on Wall Street," *NYC LGBT Historic Sites Project*, accessed June 20, 2022, https://www.nyclgbtsites.org/site/act-up-demonstration-at-the-new-york-stock-exchange/.

6. "About Us," *Mother Earth Water Walk*, accessed March 13, 2022, http://www.motherearthwaterwalk.com/?page_id=11.

7. Kate Morris, *Shifting Grounds: Landscape in Contemporary Native American Art* (Seattle: University of Washington Press, 2019), 1.

8. "Temporary Occupations," *EM-Arts*, 2004, accessed June 24, 2022, https://em-arts.org/en/independent-films/temporary-occupations.

9. Adrian Piper, "I Am the Locus (#2)," *Smart Museum of Art The University of Chicago*, accessed May 22, 2022, https://smartcollection.uchicago.edu/objects/10062/i-am-the-locus-2#.

10. Robin Cembalest, "Adrian Piper Pulls Out of Black Performance-Art Show," *ARTnews*, October 25, 2013, accessed May 22, 2022, https://www.artnews.com/art-news/news/piper-pulls-out-of-black-performance-art-show-2319/.

11. Morris, 145.

12. Barbara Lounder website, accessed May 20, 2022, http://www.barbaralounder.ca/walking-a/#id98.

13. Morris, 145.

14. "Kate Gilmore: Walk the Walk," *Public Art Fund*, accessed June 24, 2022, https://www.publicartfund.org/exhibitions/view/walk-the-walk/.

15. Courtney Fiske, "Rosemarie Castoro," *ArtForum*, accessed June 25, 2022, https://www.artforum.com/picks/rosemarie-castoro-55163.

16. Rebecca Nathanson, "How 'Carry That Weight' Is Changing the Conversation on Campus Sexual Assault," *Rolling Stone* (December 1, 2014), accessed June 25, 2022, https://www.rollingstone.com/politics/politics-news/how-carry-that-weight-is-changing-the-conversation-on-campus-sexual-assault-77543/.

17. Blake Morris, *Walking Networks* (Lanham: Rowman & Littlefield, 2020), 95.

18. Dominique Sisley, "Artist's Burka Sculpture Gets Vandalised by Drunk Racist," *Dazed*, July 25, 2016, accessed July 1, 2022, https://www.dazeddigital.com/artsandculture/article/32173/1/artist-s-burka-sculpture-gets-vandalised-by-drunk-racist.

19. *Slave Rebellion Reenactment*, accessed March 4, 2022, https://www.slave-revolt.com/.

20. Jeremy Deller, "The Battle of Orgreave, 2001," *Jeremy Deller*, accessed June 25, 2022, https://www.jeremydeller.org/TheBattleOfOrgreave/TheBattleOfOrgreave_Video.php.

21. Jeremy Deller, *Joy in People*, exhibition catalog, Hayward Gallery, London (2012): 17.

22. Candice Hopkins, "Interventions in Traditional Territories: 'Cistemaw inyiniw,' A Performance by Cheryl L'Hirondelle," *Hemispheric Institute*, accessed June 25, 2022, https://hemisphericinstitute.org/en/emisferica-21/2-1-essays/cistemaw-iyiniw-ohci.html.

23. Deborah Everett, "Alan Michelson," *Sculpture* 26, no. 4 (May 2007): 31.

24. Christy Gast, "Goldenrod Transect Performance on the High Line," accessed March 26, 2022, https://christygast.com/1676-2/.

25. Xavier Cortada, *Longitudinal Installation*, accessed July 30, 2022, https://cortada.com/gardens/longitudinalinstallation/.

26. Hamish Fulton, *Mountain Time Human Time* (Milan: Deveron Arts, 2010), 51.

27. David Begay, "Diné Worldview and Futurism: A Holistic Perspective," *Indigenous Futurisms: Transcending Past / Present / Future* (Santa Fe: IAIA Museum of Contemporary Native Arts, 2020), 54.

28. Rebecca Conroy, "Podcast Episode 5: Queer Walking Tours," *WalkingLab*, accessed May 1, 2022, https://walkinglab.org/podcast/queer-walking-tours/.

29. Conroy.

30. Conroy.

31. Lauren Sommer, "To Manage Wildfire, California Looks to What Tribes Have Known All Along," *NPR*, August 24, 2020, accessed March 26, 2022, https://www.npr.org/2020/08/24/899422710/to-manage-wildfire-california-looks-to-what-tribes-have-known-all-along.

32. Conroy.

33. "Times Beach—2017," *Teri Rueb*, accessed July 4, 2022, http://terirueb.net/times-beach-2017/.

34. Lori Waxman, *Keep Walking Intently: The Ambulatory Art of the Surrealists, the Situationists, and Fluxus* (Berlin: Sternberg Press, 2017), 222.

35. Miwon Kwon, "One Place after Another + Art and Architecture: Notes on Site Specificity," *October* 80 (1997): 88.

36. Nikos Paperstergiadis, "Everything That Surrounds," *Third Text* 15:57 (2001): 71–86, DOI: 10.1080/09528820108576945.

37. Kellie Jones, "Interview: David Hammons," *ART PAPERS*, July/August 1988, accessed May 22, 2022, https://www.artpapers.org/interview-david-hammons/.

38. Alan Michelson, "Mantle, 2018," *Alan Michelson*, accessed June 25, 2022, https://www.alanmichelson.com/mantle.

39. Kate Morris, *Shifting Grounds: Landscape in Contemporary Native American Art* (Seattle: University of Washington Press, 2019), 111–113.

40. Daniel Davis, "Most Serene Republics—Edgar Heap of Birds," National Museum of the American Indian, Smithsonian, 2012, accessed June 26, 2022, https://www.si.edu/object/most-serene-republics-edgar-heap-birds:yt_MRutY6Yy5WE.

41. Nick Stillman, "The Great White Way: Fulton Street to Reade Street, Manhattan," *The Brooklyn Rail*, June–July 2003, accessed June 26, 2022, https://brooklynrail.org/2003/06/artseen/white-way.

42. J. Halberstam, *The queer art of failure* (Durham: Duke University Press, 2011), 187.

43. Rebecca Conroy, "Podcast Episode 4: Critical and Creative Approaches to Walking in Schools," *WalkingLab*, accessed May 24, 2022, https://walkinglab.org/podcast/critical-and-creative-approaches-to-walking-in-schools/.

44. Amish Morell and Diane Borsato, *Outdoor School: Contemporary Environmental Art* (Vancouver: Douglas & McIntyre, 2021), 81.

45. Sean O'Hagan, "A Mushroom-Related Brush with Mortality: How John Cage Fell for Fungi," *The Guardian*, August 19, 2020, accessed June 26, 2022, https://www.theguardian.com/music/2020/aug/19/mushrooms-mortality-john-cage-fungi-mycology.

46. "Marcus Coates, Stoat, 1999," *Workplace*, accessed July 1, 2022, https://www.workplacegallery.co.uk/artists/9-marcus-coates/works/132/.

Chapter 9

1. Kristine Stiles, "Performance Art," *Theories and Documents of Contemporary Art: A Sourcebook of Artists' Writings* (Berkeley: University of California Press, 2012), 679.

2. Allan Kaprow, "The Legacy of Jackson Pollock," *ARTnews*, October 1958.

3. "William Anastasi, Untitled (Pocket Drawings) 1969," *MoMA*, accessed June 29, 2022, https://www.moma.org/collection/works/90658.

4. Elizabeth S. Hawley, "Shigeko Kubota," *MoMA*, accessed June 30, 2022, https://www.moma.org/artists/3277.

5. Franko B., "I Miss You," *Franko B.*, accessed June 30, 2022, http://www.franko-b.com/I_Miss_You.html.

6. Rebecca Uchill, ed., *On Procession* (Indianapolis: Indianapolis Museum of Art, 2009), 99.

7. "Lygia Pape, Divisor," *Para-Site*, May 17, 2013, accessed July 8, 2022, https://www.para-site.art/programme/lygia-pape-divisor/.

8. Eric Andersen, "The MassDress," *Festival of Fantastics Online Archive*, accessed June 30, 2022, http://www.festivaloffantastics.com/1985/05/30-persons-dress/.

9. Melanie Manchot, "Walk (Square), 2011, Single Screen, HD, 20'40"," *Melanie Manchot*, accessed June 30, 2022, http://www.melaniemanchot.net/category/walk/.

10. Robert Moor, "Tracing (and Erasing) New York's Lines of Desire," *New Yorker*, February 20, 2017, accessed June 11, 2022, https://www.new yorker.com/tech/annals-of-technology/tracing-and-erasing-new-yorks-lines-of-desire.

11. Su Ballard, Zita Joyce, and Lizzie Muller, "Editorial Essay: Networked Utopias and Speculative Futures," *Faculty of Law, Humanities and the Arts*—Papers 380 (2012), https://ro.uow.edu.au/lhapapers/380.

12. Catherine Zegher, "A Century under the Sign of Line: Drawing and Its Extension (1910–2010)," *On Line: Drawing Through the Twentieth Century* (New York City: MoMA, 2011), 100.

13. Greg Allen, "Read between the Lines: Visiting Walter De Maria's Las Vegas Piece," *Greg.org*, August 5, 2013, accessed July 2, 2022, https://greg.org/archive/2013/08/05/read-between-the-lines-visiting-walter-de-marias-las-vegas-piece.html.

14. Patricia Johanson, "Stephen Long," *Patricia Johanson*, accessed July 2, 2022, https://patriciajohanson.com/timeline/stephen_long_aerial.html.

15. Rebecca Solnit, *Wanderlust: A History of Walking* (New York: Penguin Books, 2000), 270.

16. Cynthia Morrison-Bell and Alistair Robinson, "Tim Knowles," *Walk On: From Richard Long to Janet Cardiff—40 Years of Art Walking*, catalog (Sunderland: Art Editions North, 2013), 86.

17. "My Ghost," *Jeremy Wood*, accessed July 2, 2022, https://jeremywood.net/artworks/my-ghost2016.html.

18. Karen O'Rourke, *Walking as Mapping: Artists as Cartographers* (Cambridge: MIT Press, 2013), 138–140.

19. "Francis Alÿs's Green Line & 58 Liters of Paint," *Public Delivery*, June 27, 2022, accessed July 2, 2022, https://publicdelivery.org/francis-alys-green-line/#About_the_artist.

20. "Allora & Calzadilla's Land Mark—You Never Saw Footprints like These," *Public Delivery*, June 18, 2022, accessed July 2, 2022, https://publicdelivery.org/allora-calzadilla-landmark/.

21. *Dennis Oppenheim Estate*, accessed July 2, 2022, https://www.dennis aoppenheim.org/ground-mutations.

22. *Barbara Lounder*, accessed July 2, 2022, http://www.barbaralounder.ca/walking-a/#id91.

23. Jennifer West, "One Mile Parkour Film," *High Line*, September 2012, accessed July 2, 2022, https://www.thehighline.org/art/projects/jenniferwest/.

24. "Touch," *Art Institute Chicago*, accessed July 3, 2022, https://www.artic.edu/artworks/184183/touch.

25. Kalamu ya Salaam, "The Video Artwork of Michèle Magema," *African Digital Art*, January 19, 2016, accessed July 3, 2022, http://kalamu.com/neogriot/2016/03/19/video-the-video-artwork-of-michele-magema/.

26. "Danica Phelps: Mark Down," *David Nolan Gallery*, 2009, accessed July 3, 2022, https://www.davidnolangallery.com/exhibitions/danica-phelps-mark-down?view=slider.

Chapter 10

1. Ernesto Pujol, *Walking Art Practice: Reflections on Socially Engaged Paths* (Axminster: Triarchy Press, 2018), 29.

2. Tim Cresswell, *Place: An Introduction* (New York: Wiley Blackwell, 2015), 64.

3. Amish Morrell and Diane Borsato, *Outdoor School: Contemporary Environmental Art* (Madeira Park: Douglas & McIntyre, 2021), 120.

4. Ginny Whitelaw, "Embodied Leadership: A Cure for What Ails Us?" *Forbes*, October 19, 2020, accessed March 19, 2022, https://www.forbes.com/sites/ginnywhitelaw/2020/10/19/embodied-leadership-a-cure-for-what-ails-us/.

5. Paulo Martins, "Descartes and the Paradigm of Western Medicine: An Essay," *International Journal of Recent Advances in Science and Technology* 5 (2018), 10.30750/ijarst.535.

6. Shane O'Mara, *In Praise of Walking* (New York: W. W. Norton & Company, 2019), 9.

7. O'Mara, 157.

8. Christopher Hafner, "What Is Qi? (and Other Concepts)," *Earl E. Bakken Center for Spirituality & Healing, University of Minnesota*, accessed March 19, 2022, https://www.takingcharge.csh.umn.edu/explore-healing-practices/traditional-chinese-medicine/what-qi-and-other-concepts.

9. Mary Koithan and Cynthia Farrell, "Indigenous Native American Healing Traditions," *Journal for Nurse Practitioners* 6, no. 6 (2010): 477–478, doi:10.1016/j.nurpra.2010.03.016.

10. Karein K. Goertz, "Walking as Pedagogy," *Routledge International Handbook of Walking*, ed. C. Michael Hall (Milton Park: Routledge, 2017).

11. O'Mara, 11.

12. Kerri Andrews, *Wanderers: A History of Women Walking* (London: Reaktion Books, 2020), 263.

13. Søren Kierkegaard, "Letter to Henrietta Lund [1847]," in *The Vintage Book of Walking*, ed. D. Minshull (London: Random House, 2000), 6–7.

14. George Trevelyan, *Walking* (Hartford, CT: Edwin Valentine Mitchell, 1928).

15. Andrews, 121.

16. Pujol, 15.

17. Dave Ganci, "The Marathon Monks of Mount Hiei," *Trail Runner Magazine*, accessed April 30, 2022, https://www.trailrunnermag.com/people/culture-people/the-marathon-monks-of-mount-hiei.

18. Andrews, 210.

19. "When Is a Walk a Piece of Art? When Artist Hamish Fulton Brings His Transcendental Approach to the Pedestrian to Town," *The Scotsman*, April 21, 2010, accessed February 19, 2022, https://www.scotsman.com/arts-and-culture/when-walk-piece-art-when-artist-hamish-fulton-brings-his-transcendental-approach-pedestrian-town-1723721#.

20. Rebecca Solnit, *Wanderlust: A History of Walking* (New York: Penguin Books, 2000), 276.

21. *Kay Burns*, accessed July 9, 2022, http://www.kayburns.ca/.

22. "The New Field," *Public Studio*, accessed July 9, 2022, https://www.publicstudio.ca/the-new-field.

23. Mia Keinänen, "Taking Your Mind for a Walk: A Qualitative Investigation of Walking and Thinking among Nine Norwegian Academics," *Higher Education* 71 (2016): 593–605, https://doi.org/10.1007/s10734-015-9926-2.

24. Marily Oppezzo and Daniel L. Schwartz, "Give Your Ideas Some Legs: The Positive Effect of Walking on Creative Thinking," *Journal of Experimental Psychology: Learning, Memory, and Cognition* 40, no. 4 (2014): 1142.

25. Andrews, 27.

26. Garnette Cadogan, "Walking While Black," *Literary Hub*, July 8, 2016, accessed May 15, 2022, https://lithub.com/walking-while-black/.

27. Solnit, 6.

28. Solnit, 245.

29. Andrews, 34.

30. Viv Corringham, "Shadow-Walks," accessed February 13, 2022, http://vivcorringham.org/shadow-walks.html.

31. "The Walking Reading Group: On Commons," *[SPACE]*, accessed March 4, 2022, https://spacestudios.org.uk/events/the-walking-reading-group-on-commons/.

32. Anna Dot, "Meetings on the Common Ground," *Participatory Art for Invisible Communities*, ed. Irena Sertić (Zagreb: Omnimedia, 2018), 72.

33. Anna Salleh, "We're Continually Falling while We Walk," *ABC*, September 24, 2014, accessed July 10, 2022, https://www.abc.net.au/science/articles/2014/09/24/4093109.htm.

34. Amy Sharrocks, *On Falling: A Study Room Guide on Live Art & Falling*, 2013, accessed July 10, 2022, https://www.scribd.com/document/185692718/On-Falling-A-Study-Room-Guide-on-Live-Art-falling.

35. Alyson Hallett and Phil Smith, *Walking Stumbling Limping Falling* (Axminster: Triarchy Press, 2017), 7.

36. "Jesse Darling," *Chapter NY*, 2018, accessed July 21, 2022, http://chapter-ny.com/exhibitions/past/jesse-darling/.

37. Cynthia Morrison-Bell, Mike Collier, Tim Ingold, and Alistair Robinson, *Walk On: From Richard Long to Janet Cardiff, 40 Years of Art Walking* (Sunderland: Art Editions North, 2013), 124.

38. Sofia Karamani, "Catherine Yass, High Wire, 2008," *Tate*, October 2011, accessed July 10, 2022, https://www.tate.org.uk/art/artworks/yass-high-wire-t14384.

39. "Hiwa K, Pre-Image (Blind as the Mother Tongue)," *Art Jameel Collection*, accessed July 22, 2022, https://jameelartscentre.org/collection/hiwa-k/.

40. "Martin Kersels," *Madison Museum of Contemporary Art*, accessed July 10, 2022, https://www.mmoca.org/learn/teaching-pages/martin-kersels/.

41. Lori Waxman, *Keep Walking Intently: The Ambulatory Art of the Surrealists, the Situationist International, and Fluxus* (Berlin: Sternberg Press, 2017), 238.

Appendix

1. Katherine Jane McLean, Katherine *Nose-First: Practices of Smellwalking and Smellscape Mapping* (Royal College of Art, January 2019), 84–85.

2. Ernesto Pujol, *Walking Art Practice: Reflections on Socially Engaged Paths* (Axminster: Triarchy Press, 2018), 90.

Index

ableism, 89, 90, 112, 166, 199
Aboriginal, 65, 143
Abromović, Marina, 133, 195
absurdist, 13, 108, 144, 169, 172
accessibility, 1, 52, 59, 64, 69–72, 75,
    85, 87, 90–93, 99, 110, 111, 114,
    157, 168, 182
Acconcci, Vito, 66, 95
active-listening, 72
activist, 69, 91, 94, 109, 111, 112, 136,
    157, 159, 167, 168, 172, 185, 193,
    198
Adams, Rachel, 10, 214
aerial, 180–82, 184
affordances, 151
age, 40, 65, 102, 106, 109, 184, 193
agency, 52, 72
Akomfrah, John, 162
Alastair, Brotchie, 214
Alexander, 201
Allemansträtten, 92
Allora and Calzadilla, 185, 186
Alÿs, Francis, 120, 134, 179, 181, 185,
    186
Alyson, 111, 202
Amiens Cathedral Labyrinth, 126
Anastasi, William, 176
Andersen, Eric, 180
Anderson, Laurie, 21
Andrews, Kerri, 105, 129, 193, 199

animation, 121, 122, 143
anti-art, 12, 13
Antoni, Janine, 187
Antony, Rachael, 214
Apollo 11 moonwalk, 139
app, 24, 49, 166, 184, 200
appropriation, 42, 75
architecture, 2, 5, 15, 26, 28, 35–37,
    51, 52, 62, 100, 119, 122, 134, 139,
    151, 157, 158, 160, 167, 184, 197,
    202
Ariadne, 128
Aristotle, 7, 10, 119, 199
Arnatt, Keith, 124
artforum, 18
Ashton, Rachel, 114, 195
assemblages, 123
Asylum, 113
Atkinson, Christine, 194
atmosphere, 15, 62, 121, 196
atmospheric, 36, 38, 57, 94, 106, 113,
    137
attire, 2, 108, 140, 155, 158, 159, 161,
    162, 164, 173, 181
audience, 12, 24, 28, 39, 42, 79, 83,
    95, 102, 164, 168, 177–79, 191
audio, 2, 16, 22, 25, 26, 43, 46, 51, 53,
    61, 64, 70, 76, 79–81, 87, 110, 135,
    147, 152, 154, 198, 199, 208
Aula de Teatre, 201

avant-garde, 16

B, Franko, 177, 178
Bachelard, Gaston, 149
Ball, Hugo, 27
Bashō, Matsuo, 7, 45, 197
Baudelaire, Charles, 8
Bauman, Zygmunt, 152
Baxter, Iain, 85
Baxter, Ingrid, 85
Bdote Memory Map, 98
Beeching Report, 93
bees, 195, 196
Begay, David, 165
Beitiks, Meghan Moe, 62
Belasco, Daniel, 33
Bell, Roberley, 25
Belmore, Rebecca, 160
Benítez, Francisca, 187
Benjamin, Walter, 9, 153, 154
Bernstein, Michèle, 14
Bhalla, Ataul, 164
bias, 1, 14, 55, 59, 73, 90, 108, 141,
    216
bicycle, 92, 183, 184, 200
billboard, 27, 141, 169
binaural, 80
Bing, Han, 83
bird, 48, 49
Blain, Dominique, 34
blaze, 84
blind, 52
bollards, 84
boots, 35, 67, 175
Borcilă, Rozalinda, 148
border, 8, 94, 112–15, 134, 137, 147,
    185, 187, 188
Borsato, Diane, 195, 196
boundary, 1, 14, 81, 115, 147, 158,
    167, 185
braille, 69
Brandon, Kayle, 84

breath, 147, 195, 197
Brecht, George, 17, 153
Brennan, Tim, 48
Breton, André, 12, 13, 27
Brincat, Lauren, 112
Brotchie, Alastair, 214
Brouwn, Stanley, 184
Brown, Simone, 94, 102
Brown, Trisha, 18, 24, 25, 180, 196,
    202
Brueggemann, MJ Hunter, 58
Buchanan, Beverly, 19
Buczak, Brian, 204
Buddhist, 136, 195
Buffalo, Rising, 135, 166, 169
Bullard, Brandon, 103
Bunting, Heath, 84
Bures Miller, George, 80
Burns, Brendan Stuart, 30
Burns, David Allen, 22
Burns, Kay, 197
Butler, Eric, 201

Cadogan, Garnette, 101, 198
Cage, John, 17, 112, 171
Caillebotte, Gustave, 30
cairns, 84
Calle, Sophie, 26, 66
Calzadilla, Guillermo, 185, 186
Cameron, David, 165
Camino Way, 132
Campbell, Anna, 178
cane, 109, 112, 168, 202
canvas, 9, 119, 127, 175–77, 181, 187
capitalism, 9, 14, 83, 89, 90, 149, 160
car, 39, 94, 120, 148, 151, 172
caravan, 60, 134, 135
Cardiff, Janet, 80, 214
Careri, Francesco, 1, 5, 22, 45, 67
Carlos, Laurie, 82, 83
Carlson, Andrea, 27, 99, 100, 157
Carremans, Reg, 187

Cartesian dualism, 192
cartography, 23, 68, 183
caste, 55
Castiglione, Giuseppe, 125
Castleton, Jane, 81
Castoro, Rosemarie, 160, 161
Cates, Liz (Wakáŋyaŋkéwíŋ), 144
catwalk, 177
CCTV, 95
celebrate, 11, 14, 106, 117, 118, 126, 128, 136, 137, 170
CerCCa, 60
ceremony, 99, 118, 125, 128, 136, 161, 162, 166
Certeau, Michel de, 10, 167
chalk, 40, 68, 131, 163, 182, 188
chance, 12–14, 17, 49, 53, 63, 64, 66, 86, 122–24, 131, 151, 167, 179, 181, 184
chanoyu, 125
charcoal, 180, 182
Char Dham, 131
Chartist movement, 11
Chartres Cathedral, 126
Chaulupecký, Jindřich, 40
Chavez, Cesar, 156
chemins de l'âne (donkey paths), 181
Chen, Milli, 25
children, 28, 65, 92, 98, 99, 122, 142, 143, 180
Childs, Lucinda, 18
choreography, 51, 101, 111, 178–80, 189
Christo and Jeanne-Claude, 18, 29
circumambulation, 133, 136
citizenship, 41, 89, 90, 107, 112, 113, 115
civil disobedience, 156, 181
Clark, Kara, 148
classism, 89, 90, 92
Clayton, Lenka, 45
climate, 142, 145, 164, 165

climbing, 8, 180
cloisters, 118, 119
clothing (see also 'attire'), 61, 70, 101, 105, 161, 164, 180
Cloudspotting, 110
Coates, Marcus, 172, 203
Cody, Buffalo Bill, 169
Coleridge, Samuel Taylor, 7, 8, 141
collage, 149, 177
colonialism, 60, 89, 96, 97, 100, 102, 103, 115, 137, 141, 142, 144, 156, 159, 165, 166
Columbus, Christopher, 97
commemorative, 62, 120, 137, 158, 159
commons, 90, 92–94, 124, 217
commuting, 62, 120–22, 137, 184
concerts, 17, 200
consent, 14, 65–67, 87
Cormont, Renaud de, 126
corridors, 16, 29, 147, 166
Corringham, Viv, 199, 200
Cortada, Xavier, 164
Countryside and Rights of Way (CROW) Act, 92
Coverley, Merlin, 15
COVID-19 114, 192
crawling, 157, 169, 202, 219
Cresswell, Tim, 140
Crews, Roz, 123
critique, 16, 42, 43, 66, 81, 82, 87, 147, 161, 170, 178
Crowe, Fran, 48, 49
Cullen, Sarah, 23, 176
Cumpston, Nici, 145
cup-and-rings, 127
curb, 69, 70, 110, 111
Curry, Helen, 129

Dada, 12, 13, 19, 27, 76
dance, 5, 18, 68, 128, 179, 180, 189

Davies, Bradley, 95
Davies, Bradley, 95
dawdling, 9
deaf, 50, 112
deambulation, 13, 108
Debicki, Kaitlin, 165
Debord, Guy, 14, 15
Deigaard, Lee, 123
Deitch Projects, 77
Deller, Jeremy, 162
De Maria, Walter, 10, 38, 182
Denicola, Loredana, 106
Denison, Jane, 214
Deriva Mussol, 201
dérive, 14–16, 46, 62, 79, 110, 123,
    124, 218
Derrida, Jacques, 85
Descartes, René, 192
Deveron Projects, 67, 130
Díaz Morales, Sebastián, 140
disability, 1, 2, 41, 45, 47, 71, 90, 91,
    108–12, 115, 157, 191, 199, 202
documentation, 2, 8, 16, 21, 22,
    24–26, 28, 31, 33, 35, 39, 43, 60,
    62, 69, 74, 82, 83, 85, 87, 93, 103,
    120–22, 134, 135, 140, 148, 150,
    151, 162, 176, 183, 188, 207, 208
dogs, 21, 22, 62, 120, 122–24
donkey paths (chemins de l'âne), 181
drifting, 14, 62, 66, 108, 153, 201, 218
Drobnick, Jim, 54
durational, 5, 6, 19–21, 35, 61, 78,
    112, 120, 195
D'Ignazio, Catherine, 147

Elephant trails, 181
Elkin, Lauren, 9, 106, 146, 147
Ellams, Inua, 89, 114
Emerson, Ralph Waldo, 8
Eno, Brian, 214
ephemerality, 14, 25, 54, 56, 83, 134,
    167, 168, 175, 178, 182, 197

exercising, 183, 194, 195, 199, 218

Fabergé, Henri, 194
falling, 111, 192, 198, 202–5
feminism, 55, 106, 149, 160, 161
fences, 76, 84, 128, 158
Ferguson, Bruce, 80
festival, 125, 129, 132, 133, 136
figurative, 10, 55, 63, 120, 121, 140,
    167
Filliou, Robert, 17, 102
Finlay, Alec, 200
Flanders, Elle, 198
flânerie, 8–10, 46, 62, 64, 101, 106,
    146, 218
Fleischner, Richard, 128
Fletcher, Harrell, 168, 214
Floyd, George, 30
Fluxus, 16, 17, 19, 27, 40, 46, 64, 86,
    102, 153, 177, 179
food, 5, 50, 56, 57, 71, 91, 134, 142,
    193, 216
foraging, 48, 57, 171
forests, 78, 124, 130, 153, 165
Foster, Hal, 85
Foxfire, 170
Francis III, John H., 163
Frankenthaler, Helen, 176
Fraser, Andrea, 81
Freeman, Bonnie, 165
Friedman, Ken, 17
Friedrich, Caspar David, 119
Fritz, 50, 178
Fulton, Hamish, 26, 78, 157, 158, 163,
    165, 180, 195
futurist, 100

Galindo, Regina José, 130, 177
Gallo, Rebecca, 123
Gandhi, Mohandas, 155, 156
gardens, 34, 37, 92, 118, 119, 124,
    125, 137, 142, 144

Gast, Christy, 164
gentrification, 91, 94, 95, 103, 166
Geocaching, 219
Gillespie, Patrick, 50
Gilmore, Kate, 160, 180
Give, Dillon de, 130
Glowlab, 28
Goertz, Karein K., 192
Gordon, David, 18
Graham, Dan, 128
Gran Fury, 157
Green, Kate, 145, 146
Green, Renée, 96
Gutai, 16, 19
Gutiérrez, Amanda, 104

Haeg, Fritz, 50, 178
Halberstam, Jack, 170
Hallett, Alyson, 111, 202
Hammons, David, 168
Hanh, Thich Nhat, 214
Hanska Luger, Cannupa, 157
happenings, 16, 167, 168
haptic, 52
Haussmann, Georges-Eugène, 146
Hayes, Sharon, 131
Hazlitt, Sarah Stoddart, 8, 193–95
healing, 111, 127, 192
health, 65, 99, 192, 194, 196, 205
Heap of Birds, Edgar (Hock E Aye
    Vi), 169
Hector, 161
Heddon, Deirdre, 200
hedge-maze, 125, 128
Heizer, Michael, 182
Hendricks, Geoffrey, 131
Heng, Amanda, 89, 108, 122, 172, 202
Henry, Joël, 214
Henshaw, Victoria, 47
Hersey, Tricia, 192
Hesse, Fiona, 214
heteronormativity, 166, 170

Hewlett, Robin, 86, 172, 180
Higgins, Dick, 17
high-wire, 202
hiking, 78, 197, 198, 219
Hill, Christine, 77
Hind, Claire, 214
Hiroshige, Utagawa, 30
Hock E Aye Vi (Edgar Heap of
    Birds), 169
Holt, Nancy, 18, 84
hooks, bell, 145, 149
Horodner, Stuart, 214
Horwitz, Andy, 82
Hsieh, Tehching, 120
humor, 77, 82, 86, 117, 145, 149, 172,
    173, 203, 204
Hunter, Norma D., 111
Hunter Brueggemann, MJ, 58
Husby, Larsen, 151, 185
Husserl, Edmund, 60
Hutter, Robert, 150

IDLA (Indian Defense League of
    America), 137
Idle No More Movement, 143
iLAND (interdisciplinary Laboratory
    for Art Nature and Dance), 68, 214
Iliad, 161
immigration, 29, 55, 90, 103, 104,
    113, 114, 144, 156
imperialism, 96, 97, 102, 125, 149,
    167
improvisation, 10, 74, 76, 77, 154,
    160, 180, 199, 200
Inca Trail, 131
indigenous, 2, 5, 27, 51, 89, 96–98,
    100, 103, 115, 141–43, 147, 154,
    157, 159, 165, 170, 171, 198, 216
installation, 17, 22, 25, 27, 29, 33–35,
    37, 43, 48, 60, 63, 99, 103, 104, 123,
    126, 128, 163, 164, 169, 192, 197,
    200, 202

intersectionality, 90, 107
interviews, 18, 22, 28, 134, 145, 170, 208
Isaac, Chele, 178

Jackson, Zig (Rising Buffalo), 135, 176
Jahoda, Susan, 192
Jalan Gembira, 19, 27, 93, 122
James, Lebron, 136
Jan Ader, Bas, 119
Jeanne-Claude, 18, 29
Johanson, Patricia, 182
Johnson, Walis, 104
Judson Dance Theater, 18
July, Miranda, 168, 214

K, Hiwa, 203
Kahn, Miriam, 142
kaihogyo, 195
Kailash, Mount, 131
Kanayama, Akira, 175
Kandy Esala Perahera, 136
Kaprow, Allan, 16, 61, 176
Kara, VinZula, 136, 148
Kastner, Jeffrey, 144
Kawara, On, 63
Kebede, Mihret, 113, 114, 195
Kee, Jeroen, 184
Keersmaeker, Anne Teresa De, 38, 180
kemonomichi, 181
Kern, Leslie, 106
Kersels, Martin, 203, 204
Khademi, Kubra, 89, 107, 167
Khatib, Abdelhafid, 14, 15, 102
Kierkegaard, Søren, 118, 193, 195
Kim, Christine Sun, 89, 112
Kinder Mass Trespass, 92
King Jr., Martin Luther, 156
Kinsley, Ben, 86, 172, 180
Kirkup, Wendy, 25, 95
Kline, Phil, 26

Knížák, Milan, 40
Knowles, Tim, 183, 184
Koebel, Jaime, 51
Koestenbaum, Wayne, 189
Kosugi, Takehisa, 64
Kubota, Shigeko, 177
Kwon, Miwon, 167

labyrinth, 2, 5, 6, 61, 125–30, 137, 197
Ladau, Ellen, 108, 109
Ladau, Emily, 69, 109
Laderman Ukeles, Mierle, 55
Lafon, Jordi, 201
Laing, Jennifer, 132
Lakshmana-mandal, 126
Lazard, Carolyn, 71
Lee, JeeYeun, 102–4
Lee, KangJae, 102
leisure, 2, 9, 62, 102
Lennon, John, 66
Lens, Bob, 46, 97, 192
Lewis, Glenn, 124
LGBTQ, 106, 156
library, 7, 49, 102, 200
limping, 111, 202
Lin, Maya, 78
Lippard, Lucy, 22, 76, 91, 94, 124, 132, 149–51
Lister, Anne, 8
localness, 19, 49, 62, 71, 76, 80, 82, 94, 110, 114, 124, 130, 140, 141, 149–52, 154, 199, 216, 218
Loiterers Resistance Movement, 15, 28
Loitering, 94
Long, Richard, 18, 84, 126, 182, 184, 214
Los Desfiladores Tres Puntos 22 del West Side / West Side Three-Point Marchers, 136
Lounder, Barbara, 159, 186
Luger, Cannupa Hanska, 157

Luski, Zoe, 58
L'Hirondelle, Cheryl, 162, 163

MacAlpine, Alexander, 201
MacCannell, Dean, 132
MacGregor, Gwen, 121, 183
Maciunas, George, 17, 27
Magema, Michèle, 187, 188
Malone, Karen, 144
Malpas, Jeff, 139
Manchot, Melanie, 180
Manderfeld, Rachel, 178
Mandl, Dave, 28
mapmaking, 7, 8, 13, 16, 22–24, 30,
  43, 46, 47, 51–53, 56, 59, 60, 62–64,
  68, 71, 75, 76, 79, 80, 84, 95, 98,
  103, 121, 144, 153, 154, 166–68,
  183, 184, 189, 204
maps, 19, 22, 23, 28, 29, 31, 56, 63,
  68, 70, 83, 86, 91, 92, 104, 122, 141,
  143, 167, 172, 183, 201, 218
Maraa Collective, 55
marathons, 78, 113, 114, 147, 194,
  195
marching, 11, 35, 50, 65, 92, 97–99,
  106, 112, 123, 130, 136, 137, 148,
  149, 155–57, 162, 170, 181
Maria, Walter De, 182
Marichalar-Freixa, Eva, 201
Marín, Carlos Pérez, 60, 134
Marioni, Tom, 176
Marsad Drâa, 60
Martinez, Daniel J., 136
Mattingly, Mary, 150
mazes, 125, 126, 128, 137, 153, 197
McAdam, Stuart, 93
McCann, Colum, 112
McCaslin, Matthew, 121
McCollam, Phil, 24, 127
McKenzie, Dave, 136, 137
McLean, Kate, 53, 54, 68, 216
memorials, 18, 78, 99, 132, 169, 170

memories, 21, 25, 26, 50, 54, 55, 59,
  61, 71, 80, 85, 98, 112, 118, 129,
  130, 137, 149–52, 169, 193, 198,
  208
Mendieta, Ana, 134
menhirs, 5, 6, 65
Merewether, Charles, 85, 86
Merleau-Ponty, Maurice, 60
Meseguer Zafe, Raquel, 110
Messias, Nando, 106
Métis, 162
Michelson, Alan, 163, 168
Migrating, 10, 113, 115, 219
Mildred's Lane, 217
Miller, Earl, 214
mind-body, 61, 193
mindfulness, 51, 53, 58, 69, 79, 87,
  94, 111, 192, 216
Minneapolis, 151, 185
Minnesota, 98, 99
Minos, King, 128
Minotaur, 128
monasteries, 119, 195
Monge, Lucia, 148
Monsoon, Jennifer, 214
Morales, Sebastián Díaz, 140
Morelli, François, 120
Morin, Peter, 159
Morrell, Amish, 170, 171, 194
Morris, Kate, 112, 135
Morrison-Bell, Cynthia, 214
mountaineering, 25
Murad, May, 114, 195
Murak, Teresa, 55
mushrooms, 48, 171
Mwangi Hutter, 150
Myers, Lisa, 143
Myers, Misha, 200
Mythogeography, 219

Naldi, Pat, 25, 95
Natan, Efrat, 48

Nauman, Bruce, 16, 29, 180, 197
Navarro, Eduardo, 60, 61
Nazca Plain, 126
Nearing, Guy, 171
Neo-Concrete, 179
neolithic, 5, 65
Neuhaus, Max, 112
New, Sophia, 33
Nin, Anaïs, 129, 130, 195
nomadic, 5, 134, 135, 152, 219

Obama, President, 136
Ochoa, Jorge, 148
Odell, Jenny, 49
odorphobia, 55
Okpokwasili, Okwui, 52
olfactory, 36, 53, 55, 68
olifantenpad (elephant trails), 181
Oliveros, Pauline, 50
Ono, Yoko, 17, 66, 84, 154, 181, 214
Oppenheim, Dennis, 185
Oregon Beach Bill of 1967
93
Orozco, Gabriel, 29
Oucherif, Marie, 214
O'Brian, Jean M., 98
O'Mara, Shane, 193
O'Rourke, Karen, 68

Pacific Crest Trail, 132, 194
Paik, Nam June, 17, 179
Paleolithic, 1
pandemic, 114, 123, 192
Papalia, Carmen, 52, 112, 168
Pape, Lygia, 179
parade, 2, 48, 50, 130, 136, 137, 148,
    157, 170, 178
Parkour, 186, 219
paseo, 107
Patterson, Benjamin, 17, 102, 195, 196
Paxton, Steve, 18

Pearson Clarke, Michele, 77
pedagogy, 170, 171, 173, 217
pedway, 147
Peláez, Luis Fernando, 78
Pérez Marín, Carlos, 60, 134
Peripatetic School, 7, 119
Persighetti, Simon, 68, 79, 144, 151,
    159
Pezo von Ellrichshausen, 197
Phelps, Danica, 188
phenomenology, 59–61, 64, 191
pilgrimages, 2, 61, 78, 92, 118, 120, 126,
    131–34, 137, 152, 160, 198, 219
Piper, Adrian, 158
Pistoletto, Michelangelo, 18
plato, 7
Pocahontas, 159
Polak, Esther, 184
Pollard, Ingrid, 141
Pollock, Jackson, 61, 176
Pope, Simon, 39, 64
Pope, L, 169
Porteous, J. Douglas, 53
portraits, 46, 124
Povera, Art, 16, 17
Prajapati, Sheetal, 75
pram, 111
Pratt, Richard Henry, 142
printmaking, 27, 30, 31, 143, 185
privilege, 9, 40, 41, 47, 64, 73, 75, 89,
    90, 147, 216, 217
procession, 5, 18, 38, 55, 92, 98, 106,
    136, 137, 162, 219
promenade, 26, 219
proprioception, 47
props, 2, 155, 158–61, 164, 173
prosthetic, 50, 109
prostitution, 14, 107, 194
protest, 11, 12, 25, 42, 65, 99, 118,
    136, 155–58, 160, 161, 167, 173,
    219

psychogeography, 14–16, 102, 110, 123, 219
Pujol, Ernesto, 11, 123, 141
Pythagoras, 7

Qipei, Gao, 30
Qualmann, Clare, 111, 214
questing, 131–34, 137, 219
Quincey, Thomas de, 141

Rainer, Yvonne, 18
Ramesses III, 11
Ramón, Cecilia, 198, 199
Rauschenberg, Robert, 18
Ray, Christina, 28
ready-mades, 16, 84
Reagan, Ronald, 98
Reclaim The Streets (RTS), 94
reenactment, 2, 19, 21, 22, 28, 42, 82, 99, 114, 155, 162, 163, 173, 180
refugees, 113, 114, 203
Reich, Steve, 38, 180
reprises, 21, 22, 28, 82, 83, 162, 163, 181
Ribemont-Dessaignes, George, 12
Richter, Gerhard, 176
Rickard, Jolene, 137
Right-to-Roam, 92
Rising Buffalo (Zig Jackson), 135
rites, 65, 118, 126, 128, 130, 132
ritual, 2, 6, 59, 61, 62, 68, 78, 106, 107, 117–23, 125–27, 129–31, 133, 135, 137, 142, 164, 176
Robinson, Alistair, 214
Robinson, Máiréad, 141
Robinson, Tim, 141
Rodigari, Sarah, 145
Rogers, Daniel Belasco, 33
Rose, Gillian, 149
Rose, Morag, 15, 69, 89, 90, 102
Rousseau, Jean-Jacques, 7

RTS (Reclaim the Streets), 94
Rueb, Teri, 166
running, 35, 45, 47, 62, 101, 102, 114, 128, 133, 147, 158, 162, 163, 183, 194, 195
rural, 2, 55, 57, 67, 93, 122, 130, 143–46, 149, 152, 154, 166, 191
Ruskin, John, 141
Ryan, Michael x., 121, 185

Sabri, Yasmeen, 161
Santayana, George, 10
Santiago X, 89, 100
Savage, Jennie, 80, 154
Sawatzky, Tamira, 198
Schneider, Carrie, 25, 80
Schneider, Rebecca, 83
Schrag, Anthony, 26, 132, 133
Schuerman, John, 30
Scott, Dread, 42, 162
Seamon, David, 62, 191
Semana Santa, 136
Serra, Richard, 63
settler-colonialism, 89, 97, 98, 100, 103, 113, 142, 144, 145, 166
Shalom, Todd, 11, 67, 75, 189, 214
Sharrocks, Amy, 202
shepherding, 5, 128
Shimamoto, Shozo, 16
shinrin-yoku (Japanese forest bathing), 124
Shiomi, Mieko, 17
Shiraga, Kazuo, 175
sidewalks, 17, 19, 40, 50, 57, 69, 91, 110, 111, 146, 187, 204
signage, 76, 80, 94, 110, 137, 149, 150, 154, 167, 169
Situationists, 14–16, 19, 27, 66, 79, 86, 102, 108, 153
Smellfie, 53, 54, 68
smellnotes, 54

smellscape, 53, 56
Smith, Phil, 11, 68, 79, 111, 136, 144, 151, 159, 202, 214, 219
Smith, Tony, 18
Smithson, Robert, 18, 22, 78, 132
Snowshoe, 171
Solnit, Rebecca, 9, 10, 104, 107, 118, 143, 153, 154, 183, 198, 199
Sotelo-Castro, Luis Carlos, 59
souvenirs, 22, 33, 187
SPURSE, 57
stalking, 66
Stegner, Wallace, 165
Stiles, Kristine, 175
Stingel, Rudolf, 175
Stockwell, Susan, 188
Stoddart Hazlitt, Sarah, 8, 193
Strayed, Cheryl, 132, 194
stroller, 69, 111
strolling, 15, 62
stumbling, 111, 202, 203
Sulkowicz, Emma, 161
Sullivan, Lexi Lee, 134, 214
Sun Kim, Christine, 89, 112
Surrealism, 13, 14, 17, 19, 27, 66, 108, 146, 214
surveillance, 2, 25, 67, 91, 94, 95, 102, 115, 172

Tajik, Iman, 114
Tanaka, Atsuko, 175
Tarbuck, Alice, 10
tasting, 36, 37, 45, 47, 48, 52, 54, 56–59, 153, 218
Taylor, David, 115
TCM (Traditional Chinese Medicine), 192
Thales, 7
Theseus, 128
Thomas, Aislinn, 191
Thomas, Vanessa, 58
Thompson, Brian, 29

Thoreau, Henry David, 8
Thutmose III, 11
Tiziou, JJ, 147
topography, 15, 35–37, 39, 47, 52, 57, 59, 61, 62, 70, 84, 110, 140, 159
topophilia, 141
Toppins, Aggie, 9
tourism, 2, 55, 65, 67, 76–81, 132, 141, 152, 166, 218
trails, 84, 98, 118, 130–32, 170, 178, 181, 192, 194, 197, 198
trespassing, 49, 92
Trevelyan, George Macaulay, 193
Troy towns, 126, 127
Tsen, Hui-min, 147, 157
Tuan, Yi-Fu, 139, 141, 149
Tubman, Harriet, 11
Turner, Camille, 76, 77, 81

Ulay, 133
Ulrich, Matthias, 214
utopian, 145, 147, 202

vagabond, 152
van der Werve, Guido, 133, 194
Venice Biennale, 48, 132, 133, 169
Verdier, Fabienne, 175
Villar, Alex, 158
Virdi, Jaipreet, 108

Waag Society, 184
Wakáŋyaŋkéwíŋ (Liz Cates), 144
Wakemup, Rory, 157
Walking Artists Network, 215
Walk Listen Create, 215
Walkspace, 27
walkwalkwalk, 19, 62, 150
Wanderlust, 9, 10, 107, 214
Wang, Ding, 58
Warhol, Andy, 18
Waxman, Lori, 17, 102, 131

Weiwei, Ai, 158, 180
West, Gayle Melissa, 129
West, Jennifer, 186
Westerman, Gwen, 99
wheelchair, 69, 109–11, 157
Whitelaw, Ginny, 192
williams, moira, 111
Wise, Susie, 117
Wodiczko, Krzysztof, 29, 152
Wolff, Sharne, 214
Wood, Jeremy, 184
Woolard, Caroline, 192
Woolf, Virgina, 10, 198, 219

Wordsworth, Dorothy, 8, 45, 129, 141
Wordsworth, William, 8, 141
X, SANTIAGO, 89, 100
xenophobia, 89, 90, 115, 141

Yass, Catherine, 202
Young, Austin, 22
Young, La Monte, 46, 179

Z, Pamela, 46
Zeiske, Claudia, 57
Zhen, Wanhua, 125
zines, 27, 56, 153

www.ingramcontent.com/pod-product-compliance
Lightning Source LLC
Chambersburg PA
CBHW071407170526
45165CB00001B/203